Witchcraft and Whigs

Witchcraft and Whigs

The life of Bishop Francis Hutchinson,
1660–1739

Andrew Sneddon

Manchester University Press

Copyright © Andrew Sneddon 2008

The right of Andrew Sneddon to be identified as the author of this work has been asserted by him in accordance with the Copyright, Designs and Patents Act 1988.

Published by Manchester University Press
Altrincham Street, Manchester M1 7JA, UK
and Room 400, 175 Fifth Avenue, New York, NY 10010, USA
www.manchesteruniversitypress.co.uk

British Library Cataloguing-in-Publication Data is available

Library of Congress Cataloging-in-Publication Data is available

ISBN 978 0 7190 9678 5 paperback

First published by Manchester University Press in hardback 2008

This paperback edition first published 2014

The publisher has no responsibility for the persistence or accuracy of URLs for any external or third-party internet websites referred to in this book, and does not guarantee that any content on such websites is, or will remain, accurate or appropriate.

Printed by Lightning Source

For Andy and Isa Sneddon

Would you rise in the Church, be stupid and dull,
Be empty of learning, of insolence full:
Though lewd and immoral, be formal and grave,
In flattery an artist, in fawning a slave,
No merit, no science, no virtue is wanting
In him, that's accomplished in cringing and canting;
Be studious to practise true meanness of spirit;
For who but Lord Bolton was mitred for merit?[1]
Would you wish to be wrapped in a rochet[2] – in short,
Be as poxed and profane as fanatical Hort.[3]
    (Dean Jonathan Swift, 'Advice to a parson: an epigram')[4]

---

[1] Theophilus Bolton, successively Bishop of Clonfert (1722) and Elphin (1724), and Archbishop of Cashel (1729).

[2] A surplice-like vestment worn by bishops.

[3] Josiah Hort, successively Bishop of Ferns (1721) and Kilmore (1727), and Archbishop of Tuam (1742).

[4] Jonathan Swift, *The complete poems*, ed. Pat Rogers (London, repr. 1983), p. 501; Swift never made the bench of the bishops.

Contents

Preface	page	viii
Notes on quotations		x
List of abbreviations		xi
Introduction		1

Part I England

1	Childhood and early career, 1660–c.1690	9
2	The national Church in a Suffolk parish: St James', Bury St Edmunds, 1692–1720	20
3	'A well affected man': Hutchinson and party politics, 1700–20	53
4	Angels and demons: the mental world of an eighteenth-century Anglican pastor	77
5	Hutchinson and witchcraft: *An historical essay concerning witchcraft* (1718)	93

Part II Ireland

6	The Bishop of Down and Connor and the established Church and state in Ireland, 1721–39	129
7	'Darkness must be expell'd by bringing in the light': the conversion of Irish Catholics, c.1721–34	148
8	'Improve everything that is improveable': the social, economic and cultural improvement of Ireland and the Irish, 1721–39	177

Conclusion	200
Select bibliography	206
Index	215

Preface

My interest in Bishop Francis Hutchinson began when researching a master's dissertation on early modern English witchcraft belief, at the University of St Andrews under the supervision of Professor Hamish Scott. After initial advice from Professor A. G. R. Smith, Professor James Sharpe and Dr Ian Bostridge, I embarked on a Lancaster University PhD thesis on the subject, under the supervision of Dr Robert Poole and with a scholarship provided by St Martin's College, Lancaster. My research on Hutchinson grew from a study of his witchcraft theories to an exploration of his entire life when it became apparent that not only had no one attempted to do this, but that there was enough extant primary source material to do so effectively.

The transfer of this idea into practice, first in thesis form and then in book form, has indebted me to many individuals, but first of all to my PhD supervisor, Dr Poole, without whose constant advice, patience and sharing of his wide knowledge on seventeenth- and eighteenth-century Britain this book, or indeed the thesis on which it is based, would have never been written. I would also like to thank a number of historians who read and offered their advice on various drafts of this book, namely Dr Peter Elmer, Professor David Hayton, Dr Donald Spaeth and Dr T. C. Barnard. Furthermore, my knowledge of eighteenth-century Irish economy and politics, which underlie the final chapters, has benefited greatly from discussions with my colleagues on the Leverhulme Trust-funded Irish Legislation Project, Professor Hayton, Dr John Bergin and Dr James Kelly. I would also like to thank Dr Gerald Bray for providing me with drafts of his forthcoming work on the Convocation of Canterbury and Dr Andy Wood for pointing me in the direction of Derbyshire depositions held in The National Archives, Kew.

I would like to thank the joint-editors and the editorial board of *Irish Historical Studies* for allowing me to make use of material originally published as Andrew Sneddon, 'Bishop Francis Hutchinson: a case study in the culture of eighteenth-century improvement' in *Irish Historical*

Studies, xxxv, no. 139 (May 2007). Similarly, I would like to thank the editors of *Recusant History* and *Eighteenth-Century Ireland* for allowing me to publish material from two articles: Andrew Sneddon, ' "Those crafty adversaries": Bishop Francis Hutchinson and anti-Catholic rhetoric in early Hanoverian England, c.1716–21' in *Recusant History*, xxvii, no. 4 (2005) and Andrew Sneddon, ' "Darkness must be expell'd by letting in the light": Bishop Francis Hutchinson and the conversion of Irish Catholics by means of the Irish language, c.1720–4', *Eighteenth-Century Ireland*, xviii (2004).

There are far too many people associated with academic institutions, libraries and archives who have provided invaluable assistance during the course of my research for me to be able to mention all of them. However, I would particularly like to thank the staff at the Public Record Office of Northern Ireland, who are not only erstwhile colleagues and friends, but have made my research at that institution both enjoyable and fruitful, namely Iain Fleming, Wesley Geddis, Carrie Green, Janet Hancock, Graham Jackson, Ian Montgomery and Stephen Scarth. Finally, I would like to thank my friends, who I am sure have long tired of the subject of Bishop Francis Hutchinson and the strains that producing a study of him has put on my time and temperament, in particular Neil Hamilton, John Hinder, Peter Moore, and Viv and Alan Rodgers. My immediate family (Mum, Dad, Sharon and Steve), and of course my wife Leanne, have borne the brunt of this, and to them I owe eternal gratitude.

Andrew Sneddon
Belfast

Notes on Quotations

In this book, quotations taken from contemporary manuscript and printed sources have been reproduced with the original spelling and punctuation intact, with two exceptions.

Firstly, abbreviated words have been written in full. For example 'ym,' 'wch' and 'ye' have been presented respectively as 'them,' 'which' and 'the'.

Secondly, capitalisation has been modernised. For example, a sentence that would have read in the original source as 'The judge who Tryed her and hath the Life of the Poor Woman upon his care' is reproduced here as 'The judge who tryed her and hath the life of the poor woman upon his care'.

Abbreviations

Add. MS	Additional Manuscript
A.L.B.	C.U.L., S.P.C.K. records, Abstract Letter Book
B.L.	British Library
C.C.	Christ Church, Oxford
CJ	*Journals of the House of Commons for the kingdom of Ireland*
C.U.L.	Cambridge University Library
D.R.	Church of Ireland, Down and Connor Diocesan Registry, Belfast
D.R.O.	Derbyshire Record Office
E.R.O.	Essex Record Office
H.M.C.	Historical Manuscripts Commission
LJ	*Journals of the Irish House of Lords*
L.P.L.	Lambeth Palace Library
N.R.O.	Norfolk Record Office
OldDNB	*Dictionary of national biography*
OxDNB	*Oxford dictionary of national biography*
P.R.O.N.I.	Public Record Office of Northern Ireland
R.I.A.	Royal Irish Academy
S.P.C.K.	Society for the Promotion of Christian Knowledge
S.R.O. (B)	Suffolk Record Office, Bury St Edmunds
T.C.D.	Trinity College Dublin
T.N.A.	The National Archives, Kew

Dates are presented in old style, however, the year is taken to have started on 1 January and not on 25 March, as was the custom before 1752.

Introduction

Historians who have written about Francis Hutchinson[1] have tended to study a small part of his life and his literary output as part of larger studies on other subjects. Bishop Hutchinson is thus many things to many historians. To some he represents the archetypal eighteenth-century Protestant bibliophile,[2] to others the type of clerical, social and economic improver and antiquarian that flourished in Ireland in the early eighteenth century.[3] Despite this interest in his life in Ireland, most academics have been drawn to his life and work on account of his seminal, sceptical witchcraft tract, the *Historical essay*, published in London in 1718. Their interpretations of why Hutchinson rejected traditional witchcraft beliefs in this book reflect the changing face of the historiography of decline in educated belief in witchcraft.

The view that the English educated elite, if not the majority of the population, had rejected witchcraft by the early eighteenth century because they now, as inheritors of the advances in knowledge collectively known as the 'Scientific Revolution', subscribed to a view of the universe which left little room for the machinations of immaterial forces such as witchcraft and magic, enjoyed a central place in the historiography of

---

[1] Despite an extensive search conducted over a number of years, it has proven impossible to track down a portrait of Bishop Hutchinson. There is no doubt that one existed in the past. The Belfast-born poet and broadcaster, Louis MacNeice, wrote the following in 1938 of his father's house (Bishop's house) in Malone Road, Belfast: 'in the dining-room were oil portraits in heavy gilt mitre-topped frames. Dr Hutchinson, of the early eighteenth-century, self-possessed, in a heavy wig to his shoulders, a man who knew the world' in Alan Heuser (ed.), *Selected prose of Louis MacNeice* (Oxford, 1990), pp. 62–3.

[2] Gordon Wheeler, 'Bishop Francis Hutchinson: his Irish publications and his library' in John Gray and Wesley McCann (eds), *An uncommon bookman: essays in memory of J. R. R. Adams* (Belfast, 1996), pp. 140–58.

[3] T. C. Barnard, 'Improving clergymen, 1660–1760' in Alan Ford, James McGuire and Kenneth Milne (eds), *As by law established: the Church of Ireland since the Reformation* (Dublin, 1995), p. 138; idem, 'Protestants and the Irish language: c.1675–1725' in *Journal of Ecclesiastical History*, xliv (1993), 265.

decline until recently.[4] For one such historian, Wallace Notestein, Francis Hutchinson was the personification of this educated, rationalist outlook for which witchcraft no longer held any attraction.[5] This triumphalist approach, however, lost much of its appeal by the last decade of the twentieth century. It is now generally accepted that the impact of the 'Scientific Revolution' had been over-estimated because it failed to alter the mental world of the educated as rapidly or totally as once thought.[6] As Ian Bostridge recently put it: 'the mechanical philosophy left too much of the old world of spirits and wonders intact to have acted as reason's exorcist in the casting-out of witchcraft'.[7]

Since the mid-1990s, historians of witchcraft have adopted a more complex approach to decline. James Sharpe regards the rejection of witchcraft belief by the educated as a result of a number of intellectual, religious and cultural shifts occurring within their mental world; shifts that deprived witchcraft of the context in which it had thrived during the previous century or so. Ian Bostridge, on the other hand, argues that witchcraft belief became marginalised by educated culture because by the late 1710s it had become ideologically redundant, especially in establishment Whig circles. This was because, by that time, witchcraft was no longer required (or indeed able) to perform its original political function of forging Christian unity by bolstering the idea of a sacral confessional state.[8]

The view of decline adopted by a witchcraft historian has invariably informed their view of Hutchinson. Sharpe suggests that Hutchinson's witchcraft scepticism was the result of two things: his desire to distance himself from a belief system increasingly considered by the elite as part of vulgar, popular culture; and his disinclination to view the universe as a place where immaterial forces regularly impinged on the day-to-day workings of the temporal world. Bostridge, on the other hand,

---

[4] Salient examples of this can be found in Keith Thomas, *Religion and the decline of magic: studies in popular beliefs in sixteenth and seventeenth century England* (London, 1971, repr. 1973), p. 577, and Brian Easlea, *Witch-hunting, magic and the new philosophy: an introduction to the debates of the Scientific Revolution, 1450–1750* (Brighton, 1980), pp. 197–207.

[5] Wallace Notestein, *A history of witchcraft in England from 1558 to 1718* (Washington, 1909), p. 343.

[6] James Sharpe, *Instruments of darkness: witchcraft in England 1550–1750* (London, 1996), pp. 256–70; idem, *Witchcraft in early modern England* (London, 2001), pp. 78–9; Stuart Clark, *Thinking with demons: the idea of witchcraft in early modern Europe* (Oxford, 1997), pp. 296, 298–9.

[7] Ian Bostridge, *Witchcraft and its transformations c.1650–c.1750* (Oxford, 1997), p. 4.

[8] See Chapter 5.

argues that Hutchinson rejected witchcraft because he regarded it as a salient example of religious enthusiasm and as such inimical to his Whiggish vision of a polite, ordered, commercial society.[9]

Yet this interest in Hutchinson has not as yet yielded a full biographical study to explore his life, thought and career in its entirety, both in Britain and Ireland. The lack of such a study is all the more lamentable given the relatively large amount of primary manuscript and printed source material relating to Hutchinson that is still extant, as a cursory perusal of the footnotes and bibliography of this book will confirm. Hutchinson left over thirty published books, pamphlets and sermons to posterity, on a wide variety of subjects, not only on witchcraft but also on economic improvement, astrology, prophecy, angels and the Irish language. Furthermore, archives and repositories, in England and Ireland, hold numerous letters by and to him, from luminaries such as the Archbishop of Canterbury, William Wake and the Ulster-born physician, collector and member of the Royal Society, Sir Hans Sloane. In addition, the Public Record Office of Northern Ireland has in its possession Hutchinson's account and commonplace books for the 1720s and 1730s, a long with his will and a manuscript copy of his highly influential Anglican catechism, written in Irish and English, and published in Belfast in 1722.

Tracing his life from his relatively humble origins to the splendour of the Irish episcopacy, this book will suggest that Hutchinson dedicated his life firstly to protecting the position of the established Church within society, and secondly to forging and maintaining the political hegemony of the Whig and Hanoverian regime, first in England and then in Ireland. It will be suggested that the way he defended these ideals and institutions was in the manner of a moderate, principled, career-minded, Latitudinarian-Whig reformer.[10] Furthermore, it was this outlook that fuelled his third main concern in life, the social and economic improvement of Ireland.

The second son of Edward Hitchinsonne (b. 1625) and Mary Tallents, Francis Hitchinson was born on 2 January 1660 and baptised six days later at St Margaret's church, Carsington.[11] Carsington was a

---

[9] Ibid.
[10] In the post-Revolution Church of England, Latitudinarians were a relatively small group of influential clergymen closely associated with promoting the new science, the Whig interest and rational religion.
[11] Carsington Parish Register, 1592–1640 (Derbyshire Record Office [hereafter D.R.O.], Church of England parish registers, D2681, A/PI 1/1); Carsington Parish Register, 1653–1701 (D.R.O., Church of England parish registers, D2681, A/PI 1/2). Before the 1680s, the Hutchinson family name is spelled as either Hitchinsonne or Hitchinson in the Carsington parish registers.

rural hamlet that lay in a wooded valley in the midst of one of the most populous, industrially developed and prosperous areas of Derbyshire.[12] Francis had three brothers and three sisters: John (b. 1655, d. 1689); Phillip (b. 1664, d. 1677); Samuel (b. 1666, d. 1748); Sarah (b. 1654, d. 1654); Mary (b. 1657, d. 1732); and Ellinor (b. 1662).[13] Their father, Edward, was the son of a husbandsman, William Hitchinsonne, who, like his son and grandchildren, was born in Carsington.[14]

Details of Hutchinson's education remain a mystery. However, in 1677, he matriculated as a pensioner at St Catharine Hall, Cambridge. He gained a BA there in 1681 and an MA three years later. He was ordained deacon in 1683 and priest in 1684. His first clerical appointment was as lecturer or reader in the parish of Widdington, Essex. In 1688, he was made rector of Quendon, Essex, before being appointed to the vicarage of Hoxne in Suffolk in 1691 and the perpetual curacy of St James', Bury St Edmunds, Suffolk, in 1692. In 1706 he became rector of Passenham, Northamptonshire.[15]

In his main parish of residence from 1692 to 1720, St James' in Bury St Edmunds, Hutchinson was a model pastor. He initiated and sustained a programme of pastoral improvement there in conjunction with the Society for Promoting Christian Knowledge (S.P.C.K.), for whom he was the corresponding member for the County of Suffolk between 1700 and 1721. Hutchinson's Low-Church Latitudinarianism informed his theology, his attitude to the problem of Protestant Dissent and the part he played, while diocesan proctor for the archdeaconry of Suffolk and Sudbury, in the politically charged 1701–2 session of the Convocation of Canterbury (the national synod of the Church of England).[16]

A prolific and accomplished author, his pen was mainly utilised in defence of the Whig party: he not only supported the Whig stance on the great party issues of the day, but used his longer tracts to promulgate

---

[12] Gladwyn Turbett, *A history of Derbyshire* (3 vols, London, 1999), iii, 1132–53.
[13] Carsington Parish Register, 1653–1701 (D.R.O., D2681, A/PI 1/2); Carsington Parish Register, 1687–1719 (D.R.O., Church of England parish registers, D2681, A/PI 1/3); Bernard Burke, *A genealogical and heraldic dictionary of the peerage and baronetage of the British Empire* (London, 1856); Bishop Francis Hutchinson's commonplace book, 1721–30 (P.R.O.N.I., Down Diocesan Papers, MS DIO/1/22/1, p. 4 [1st pagination]). This commonplace book is split into three sections and has a peculiar pattern of pagination: the first section has no pagination, whilst the middle section has its own pagination, as does the final section. Thus, in order to avoid confusion, the first section is referred to as unpaginated, the second section as 1st pagination and the third section as 2nd pagination.
[14] Carsington Parish Register, 1592–1640 (D.R.O., D2681, A/PI 1/1).
[15] See Chapter 1.
[16] See Chapter 2.

mainstream Whig ideology and anti-Catholic propaganda. The *Historical essay*, for example, was in part a defence of the 'Whiggish' social and cultural ideology of politeness and sociability. After the Hanoverian succession, his reputation as a dependable Whig and the patronage of the influential ensured his swift rise through the ranks of the clergy. He was successively appointed royal chaplain in 1715 and Bishop of Down and Connor in 1720 by George I, on the recommendation of leading Whig ministers and ecclesiastical advisers.[17]

In Ireland, Hutchinson continued to defend the Whig and Hanoverian regime. Almost immediately he embarked on a crusade to neutralise the threat he believed the Catholic majority posed to it by trying to convert them, over a nine-year period, to Protestantism, using, primarily, the medium of Irish. After these schemes failed, he returned to his earlier career as a Whig apologist, exchanging blows with their then parliamentary opposition, the Irish 'patriot' party, both in print and in the Irish House of Lords. Hutchinson was also among a small group of pamphleteering and projecting clergy and landowners dedicated to the social, cultural and economic improvement of Ireland.[18]

Hutchinson married three times. Some time before 1701, he married Dame Mary Crofts Read, widow of Sir Charles Crofts Read of Berdwell in Suffolk and daughter to Sir Thomas Hewit of St Martin's and Margaret Hillersdon (daughter of Sir William Lytton of Knebworth).[19] After the death of Dame Mary, Hutchinson married Peregrine North (widow of William Hanmer of Hawsted, Suffolk) in Bury St Edmunds on 15 April 1707. He took a third wife, Anne, at an unknown date, but probably before he left for Ireland in 1721. Anne was the sister of the wife of Anthony Chapman of Newport Pagnell, Buckinghamshire, and aunt of Rev. Robert Chapman and of Mrs Judith Chapman. Anne died at an advanced age on 14 September 1758 in Grafton Street, Dublin. Francis and Anne were parents to one daughter, Frances, and one son, Thomas, who predeceased his father.[20]

---

[17] See chapters 3 and 6.
[18] See chapters 6, 7 and 8.
[19] Thomas Tarver and his wife Bridget vs. Richard Thelwall, 1710 (The National Archives, Kew [hereafter T.N.A.], Records of Exchequer, E134/9Anne/TRIN10); Nathaniel Salmon, *The history of Hertfordshire, describing the county, and its antient monuments, particularly the Roman* . . . (London, 1728), p. 261.
[20] [Ulster Historical Foundation] *Clergy of Down and Dromore* (Belfast, 1996), part 2, p. 21; Sir Stephen Leslie (ed.), *Dictionary of national biography* [hereafter OldDNB] (63 vols, Oxford, 1885–1901), x, 338–9; Sir John Cullum, *The history and antiquities of Hawsted, in the county of Suffolk* . . . (London, 1784), p. 70.

Hutchinson died on 25 June 1739. He was buried two days later under the chancel at the Portglenone chapel of ease, which he had built at his own expense a few years earlier.[21] The fact that he did not want to have his body sent back to Derbyshire, unlike his sister Mary, whose body was exhumed and sent to England in 1732, attests to the affection he had for his new homeland.[22]

---

[21] R. M. Sibbet, *On the shining Bann, records of an Ulster manor, for all touring in Northern Ireland* (Belfast, 1928), pp. 171–4.

[22] Hutchinson's commonplace book, 1721–30 (P.R.O.N.I., MS DIO/1/22/1, p. 4 [1st pagination]).

Part I
England

1

Childhood and early career, 1660–c.1690

The biographical articles of nineteenth-century reference works (and subsequent revised editions) such as the *Dictionary of national biography* have been the only guides available to those interested in Hutchinson's early clerical career and family background.[1] Despite the fact that his life before 1700 is sparsely covered by the extant primary source material,[2] it is nonetheless possible to expand on what has already been written in order to throw more light on the social status and political leanings of Hutchinson and his family in the late seventeenth century. This, in turn, provides a background for the examination of Hutchinson's religious and political outlook as well as his clerical career after the Glorious Revolution, subjects discussed at length in chapters 2 and 3.[3]

I

During the course of his life, Hutchinson's father, Edward, became a relatively wealthy yeoman farmer and can be regarded as being of the

---

[1] Bernard Burke, *Genealogical and heraldic dictionary*; J. and J. A. Venn, *Alumni Cantabrigienses: A biographical list of all known students, graduates and holders of office at the University of Cambridge, from the earliest times to 1900*, part 1 (4 vols, Cambridge, 1922–7), iii, 169; Leslie, *OldDNB*, x, pp. 338–9; Toby Barnard, 'Hutchinson, Francis (1660–1739)' in H. C. G. Matthew and Brian Harrison (eds), *Oxford dictionary of national biography* (Oxford, 2004), hereafter *OxDNB*.

[2] In contrast to his later life, he was not a member of any society or official body and had only penned two sermons: Francis Hutchinson, *A sermon preached at Beccles in Suffolk before the Right Reverend Father in God, John, Lord Bishop of Norwich, at the second session of his Lordship's primary visitation held there, May 27. 1692. By Francis Hutchinson, M.A. vicar of Hoxne. Imprimatur, Aug. 3. 1692* (London, 1692) and *A sermon preached at the publick commencement at Cambridge. Sunday in the afternoon July iij 1698. By Francis Hutchinson, D.D. preacher at St James's in Bury St Edmunds* (Cambridge, 1698). Furthermore, there is no extant correspondence written by or about Hutchinson before 1700.

[3] For biographical details of the Hutchinson family of Carsington, Derbyshire, see Introduction, pp. 3–6.

'middling' rank in seventeenth-century English society. Yeoman status was usually afforded to those who farmed more than 50 acres, although the actual amount worked varied greatly. Lesser yeoman farmers earned between £40 and £50 a year, but their wealthy counterparts could earn between £100 and £200. Husbandsmen, like Edward's father, usually farmed between 5 and 50 acres and fell below the country gentry, urban professionals and yeomanry in the social hierarchy but above the mass of the common people, which included labourers and cottagers. An early seventeenth-century husbandsman who ploughed 30 acres of land could be expected to earn an annual net profit of £14 or £15.[4]

Unfortunately, probate inventories for Edward Hutchinson are no longer extant. It is thus hard to gauge his wealth with any real accuracy. In a deposition taken in 1696 (by the clerk of a commission of local gentlemen empowered to examine a tithe dispute between the minister of Carsington, Nathaniel Boothouse, and a wealthy Presbyterian farmer and lead merchant, Robert Heaward), Samuel Hutchinson, Francis's younger brother and one of the deponents called by the commission, was described as a yeoman. He is also recorded as having stated to the clerk that he was, at the start of the dispute in 1692, still living with his father and managing several lands for him.[5] The deposition fails to mention the acreage of land that Samuel worked and his father owned.

The hearth-tax returns of Michaelmas 1664 for Hopton and Carsington, which both lay in Wirksworth hundred, state that Edward Hutchinson (or Hutcheson as it is spelled in the returns) paid tax on two hearths. This indicates that he owned property commensurate with the income of a moderately wealthy yeoman.[6] The hearth-tax revenue was first granted by Parliament to Charles II in 1662 and was levied, except for those exempt due to poverty, at a rate of 2 shillings per annum for every hearth-fire or stove. Occupiers taxed on one hearth were likely to be poor craftsmen, husbandsmen or the labouring poor; those liable for two or three hearths were usually craftsmen, tradesmen or yeoman farmers.[7]

The Hutchinsons were not only of the middling sort, but also communicants of the Church of England. Francis's father was even sworn in as churchwarden in St Margaret's parish in Carsington on 11 March

---

[4] Keith Wrightson, *English Society, 1580–1680* (6th edn, London, 2000), pp. 27–33.
[5] Depositions: Nathaniel Boothouse vs Robert Hayward, 1696 (T.N.A., Records of Exchequer, E134/8WM3/EAST 11).
[6] *Derbyshire hearth tax assessments 1662–70*, ed. David G. Edwards (Chesterfield, 1982), p. 195.
[7] Roger Fieldhouse, 'The hearth tax and other records' in Alan Rogers (ed.), *Group projects in local history* (Kent, 1977), pp. 72–3, 80.

1656.[8] Nonetheless, Francis Hutchinson and his brother Samuel were on friendly terms with members of the Derbyshire Protestant dissenting community, which was unusually large in that part of the county where Carsington lay.[9] Between 1694 and 1696, Samuel, along with his cousin John Hutchinson, submitted several depositions supporting Heaward's refusal to pay tithes to Boothouse.[10]

Francis Hutchinson himself was close to his maternal uncle, Francis Tallents, the celebrated historian and ejected Puritan minister, who directed his historical studies and whom he regarded as a 'man of great sincerity'.[11] In the early 1680s, when Hutchinson was still studying at Cambridge, Tallents sent his nephew a draft copy of his series of chronological tables, *A view of universal history* (1685), which Tallents had began writing in the 1640s for the use of his pupils at Magdalene college, Cambridge.[12] Tallents had given Hutchinson instructions to 'take a copy of the chief parts of it' to be a guide to him in 'reading history'.[13] When the time came for it to be published, Tallents sent Hutchinson with copies of it to be proofread by Dr William Beveridge, later Bishop of St Asaph, Dr Richard Kidder, later Bishop of Bath and Wells, and Dr Edward Stillingfleet, later Bishop of Worcester.[14]

Given the attitude of Hutchinson and his brother to Protestant dissenters it is highly likely they became supporters of the Whigs, when, during the Exclusion crisis of 1679–81, that party was formed and became associated with both the toleration of non-conformity and the exclusion of James, Duke of York, from his title to the thrones of the kingdoms of Ireland, Scotland and England. Hutchinson bragged about his Whig heritage in 1720, when trying to persuade the chief ecclesiastical adviser to the Whig ministry and George I – the Archbishop of Canterbury, William Wake – that he was politically acceptable to the new Whig and

---

[8] Carsington parish register, 1653–1701 (D.R.O., D2681, A/PI 1/2).

[9] Richard Clark, 'Anglicanism, recusancy and Dissent in Derbyshire 1603–1730' (PhD thesis, Oxford University, 1980), pp. 1–29, 172, 208–12.

[10] Nathaniel Boothouse vs Robert Hayward, 1695 (T.N.A., Records of Exchequer, E134/6&7WM3/ HIL15); Nathaniel Boothouse vs Robert Hayward, 1694 (T.N.A., Records of Exchequer, E134/6W&M/ MICH10); Nathaniel Boothouse vs Robert Hayward, 1696 (T.N.A., Records of Exchequer E134/8Wm3/ East 11); Carsington Parish Register, 1653–1701 (D.R.O., D2681, A/PI 1/2).

[11] Francis Hutchinson, *A Defence of the antient historians: with a particular application of it to the history of Ireland and Great-Britain* (Dublin, 1734), p. 33. The introduction to this book was published the year before as Francis Hutchinson, *A Defence of the antient historians: with a particular application of it to the history of Ireland and Great-Britain* (Dublin, 1733).

[12] Ibid., p. 33; C. D. Gilbert, 'Tallents, Francis (1619–1708)' in *OxDNB*.

[13] Hutchinson, *Defence of antient historians*, p. 33.

[14] Ibid., p. 34.

Hanoverian regime and thus worthy of high preferment: 'I have been steady in the true interest of king and nation from the begginning of my life, as my father and friends were before me'.[15]

II

The fact that Hutchinson was admitted a 'pensioner' to Cambridge in 1677 – and neither a 'sizar' nor a 'fellow commoner' – lends weight to the assertion made earlier that his family were of the middling sort. The fact that they could pay for their son to attend university also attests to their secure financial position. This was, after all, a time when a university education was becoming increasingly expensive. He matriculated the following year, graduating BA in 1681 and MA in 1684.[16] In common with the majority of prospective clerical candidates in this period, Hutchinson had stayed on at university to take his MA in order to increase his career prospects and bridge the gap between receiving his BA and reaching the legal age at which one could enter deacon's orders, which was 24. The Cambridge MA contained more theology than the undergraduate degree, which specialised in ancient and modern philosophy, literature, geometry, rhetoric and astronomy. Owing to the rising costs of university fees in the latter half of the seventeenth century, it was usually students from the gentry and professional middling orders who took an MA.[17]

Hutchinson's affiliation with Cambridge did not end with completion of the MA; in July 1698 he commenced DD.[18] Doctorates in that period were conferred on those who had either completed some formal written exercises or had been recently elevated to a senior position in the Church. Consequently, the award of a DD fails to give much indication to historians of the intellectual powers of the recipient.[19] As Hutchinson was still of the lower clergy in 1698, it is highly likely that he gained his doctorate through scholarly exertion rather than the exercise of

---

[15] Francis Hutchinson to William Wake, 14 April 1720 (Christ Church, Oxford [hereafter C.C.], Wake Letters, vol. 21, no. 215).

[16] Venn, *Alumni Cantabrigienses*, iii, 169; William Gibson, *A social history of the domestic chaplain, 1530–1840* (London, 1997), p. 65.

[17] John H. Pruett, *The parish clergy under the later Stuarts: the Leicestershire experience* (Illinois, 1978), pp. 39–41; Geoffrey Holmes, *Augustan England: professions, state and society, 1680–1750* (London, 1982), p. 85; Norman Sykes, *Church and state in England in the eighteenth century* (Cambridge, 1934), p. 196.

[18] Venn, *Alumni Cantabrigienses*, iii, 169.

[19] Vivien Barrie-Curien, 'Clerical recruitment and career patterns in the Church of England during the eighteenth century' in W. M. Jacob and Nigel Yates (eds), *Crown and mitre, religion and society in northern Europe since the Reformation* (Suffolk, 2003), p. 102.

patronage. Furthermore, the sermon that he delivered at his commencement was deemed worthy of publication.[20] Hutchinson was extremely proud of this sermon and 36 years after it was first published he reprinted it at the back of the *Defence of the antient historians* (1734).[21]

III

While still at Cambridge, Hutchinson was ordained deacon (on 23 September 1683) and then priest (on 24 February 1684) by the Bishop of London, Henry Compton.[22] This unusually rapid progression from university to deacon to priest was the result of having a lecturer's position waiting for him in the rectory of Widdington, which lay in the county of Essex and constituted part of the Diocese of London.[23] The 33rd Canon of the Canons of 1604 stated that a Bishop had to be satisfied that a prospective ordinand had a title to a living before he could be ordained.[24] It was Hutchinson's association with fellow St Catharine's pensioner, Thomas Twisleton, that gained him this appointment.[25] Twisleton was the nephew of the lay patron of Widdington, John Turner of Widdington Hall, Essex. Twisleton was instituted rector of the parish of Widdington on 25 March 1684.[26] Hutchinson was appointed lecturer two months later, on 7 May 1684.[27]

In that period rectors received for themselves the goods or money yielded from the greater tithes, which, Geoffrey Holmes suggested, made the country rectory for many Anglican parsons 'the height of their ambition'.[28] The pastoral duties laid upon rector, vicar and perpetual curate were virtually the same but most vicars received, along with their stipend, the small tithes attached to the living. Vicars also received fees for performing christenings, burials, and marriages and from rents collected

---

[20] Hutchinson, *Sermon preached . . . 3 July 1698*.
[21] Hutchinson, *Defence of antient historians*, pp. 224–64.
[22] Bishop of London's ordination registers, 1675–1809 (Guildhall Library, Diocese of London records, MS 9535/3, fos. 37, 39–40).
[23] Consistory Court records (Corporation of London, London Metropolitan Archives, Diocese of London records, DL/C/345, fo. 239ʳ).
[24] Sykes, *Church and state*, p. 199.
[25] Venn, *Alumni Cantabrigienses*, iv, 282.
[26] Richard Newcourt, *Repertorium ecclesiasticum parochiale Londienense: an ecclesiastical parochial history of the diocese of London* (2 vols, London, 1708–10), ii, 661; Phillip Morant, *The history of and antiquities of the county of Essex* (2 vols, London, 1768), ii, 566–7.
[27] Consistory court records (Corporation of London, London Metropolitan Archives, Diocese of London records, DL/C/345), fo. 239ʳ.
[28] Holmes, *Augustan England*, p. 97.

from glebe lands. Perpetual curates were licensed by their Bishop, but were normally nominated and paid a stipend by the impropriator or lay rector. These curates were perpetual in the sense that only their Bishop could remove them from their livings. Stipendiary curates were appointed by the incumbent of the living, who was responsible for their stipend. Temporary curates or lecturers were paid and employed by a rector or vicar to assist them.[29] By the late seventeenth or early eighteenth century, 17% of vicarages and rectories were worth under £50 a year, 60% between £80 and £200, and 13% were worth £200 or more. In most areas of England, £50 to £80 a year was the minimum amount needed to maintain the lifestyle of a member of the middling sort, while an income of £200 or above placed one within the ranks of the lesser gentry.[30]

Most assistant or stipendiary curates in the late seventeenth or early eighteenth century were paid between £30 and £40 per annum.[31] The rectory of Widdington gave Twisleton a healthy annual income. The holder was still liable to pay first fruits and tenths, meaning that the living was worth more than £50 per year. In 1704, in attempt to tackle the problem of clerical poverty, Parliament passed the Bounty Act, exempting incumbents whose livings were worth less than £50 per year from paying first fruits and tenths. First fruits and tenths were ecclesiastical taxes, which the government had been collecting from the clergy since the reign of Henry VIII.[32] Hutchinson's lecturer's position, on the other hand, represented the very bottom rung on the ladder of preferment and thus is likely to have afforded him an income even lower than that of a curate.[33]

The fact that Twisleton was appointed rector over Hutchinson is not surprising. At that time the Anglican clergy was an overcrowded and extremely competitive profession, with the supply of graduates seeking presentment constantly outstripping the number of available livings of even the most moderate means. Connection and nobility of birth were the two main characteristics that marked out the winners from the losers in the lottery of preferment in that period. As a result, many young clergymen of noble birth and good connection went straight from priest's

---

[29] J. S. Purvis, *An introduction to ecclesiastical records* (London, 1953), pp. 17–19.

[30] Donald Spaeth, *The Church in an age of danger: parsons and parishioners, 1660–1740* (Cambridge, 2000), pp. 35, 38–40.

[31] Ibid., p. 38.

[32] John Ecton, *Liber valuorum and decimarum thesaurus rerum ecclesiasticarum: being an account of the valuations of all the ecclesiastical benefices . . . in England and Wales, as they now stand chargeable with, or lately were discharged from the payment of first-fruits and tenths* (London, 1728), p. 216.

[33] Holmes, *Augustan England*, pp. 83–6, 90–1, 95.

orders to good country rectories or wealthy vicarages, whilst a lucky few gained high office straight away. Those of low birth or little connection were usually left to fight over the curate's and lecturer's positions.[34]

Hutchinson remained lecturer at Widdington until 13 July 1688, when John Turner, obviously content that Hutchinson's character and abilities were adequate for the undertaking, presented him to the rectory of Quendon, a parish that lay within the Diocese of London and the county of Essex.[35] The parishes of Quendon and Widdington both formed part of Turner's two estates, those of Widdington Hall and Newham Hall.[36] In the late seventeenth and early eighteenth centuries, most lay patrons were of lesser gentry stock and usually were able to present ministers only to the two or three parishes that lay within their estates.[37] Quendon was the lesser of the two livings controlled by Turner, as it was exempt from payment of first fruits, being worth less than £50 a year. It nonetheless represented a vast improvement on the income of his previous position.[38]

Hutchinson served the parish of Quendon until early 1691, when he resigned his post in order to become vicar of Hoxne in Suffolk.[39] Canon law forbade the holding of two benefices that were more than 30 miles apart or lay in different dioceses.[40] He was presented to the vicarage of Hoxne by its lay patron, William Maynard – eldest son of a confirmed Tory, Baron Maynard – and was instituted and inducted to it on 12 February 1691.[41] William Maynard was of the Whig interest; his son, Thomas Maynard, became Whig MP for the constituencies of Eye (1710–15) and West Looe (1715–22).[42] It is likely that it was Hutchinson's political acceptability that attracted the patronage, which lasted well into the next century, of the Whiggish Maynard. There is

---

[34] Ibid., p. 97.

[35] Newcourt, *Repertorium ecclesiasticum*, ii, 477. Newcourt actually states that Hutchinson took up the rectory of Quendon on 13 July 1668. The year is an obvious typographical error.

[36] Morant, *Essex*, ii, 566–7, 581.

[37] W. M. Jacob, *Lay people and religion in the early eighteenth century* (Cambridge, 1996), pp. 28, 23.

[38] John Ecton, *Liber valorum and decimarum; being an account of the valuations and yearly tenths of all such ecclesiastical benefices in England and Wales, as now stand chargeable with the payment of first-fruits and tenths* . . . (London, 1711), p. 233.

[39] Quendon parish registers of baptisms, marriages and burials, 1687–1735 (Essex Record Office [hereafter E.R.O.], Parish Records, D/P 269/1/1); Archdeaconry of Colchester, visitations, 1685–90 (E.R.O., Archdeaconry Records, D/AC/V10).

[40] Sykes, *Church and state*, p. 148.

[41] Consignation book, 1692 (Norfolk Record Office [hereafter N.R.O.], Norwich diocese, visitation records, DN/VSC 4/8, fo. 47); Eveline Cruickshanks, David William Hayton and Stuart Handley, *The House of Commons, 1690–1715* (5 vols, London, 2002), iv, 779.

[42] Cruickshanks, Hayton and Handley, *The House of Commons, 1690–1715*, ii, 548; idem, iv, 779–80.

certainly no evidence of any personal connection between the two men before 1691. It is also improbable that Maynard would have appointed a man deep in Tory or High-Church notions, especially at a time when politics was becoming increasingly polarised across party lines.[43]

Furthermore, despite having been educated at Cambridge at a time when it was becoming a seminary for High-Churchmen,[44] he was nonetheless by this time a professed Whig.[45] The question also has to be mooted as to whether a Low-Church Whig, such as the newly appointed Bishop of Norwich, John Moore, would have asked Hutchinson to preach a sermon on the occasion of his primary visitation if he had been a High-Church Tory.[46] Hutchinson's sermon also exemplifies the new sermon style favoured by Latitudinarians in the later seventeenth and early eighteenth centuries.[47] If Maynard, or indeed Moore, were in any doubt in the 1690s as to Hutchinson's commitment to the Low-Church Whig cause, this would be vanquished during succeeding decades by his political activism.[48]

Upon appointment to the parish of Hoxne, Hutchinson immediately took up residence in a small cottage he rented there.[49] Hoxne at that time was a remote country parish, with about 127 households supported by an agrarian economy.[50] The two livings that Maynard controlled, and in turn presented Hutchinson to, lay on his estates of Hoxne Hall in Suffolk and Passenham in Northamptonshire, of which more will be said later.[51] Hoxne was a relatively poor living, which in common with Quendon was exempt from payment of first fruits and tenths.[52] A year

---

[43] See Chapter 3 for a discussion of the politics of party in late seventeenth- and early eighteenth-century England.

[44] John Gascoigne, *Cambridge in the age of Enlightenment: science, religion and politics from the Restoration to the French Revolution* (Cambridge, 1989), pp. 27–30, 33, 39.

[45] See pp. 11–12 above.

[46] Hutchinson, *Sermon preached . . . 27 May 1692*; Peter Meadows, 'Moore, John (1646–1714)' in OxDNB.

[47] See Chapter 2, pp. 27–9.

[48] See chapters, 2, 3, 6 and 7.

[49] Consignation book, 1691 (N.R.O., Norwich diocese, visitation records, DN/VIS 9/1); Bishop Francis Hutchinson's commonplace book, 1731–9 (Church of Ireland, Down and Connor, Diocesan Registry, Belfast [hereafter D.R.], un-pressmarked), p. 495; Francis Hutchinson to Bishop John Moore, 16 June 1694 (County Record Office, Cambridge, letter book of originals addressed to Dr John Moore, 17/C1).

[50] *A survey of Suffolk parish history: east Suffolk*, Vol. 1, A-H (Ipswich, 1990), Hoxne.

[51] Richard Romney Sedgwick, *The history of Parliament: the House of Commons, 1715–54* (2 vols, London, 1970), ii, 249.

[52] John Ecton, *Valor beneficiorum, or a valuation of all ecclesiastical preferments in England and Wales to which is added, a collection of choice presidents, relating to ecclesiastical affairs* (London, 1695), p. 304.

later, in early 1692, Hutchinson was presented to the perpetual curacy of St James' in Bury St Edmunds.⁵³ It is likely that Maynard helped Hutchinson get this position, probably as a way to compensate for the low income provided by Hoxne. Indeed, the promise of further patronage may have been the extra incentive Hutchinson needed to entice him to leave his low-paid Essex rectory to take up an equally low-paid living in Suffolk. The Maynards were firm friends of the Macros of Bury St Edmunds.⁵⁴ The head of the Macro family, Thomas Macro, was a vehement Whig, a wealthy apothecary and an influential member of the town corporation.⁵⁵ He was thus in a position to recommend Hutchinson be appointed. The corporation, the chief burgess and the aldermen of Bury St Edmunds, constituted the lay rectors for the two rectories of St James' and St Mary's. Unlike some lay rectors in this period, the corporation was extremely fair in its treatment of its curates, since the income from the small and large tithes amounted to little more than the £80 per annum they paid them.⁵⁶

Fairly soon after his appointment to St James', Hutchinson moved from Hoxne to Bury St Edmunds, a place where he lived and worked for the next for 28 years or so.⁵⁷ He bought a smart town house soon afterwards, which he sold in 1729 for £220 after renting it out for a number of years for £18 per annum.⁵⁸ Hutchinson had good reason to move to Bury St Edmunds. In the generation after the Glorious Revolution, even a relatively small town such as Bury St Edmunds – in common with all English resort towns in that period, and in contrast to Hoxne – was crowded with nobility and gentry, whose spending funded the service-based economy of the town. With their organised social life, broad

---

⁵³ Consignation book, 1692 (N.R.O., Norwich visitation records, DN/VSC 4/8, fo. 55ʳ).

⁵⁴ Susan Macro to her daughter, 20 Oct. 1715 (Suffolk Record Office, Bury [hereafter S.R.O. (B)], Transcripts of letters of Susan Macro to her daughter (1713–18), P733/1, p. 32); Susan Macro to her daughter, 7 June 1716 (S.R.O. (B), P733/1, p. 44); Susan Macro to her daughter, 4 Apr. 1717 (S.R.O. (B) P733/1, p. 56).

⁵⁵ Patricia E. Murrel, 'Suffolk: the political behaviour of the county and parliamentary borough from the Exclusion Crisis to the accession of the House of Hanover' (PhD thesis, University of Newcastle upon Tyne, 1982), p. 25.

⁵⁶ Francis Hutchinson, *A defence of the clergy's liberty, in the choice of their proctors for Convocation: . . . In a letter to the reverend the clergy of the archdeacon of Sudbury* (London, 1710), p. 9; Browne Willis, *Parochiale Anglicanum: or, the names of all the churches and chapels within the dioceses of Canterbury, Rochester, London, Winchester, Chichester, Norwich, Salisbury, Wells, Exeter, St David's, Landaff, Bangor, and St Asaph . . . With an account of most of their dedications, their patrons . . .* (London, 1733), p. 101.

⁵⁷ Hutchinson's life in Bury St Edmunds is explored in detail in chapters 2, 3 and 5.

⁵⁸ Hutchinson commonplace book, 1721–30 (P.R.O.N.I., MS DIO/1/22/1), p. 17 [1st pagination], p. 57 [2nd pagination].

streets and specialist shops, resort towns made for a society almost as 'polite' as that of London.⁵⁹

Although Hutchinson was now perpetual curate at St James', William Maynard had not forgotten him and he was instituted to the rectory of Passenham, in the Diocese of Peterborough, on 13 November 1706.⁶⁰ In accordance with canon law, he relinquished his other ecclesiastical living, Hoxne. He was allowed to remain in possession of his perpetual curacy in Bury St Edmunds because at that time curacies were not considered ecclesiastical benefices. The curate Hutchinson was employing to serve Hoxne for him, Nathaniel Frith, was, upon Hutchinson's appointment to Passenham, made vicar of Hoxne in early 1707 by Thomas Maynard.⁶¹

Passenham was a less valuable living than it appeared on paper. The court Whig and established Oxford scholar, Richard Meadowcourt, refused to take over the living when he was offered it in 1720 for this very reason.⁶² Hutchinson thus remained rector of the living until the vacancy was filled in 1727 by John Jenkins, another alumnus of St Catharine's College, Cambridge.⁶³ Meadowcourt explained to the then patron of the living, William Wake,⁶⁴ that the rectory was in theory worth £200 per annum but in practice yielded around £120 per annum, which was less than he earned from his fellowship at Merton college. The £80 deficit between the projected and actual income was due to a number of necessary expenses. Meadowcourt complained that the parish of Passenham was so 'unhealthy' that it made residence an impossibility, which in turn necessitated the employment of a curate.⁶⁵ The parish of Passenham consisted of 120 households by the early

---

⁵⁹ John James Raven, *History of Suffolk* (London, 1895), p. 239; Rosemary Sweet, *The English town 1680–1840: government, society and culture* (London, 1999), pp. 22–4, 194.

⁶⁰ Henry Isham Longdon, *Northamptonshire and Rutland clergy from 1500* (16 vols, Northampton, 1940), vii, 179.

⁶¹ Consignation book, 1706 (N.R.O., Norwich visitation records, DN/VSC 5/9).

⁶² Longdon, *Northamptonshire and Rutland clergy*, p. 179; Lord Hardwicke to Lord Carteret, 9 June 1721 (British Library [hereafter B.L.], Additional Manuscript [hereafter Add. MS] 36134, fo. 54); Hutchinson resigned the perpetual curacy of Bury St Edmunds in 1720: Historical Manuscripts Commission [hereafter H.M.C.], *14th Report*, appendix, Part VIII: The manuscripts of Lincoln, Bury St Edmunds, and Great Grimsby corporations; land of the deans and chapters of Worcester and Lichfield (London, 1895), p. 154.

⁶³ Longdon, *Northamptonshire and Rutland clergy*, vii, 9, 179.

⁶⁴ The right of presentment to a living passed from the patron (in this case William Maynard) to the crown if the last incumbent had been raised to the episcopate.

⁶⁵ Richard Meadowcourt to Archbishop William Wake, 18 May 1722 (C.C. Wake Letters, vol. 22, nos. 135–6).

eighteenth century, but the majority of the residents were extremely poor.[66] Hutchinson had chosen not to reside in Passenham and had paid his curate a respectable £40 per annum.[67] Meadowcourt argued that, because of Hutchinson's precedent, he too would have to pay his curate this amount or more, an expense he found particularly objectionable. He was also concerned that £40 per year had to be found to cover the cost of poor-relief taxes and 'the continual expense of keeping a very large, and ruinous house in repair'.[68]

The above exposition of Hutchinson's early life makes this by necessity the most impressionistic of all the chapters in this book. It is nonetheless fairly clear that his upbringing did much to shape his political and religious outlook as well as his career. Hutchinson's family may have been of relatively humble social standing, as part of the middling orders, but they were nonetheless wealthy enough to start their son on the road to a career in the Church by sending him to Cambridge University. However, this social status meant that his rapid progression from the deacon's orders to his first clerical appointment had to be bought with the coin of social connection that he himself had earned while at university. It was his diligence in his lowly position of lecturer of Widdington that persuaded the patron of this living to promote him to the, albeit poor, rectory of Quendon.

From 1691 onwards it was Hutchinson's political acceptability to a Whig patron, William Maynard, which ensured his steady rise in income and clerical status. During the two decades after the Glorious Revolution, Hutchinson was appointed to all of the livings under Maynard's control in Suffolk and Northamptonshire. Maynard also used his friendship with a leading member of the Bury St Edmunds town corporation to gain Hutchinson an attractive perpetual curacy there. Hutchinson's tolerant attitude to Protestant Dissenters and Whiggism, readily apparent in his numerous writings from the early eighteenth century, was likely to have been fostered during childhood and adolescence, as this was a political outlook shared by his family.

---

[66] 'Passenham' in *A history of the County of Northamptonshire: the hundred of Cleley* (2002), v, 208–45 (www.british-history.ac.uk/report.asp?compid=22787), accessed 24 April 2006.
[67] Richard Meadowcourt to Archbishop William Wake, 18 May 1722 (C.C., Wake Letters, vol. 22, nos. 135–6).
[68] Ibid.

2

The national Church in a Suffolk parish: St James', Bury St Edmunds, 1692–1720

The Church of England c.1689–c.1833: from toleration to Tractarianism is widely regarded as one of the best general surveys of the national Church in the long eighteenth century. One of its main contentions is that the Church of England in this period was a vigorous, dynamic and relatively well-run institution.[1] A complementary work, *The national Church in local perspective*, published ten years later, lent even more weight to this argument by demonstrating – through examination of a wide range of localities, from parish to county to principality – that regional and local diversity in this period affected almost every aspect of the national Church, from diocesan and parochial administration to how the clergy reacted to Catholic and Protestant Dissent, without that diversity destroying the Church's homogeneity, its effectiveness as an institution or its central position in the religious life of the nation. However little attention was paid in this survey, or indeed by church historians in general, to the plight of the national Church in Suffolk, at diocesan, county or parish level.[2]

This chapter aims to help fill this historiographical lacuna by examining the parish of St James', Bury St Edmunds between 1692 and 1720, when Hutchinson was perpetual curate. It suggests that, largely through his reforming efforts, the established Church in Bury St Edmunds was well run in terms of pastoral administration. It also vividly illustrates the way the directives of the national Church, formulated at the centre by

---

[1] John Walsh, Colin Haydon and Stephen Taylor (eds), *The Church of England c.1689 to c.1833: toleration to Tractarianism* (Cambridge, 1993) [hereafter *Toleration to Tractarianism*].

[2] Jeremy Gregory and Jeffrey S. Chamberlain (eds), *The national Church in local perspective: the Church of England and the regions, 1660–1800* (Cambridge, 2003).

national bodies such as the Society for Promoting Christian Knowledge (S.P.C.K.), were interpreted by reforming ministers such as Hutchinson.

I

By the time Hutchinson gained the perpetual curacy of St James' in Bury St Edmunds in 1692, he had been a lower clergyman for eight years. However, it is not until this time that primary material becomes full enough to allow the question to be posed: how well, and in what ways, did Hutchinson perform his clerical duty? Providing answers to this question will be the focus of this section. It will be argued below that Hutchinson was an exemplar of the reforming clergyman increasingly prevalent in post-Revolution England. Hutchinson was convinced that the best way to raise the status and authority of the Church of England in post-Toleration Act England was to draw Dissenters back into the Anglican fold. In true Low-Church fashion, he believed this could be accomplished by voluntary means, primarily through increased pastoral efforts on the part of parish clergy such as himself. His own pastoral improvement programme had two main elements: the provision of a high standard of public worship and the implementation of a number of educational strategies designed to increase popular understanding of the Anglican faith, both completed under the advice and supervision of the S.P.C.K. in London.

In the late seventeenth and early eighteenth century, a sense of 'calling' continued to draw young men into an extremely competitive profession, and most clergymen, at all levels, felt a sense of loyalty to the established Church.[3] This loyalty manifested itself in an almost universal commitment to protecting its authority and status, a task that seemed all the more urgent after the passing of the Toleration Act in 1689. This Act allowed six or seven hundred Protestant dissenting congregations to spring up in competition with the Church, which up to that point had enjoyed a legal monopoly over the religious life of the nation.[4] In the decades immediately following the Revolution, High- and Low-Churchmen

---

[3] Holmes, *Augustan England*, pp. 84–5.

[4] John Walsh and Stephen Taylor, 'Introduction: the Church and Anglicanism in the "long" eighteenth century' in Walsh, Haydon and Taylor, *Toleration to Tractarianism*, pp. 58–60; Gordon Rupp, *Religion in England 1688–1791* (Oxford, 1986), pp. 72–6; George Every, *The High-Church party, 1688–1718* (London, 1956), pp. 75–82; Geoffrey Holmes, *The trial of Dr Sacheverell* (Suffolk, 1973), pp. 21–8; G. V. Bennett, *Tory crisis in Church and state, 1688–1730: the career of Francis Atterbury, Bishop of Rochester* (Oxford, 1975), pp. 11–19; idem, 'Conflict in the Church' in G. Holmes (ed.), *Britain after the Glorious Revolution, 1689–1714* (London, 1978), pp. 162–5.

displayed a marked difference in their approach to the problem of Dissent.[5] As Stephen Taylor and John Walsh have argued, the adherents of the High-Church tradition were more ready to accept the need for the Church to 'attempt to retain what it could of its old coercive power, tightening up the discipline of the Church courts and curtailing the toleration of Dissenters to the bare minimum'.[6] On the other hand, they continue, Low-Churchmen were more likely to 'accept the Toleration Act as irrevocable and seek to win back dissidents by persuasion, through voluntary societies and missionizing'.[7] Different pastoral strategies were not the only differences that existed between High and Low-Churchmen, they could also hold divergent views on doctrine, worship and ecclesiology.[8]

Given his family's close ties with the Derbyshire dissenting community and given that he now lived in Suffolk, Hutchinson would have found it very difficult to ignore the problem of Dissent.[9] In the early eighteenth century it was an issue which dominated the political life of Suffolk, partly because it contained a disproportionately high number of Protestant non-conformists.[10] Its Catholic population was by contrast very small.[11] In the north of England, large, self-contained Catholic communities prospered, whereas in early eighteenth-century East Anglia Catholicism remained a non-conformity of the gentry.[12] Hutchinson's attitude to Protestant Dissent was essentially that of a Low-Church Whig. He was not only an unstinting supporter of the Toleration Act of 1689 and recognised the validity of other Reformed national Churches,[13] but he also supported voluntary rather than coercive methods as a way to combat the growth of Protestant Dissent. The clergy of the Church of England, he opined in 1707, must 'get ground of . . . draw over and gain upon our dessenters'.[14]

---

[5] Holmes, *Dr Sacheverell*, pp. 28–33.
[6] Walsh and Taylor, 'Introduction', p. 46.
[7] Ibid.
[8] Ibid., pp. 30, 36–41.
[9] See p. 11 above.
[10] See p. 56 below.
[11] See p. 34 below.
[12] B. Gordon Blackwood, 'Lancashire Catholics, Protestants and Jacobites during the 1715 rebellion' in *Recusant History*, xxii (1994), 49–50; Haydon, *Anti-Catholicism*, p. 77; Robert Hole, 'Devonshire Catholics, 1676–1688' in *Southern History*, xvi (1994), 87.
[13] See p. 67 below.
[14] Francis Hutchinson, *A sermon preached at St Edmund's-Bury, on the first of May, 1707. Being the day of thanksgiving for the union of England and Scotland* . . . (London, 1707), p. 16.

There were, in Hutchinson's view, two main ways to achieve this end: through increased pastoral effort on the part of the parish clergy and by the comprehension of moderate Dissenters achieved by altering and amending the Church's liturgy and canons. Comprehension had been raised in Parliament several times during the course of the 1660s, 1670s and 1680s, with little success. After the Glorious Revolution it became associated with Latitudinarian churchmen, especially newly appointed bishops such as John Tillotson, Archbishop of Canterbury, Edward Stillingfleet, Bishop of Worcester, and Gilbert Burnet, Bishop of Salisbury.[15] Latitudinarian support of comprehension was a consequence of a shared theological position.[16]

They believed that in order to promote greater unity among all Protestants, the established Church should concentrate on the essential doctrines of Christian religion that united rather than those which divided. These essentials, which were necessary for salvation, could be found in the Scriptures, with individuals being left to decide for themselves the validity of doctrinal inessentials. Latitudinarians also believed that the Scriptures were accessible to everyone, no matter what their training. Sacerdotalism, the elevation of the sacraments of the Church beyond what is warranted in the Bible, was frowned upon. Latitudinarians also mooted that faith should be founded on reason as well as revelation. How far a Latitudinarian was prepared to go to in the pursuit of this aim varied greatly. Benjamin Hoadly, Bishop of Worcester, and a small minority of clerical intellectuals were determined to strip away all doctrine that did not bear the examination of reason, leaving only the true essentials. Revealed religion, however, remained the standard rule of faith for most Latitudinarians, who were content to offer some latitude on accepted doctrine in order to stay within the realms of Christian orthodoxy, while avoiding controversial areas such as the truthfulness of the Trinity.[17]

---

[15] John Spurr, *The Post-Reformation: religion, politics and society in Britain 1603–1714* (Harlow, 2006), pp. 157, 165–6, 187–9, 204.

[16] For a study that challenges the notion that Latitudinarianism represented a definite theological position with definable principles and doctrines, see John Spurr, ' "Latitudinarianism" and the Restoration Church' in *Historical Journal*, xxxi, no. 1 (1988), 61–2.

[17] Every, *High-Church party*, pp. 2–3; Martin Fitzpatrick, 'Latitudinarianism at the parting of the ways: a suggestion' in Walsh, Haydon and Taylor (eds), *Toleration to Tractarianism*, pp. 209–13; John Gascoigne, 'Anglican latitudinarianism and political radicalism in the late eighteenth century' in *History*, lxxi (1986), 22–4; Margaret C. Jacob, *The Newtonians and the English Revolution, 1689–1720* (New York, 1976), pp. 15–21; Walsh and Taylor, 'Introduction', pp. 36–40.

Hutchinson was an advocate of comprehension as well as reasonable religion. He called for changes in the 'canons, articles, and laws' of the established Church to enable the 'the door of communion' to be opened 'as wide' as possible.[18] Unfortunately he gave no indication what form these changes should take, being convinced this was a decision best left 'to churches and councils, and law-makers'[19] and men 'favour'd with the ears and secrets of Princes'.[20] Although Christianity, he declared in 1718, had been 'so often and wonderfully attested both by miracles, and God's Providence', the 'apostle St Paul' nonetheless required men to 'be ready to render a reason' for their beliefs.[21] A moderate Latitudinarian, Hutchinson was willing to scrutinise some accepted doctrines, such as the existence of angels,[22] but regarded others, such as the Trinity, as being beyond the 'short plummet' of man's reason.[23] He even censured those hotter Latitudinarian intellectuals who did so.[24] However, rather than regard such men's activities as bordering on heretical as other High-Church clerics might have done, Hutchinson attributed their transgressions to over-zealous intellectual inquisitiveness:

> this age ... is very inquisitive about the truth of religion, and very prying into its foundations ... [and though] the enquiries that are made so frequently, and sometimes too irreverently, I am willing to hope, do not proceed from any aversion to religion ... but rather from its increase of learning, that dives and searches after the bottom of all things.[25]

Hutchinson, a hagiographer of Tillotson (*The Life of the Most Reverend Father in God John Tillotson* was published in 1717), was particularly concerned to refute allegations that Tillotson had been a Socinian or had in any way strayed outside the remits of the articles

---

[18] Francis Hutchinson, *A compassionate address to those papists, who will be prevail'd with to examine the cause for which they suffer. In five letters...* (London, 1716), p. 19.
[19] Ibid.
[20] Ibid., p. 20.
[21] Francis Hutchinson, *An historical essay concerning witchcraft with observations upon matters of fact; tending to clear the texts of the sacred Scriptures, and confute the vulgar errors about that point. And also two sermons: one in proof of the Christian religion; the other concerning good and evil angels* (1st edn, London, 1718), p. 231.
[22] Hutchinson, *Historical essay*, Sermon II: Concerning angels, pp. 255–7.
[23] Francis Hutchinson, *The certainty of Protestants a safer foundation than the infallibility of Papists* (Dublin, 1738), p. 19.
[24] Francis Hutchinson, *Advices concerning the manner of receiving popish converts, and encouraging both priests and others to live in unity with the Church of Ireland... In a letter to a reverend clergy-man of the diocese of Down and Connor* (Dublin, 1729), pp. 9–10.
[25] Hutchinson, *Historical essay*, Sermon I: The Christian religion demonstrated, p. 231.

and liturgy of the established Church.[26] Hutchinson also defended Tillotson against High-Church claims that he had dispensed the sacrament of Holy Communion to seated communicants only. He suggested that such practices were a matter of individual choice, as the Scriptures did not specify the way in which the sacraments were to be administered.[27] This critique of sacerdotalism may have been rooted in the fact that Hutchinson saw it as a further obstacle to comprehension. Stillingfleet was certainly convinced that making those taking communion kneel made comprehension more difficult.[28]

Increased pastoral effort by the parish clergy was also generally regarded as an effective way to draw Dissenters back into the Anglican fold. In the decades immediately following the Glorious Revolution, it was a common concern of High- and Low-Church men alike to raise pastoral standards. In stark contrast to comprehension, which was the province of the Low-Churchman, even High-Churchmen saw the benefit of pastoral reform as a way to deal with Dissent and raise the authority of the established Church in society.[29] Furthermore, as Gregory points out, the 'clergy saw themselves as continuing, and in some cases fulfilling, the Reformation ideals of spreading Anglicanism and Christianity to the "dark corners of the land".'[30]

Hutchinson was not content to advise others to do what he would not do himself and consequently threw himself into the task of pastoral improvement in his parish. His improvement programme took two main forms. Firstly, he set out to provide an extremely high standard of public worship, which by contemporaneous standards was reached by maintaining regular services and Holy Communions, and through the delivery of regular sermons. The canonical standard of public worship in England and Wales was that of two services on a Sunday, which

---

[26] Francis Hutchinson, *The life of the Most Reverend Father in God John Tillotson... Compiled from the minutes of the Reverend Mr. Young... with many curious memoirs communicated by the late Right Reverend Gilbert, Lord Bishop of Sarum* (London, 1717), pp. 9–10, 22–3, 53. This volume of 84 pages should not be confused with another version, issued in the same year by the same publisher (E. Curll), but printed in larger type, containing 221 pages and a few corrections and additions.

[27] Ibid., pp. 8–9.

[28] John Marshall, 'The ecclesiology of the latitude-men 1660–1689:Stillingfleet, Tillotson and "Hobbism"' in *Journal of Ecclesiastical History*, xxxvi (1985), 419.

[29] Jeremy Gregory, *Restoration, reformation and reform, 1660–1828: archbishops of Canterbury and their diocese* (Oxford, 2000), pp. 234, 91, 233, 283–4. For a study that stresses the partisanship of the issue of pastoral and clerical reform, see Donald Spaeth, '"The enemy within": the failure of reform in the diocese of Salisbury in the eighteenth century' in Gregory and Chamberlain, *The national Church in local perspective*, pp. 121–44.

[30] Gregory, *Restoration, reformation and reform*, p. 234.

included a sermon in the morning and prayers at evensong. Although most parishes did indeed provide Sunday services, this ideal was not met in many places. In the Diocese of London, for example, only 50 per cent of parishes offered two services. The canons also stated that Communion had to be administered at least three times a year, a target most English parishes easily reached. It was also seen as part of the duty of a eighteenth-century cleric to lead a moral and pious life since this was perceived as one of the main ways in which the clergy could teach their flocks morality and virtue.[31] Consequently, moral lapses such as drunkenness, profanity, fornication and gambling were dealt with by the bishop at his visitations.[32] During the eighteenth century, the visitation process was increasingly used by archbishops and bishops to monitor pastoral provision, as well as to shape the structure of the Church in their dioceses.[33] In the Diocese of Norwich in the eighteenth century, a primary visitation was called by each new bishop and every seven years thereafter.[34]

In April 1701, Hutchinson wrote to the S.P.C.K. in London to inform them that he was maintaining 'monthly sacraments'.[35] Towns were more likely to have frequent communions than small villages, simply because they possessed larger congregations and so there was a higher demand.[36] Unfortunately, there are no extant records to establish exactly how frequent church services were in Bury St Edmunds between 1692 and 1720. However, the available evidence suggests that Hutchinson provided regular services. Extant visitation and Act books of successive bishops of Norwich (John Moore and Charles Trimnell) show that Hutchinson was never presented to his bishop by a churchwarden for neglect. Furthermore, on the rare occasion that Hutchinson had to attend court to fulfil his chaplaincy duties, he ensured that Dr Cox Macro assisted his curate in running his Sunday service.[37]

---

[31] Taylor and Walsh, 'Introduction', p. 14; Spaeth, *Church in an age of danger*, p. 109; J. Gregory and J. S. Chamberlain, 'National and local perspectives on the Church of England in the long eighteenth century' in *The national Church in local perspective*, p. 21.

[32] Spaeth, *Church in an age of danger*, pp. 112–32.

[33] Jeremy Gregory, 'Archbishops of Canterbury, their diocese, and the shaping of the National Church' in Gregory and Chamberlain, *The national Church in local perspective*, p. 41.

[34] W. M. Jacob, 'Church and society in Norfolk, 1700–1800' in ibid., p. 180.

[35] Francis Hutchinson to John Chamberlayne, 25 Apr. 1701 (Cambridge University Library [hereafter C.U.L.], S.P.C.K. records, Correspondence, 1699–1701, p. 286).

[36] W. M. Jacob, *Lay people and religion in the early eighteenth century* (Cambridge, 1996), pp. 60–1.

[37] Thomas Macro to John Wilson, 2 Aug. 1716 (S.R.O. (B), P733/1, p. 46); Susan Macro to her daughter, 20 Sept. 1716 (S.R.O. (B), P733/1, p. 48); Nicholas Clagett to Cox Macro, 29 Oct. (BL, Add. MS 32556, fo. 144); see p. 32 below for a summary of Hutchinson's royal chaplaincy.

Hutchinson's services were not only frequent, but also well attended. Despite the pessimistic claims of contemporaneous parish clergy in the late seventeenth and early eighteenth centuries, sparse congregations were the exception rather than the rule. Good preachers such as Tillotson were especially likely to fill their churches. This is unsurprising given that parishioners expected regular sermons in their parish church and demanded that they be of a high quality.[38] In 1701 Hutchinson informed the S.P.C.K. that he was keeping 'full congregations'.[39] The high quality of his sermons probably played a prime role in this achievement. Both clerical and lay audiences were fulsome in praise of his sermons[40] and he had been asked to preach at important occasions such as Episcopal visitations, assize sessions and before the town corporation.[41]

The success of Hutchinson's sermons was probably due to his adoption of a style that was highly fashionable at the time. Isabel Rivers argues that, in the Restoration period, leading Latitudinarian clergymen developed 'a collective language and rhetorical method which by the end of the century had largely succeeded in ousting the rival language of non-conformity and establishing itself... as the standard for rational public discourse'.[42] The new-style sermons contained a paucity of metaphor and rich imagery, and were marked by a simplicity of diction. They employed simple rather than complex sentences and avoided the use of Latin and Greek or esoteric, complex words, terms or phrases.[43] This new style was used in controversial works and treatises, handbooks but most of all in sermons; it was pioneered through the theorising of Benjamin Wilkins and then, by example, through the highly successfully sermons of John Tillotson.

The Latitudinarian move to a simpler, clearer, more rational and structured style of sermon was born of the need to distance themselves

---

[38] Jacob, *Lay people and religion*, pp. 54–5, 3, 63–7; Spaeth, *Church in the age of danger*, pp. 189–90; Norman Sykes, 'The sermons of Archbishop Tillotson' in *Theology*, lviii (1955), 298.

[39] Francis Hutchinson to John Chamberlayne, 25 Apr. 1701 (C.U.L., S.P.C.K. Correspondence, 1699–1701), p. 286.

[40] For examples of this, see Chapter 3 and Hutchinson, *Sermon preached... 27 May 1692*, sig. A2^v.

[41] Francis Hutchinson, *Sermon preached... 27 May 1692*; idem, *Sermon preached... 3 July 1698*; idem, *A sermon preach'd at the assize at Bury St Edmunds in Suffolk, March the 25th, 1707* (London, 1707); idem, *Sermon preached... 1 May 1707*; Visitation processes, 1706 (N.R.O., Norwich diocese, visitation records, DN/VIS/10/1).

[42] Isabel Rivers, *Reason, grace, and sentiment: a study of the language of religion and ethics in England, 1660–1780* (2 vols, Cambridge, 1991–2000), i, 38.

[43] Sykes, 'Sermons of Abp Tillotson', pp. 297–8; Rivers, *Reason, grace, and sentiment*, pp. 53–9; E. M. Batley, 'Archbishop John Tillotson and Johann Gottfried Lessing: the ideal of an objective prose style' in *Eighteenth Century Studies*, iii (1971), 319–20, 322–3, 326.

from the baroque, complex, sometimes classical language and imagery of the metaphysical preachers such as John Donne, as well as from the 'enthusiastical' cant and speculative subject matter of the early seventeenth-century Puritan preachers. The language of the new science and the need to appeal to the polite audiences of the fashionable London parishes also had a great influence on them. This change was also intimately related to the endeavour by clergymen to inculcate into their parishioners an understanding of the Christian faith: they believed that, because this new plain style was easier to understand, it provided a perfect vehicle for the dissemination of essential Christian truths and doctrines among the masses. The new style was increasingly adopted during the final years of the seventeenth century and became the hallmark of the eighteenth-century sermon. By contrast, learned and complex sermons were increasingly deemed inappropriate for the parish church.[44]

Hutchinson not only admired Tillotson, but was also heavily involved with attempts to educate the poor in his parish.[45] It is therefore unsurprising that Hutchinson's sermons of the period of 1692–1720 were written in the new sermon style.[46] This style is readily apparent in a visitation sermon Hutchinson preached before the Low-Church Whig Bishop of Norwich, John Moore, in 1692:

> When God himself was pleased to speak from Sinai with thunder and lightening, flames and smoak, to the midst of heaven, they all promised, even the mixt multitude, that they would obey whatsoever he shou'd command them.[47]

Hutchinson was able to indulge more in his intellectual and literary pretensions when preaching in front of academic audiences. In 1698 Hutchinson, in a sermon given at his commencement of doctor of divinity at Cambridge, included some rich, metaphorical descriptions of creation and an exposition on natural philosophy and natural theology.[48]

---

[44] Jacob, *Lay people and religion*, pp. 48–9; Sykes, 'Sermons of Abp Tillotson', pp. 297–99; Rivers, *Reason, grace, and sentiment*, pp. 53, 56–9; Jeremy Gregory, 'The eighteenth-century reformation: the pastoral task of Anglican clergy after 1689' in *Toleration to Tractarianism*, p. 75; Spaeth, *Church in the age of danger*, p. 53.

[45] See pp. 31–6 below.

[46] Hutchinson, *Sermon preached . . . 27 May 1692*; idem, *Sermon preached . . . 3 July 1698*; idem, *Sermon preached . . . 25 Mar. 1707*; idem, *Sermon preached . . . 1 May 1707*.

[47] Hutchinson, *Sermon preached . . . 27 May 1692*, p. 18.

[48] Hutchinson, *Sermon preached . . . 3 July 1698*, pp. 1–14; for Hutchinson's views on natural philosophy and theology, see Chapter 4 below.

Sermons written in the new style were also highly structured. Tillotson's sermons followed a strict pattern, which Hutchinson applied to his own works: a piece of text is introduced, explained, then set in its wider context.[49] This is followed by an exposition of a series of propositions arising from the text.[50] The text was then applied to the particular congregation being addressed, which was presented in named and numbered divisions. Possible objections to the argument were also answered sequentially: firstly, secondly, thirdly.[51] It was in this third section that Tillotson, and thus Hutchinson, demonstrated the final aspect of the new style: the use of a rational argument backed up with evidence.[52] In his 1698 sermon, Hutchinson used deductive reasoning, scriptural justification and occasional appeals to common sense to justify three parts of Christian doctrine: that man had an immortal soul, that heaven and hell existed, and that afterlife punishment and rewards were part of this reality.[53]

Historians who have taken a pessimistic view of the clergy's provision of public worship have seen the increase of pluralism in the late seventeenth and early eighteenth century as an indication of declining standards. Most parochial pluralists did not employ curates and chose instead to juggle both livings themselves. Although the English godly elite frowned on this practice, preferring that pluralists and absentees employed curates to help them, there is scant evidence to suggest that it led to pastoral neglect.[54] Hutchinson, from 1692 to 1697, served Bury St Edmunds and Hoxne by himself with the exception for a brief period in September 1694 when he hired Thomas Poke as a lecturer in the latter parish. In May 1697 Hutchinson began employing a full-time curate for the parish of Hoxne, Edmund Beeston, who was also rector of Sproughton, Suffolk. Beeston served at Hoxne until at least October 1703,

---

[49] Sykes, 'Sermons of Abp Tillotson', p. 299; Hutchinson, *Sermon preached . . . 27 May 1692*, pp. 1–4; idem, *Sermon preached . . . 3 July 1698*, pp. 1–2; idem, *Sermon preached . . . 25 Mar. 1707*, pp. 1–2; idem, *Sermon preached . . . 1 May 1707*, pp. 2–3.

[50] Sykes, 'Sermons of Abp Tillotson', p. 299; Hutchinson, *Sermon preached . . . 27 May 1692*, pp. 4–5; idem, *Sermon preached . . . 3 July 1698*, pp. 2–4; idem, *Sermon preach'd . . . 25 Mar. 1707*, pp. 2–3; idem, *Sermon preached . . . 1 May 1707*, pp. 4–5.

[51] Sykes, 'Sermons of Abp Tillotson', p. 299; Hutchinson, *Sermon preached . . . 27 May 1692*, pp. 5–26; idem, *Sermon preached . . . 3 July 1698*, 4–23; idem, *Sermon preached . . . 25 March 1707*, pp. 3–19; idem, *Sermon preached . . . 1 May 1707*, pp. 5–16.

[52] Sykes, 'Sermons of Abp Tillotson', p. 298; Rivers, *Reason, grace, and sentiment*, pp. 51–2, 54–5.

[53] Hutchinson, *Sermon preached . . . 3 July 1698*, pp. 3, 5, 20, 11–14, 7–8, 22.

[54] Spaeth, *Church in an age of danger*, pp. 30–1, 39, 115–16; Taylor and Walsh, 'Introduction', pp. 7–9.

but by 1706 he had been replaced by Edward Bosworth.[55] Unfortunately, we do not know what either man was paid. Nathaniel Frith became Hutchinson's assistant curate at Bury St Edmunds in September 1701 and remained there until he became vicar of Hoxne in January 1707.[56] By the time Bishop Trimnell held his primary visitation on 26 October 1709, John Brinkely had replaced Frith as Hutchinson's curate. Brinkely remained Hutchinson's assistant until he went to Ireland in 1721.[57] Hutchinson also employed a curate in Passenham between 1706 and 1720.[58]

Hutchinson strove to live as blameless a life in Bury St Edmunds as was possible. The presentments made by churchwardens at Episcopal and Archdeaconry visitations for the vicarage of Hoxne, the curacy of St James' during the late seventeenth and early eighteenth centuries, reveal that Hutchinson was not brought before the Church courts for any type of moral offence. He was furthermore admitted to the S.P.C.K., a society which operated a rigorous selection policy to ensure that only religious men of proven good characters joined its ranks.[59] Consequently, Hutchinson could state in 1707, without hypocrisy, that a nation could be lifted to 'true virtue' with the help of 'the good influence of many pious and shining examples of good men and women'.[60]

The second way in which Hutchinson tried to increase the standard of pastoral care in his parish was through the implementation of a number of educational initiatives. In the seventeenth and early eighteenth centuries, the parish clergy developed a number of educational strategies designed to inculcate in their parishioners an understanding of their

---

[55] Visitation processes, 1706 (N.R.O., Norwich diocese, visitation records, DN/VIS/10/1); Court call book, October 1690 (Suffolk Record Office, Ipswich [hereafter S.R.O.(I)], Archdeaconry records, FAA/2/16); Court call book, September 1693 (S.R.O.(I), FAA/2/17); Court call book, September 1694 (S.R.O.(I), FAA/2/17); Court call book, April 1695 (S.R.O.(I), FAA/2/18); Court call book, May 1696 (S.R.O.(I), FAA/2/18); Court call book, May 1697 (S.R.O.(I), FAA/2/19); Court call book, September 1699 (S.R.O.(I), FAA/2/20); Court call book, September 1701 (S.R.O.(I), FAA/2/20); Court call book, April 1702 to October 1703 (S.R.O.(I), FAA/2/21); Venn, *Alumni Cantabrigienses*, i, 126, 185.

[56] Consignation books, 1709 (N.R.O., Norwich diocese, visitation records, DN/VSC/5/10, p. 256); Consignation books, 1706 (N.R.O., DN/VSC 5/9).

[57] Consignation books, 1709 (N.R.O., DN/VSC 5/10, p. 263); Visitation processes, 1709 (N.R.O., DN/VIS/11); Visitation Call Book, 1710 (S.R.O. (B), Diocese of Norwich, Archdeacon's records, E14/2/2); Minutes and accounts, 1706–26 (S.R.O. (B), Church charity school records, FL 545/11/11, pp. 22, 25, 32, 39, 44–9, 52, 55, 57–68).

[58] See pp. 18–19 above.

[59] William A. and Phyllis W. Bultman, 'The roots of Anglican humanitarianism: a study of the membership of the S.P.C.K. and the S.P.G., 1699–1720' in *Historical Magazine of the Protestant Episcopal Church*, xxxiii (1966), 14.

[60] Hutchinson, *Sermon preached . . . 25 Mar. 1707*, p. 17.

Anglican faith. They distributed religious tracts and proselytising material, catechised their flocks and founded charity schools. Furthermore, as in Hutchinson's case, they often conducted these programmes under the guidance of the S.P.C.K.[61]

The S.P.C.K. was a non-partisan, predominately clerical, voluntary body formed in 1698 to ensure the continued dominance of the established Church in an age of uncertainty. This non-partisan aim ensured that both High- and Low-Churchmen were eager to join it.[62] On 10 October 1700, Hutchinson joined the S.P.C.K. as one of the corresponding members for the town of Bury St Edmunds.[63] The fact that the S.P.C.K. had the good of the Anglican Church at its heart would have ensured Hutchinson's support, but the fact that the Archdeacon of Norfolk, and his future diocesan, Trimnell, were also members may have acted as an extra spur.[64] There were two types of members of the S.P.C.K., residing members and corresponding members: by the early eighteenth century there were around 100 of the former and 450 of the latter. Residing members were usually powerful laymen; they paid an annual subscription and lived in London where the Society's headquarters were located. They were allowed to hold office in the Society, as well as vote at its meetings. Corresponding members, such as Hutchinson, were largely drawn from the ranks of the active and intellectual parish clergy. Each English county usually contained four or five corresponding members who were informed of the Society's activities through annual reports and circular letters; they also received packages of religious literature, which they were expected to distribute throughout their district. They were also instructed to send news to the secretary of the Society concerning the function of local charities, were authorised to collect funds for the Society and to petition directly for its assistance in local projects. Although corresponding members could attend meetings of the S.P.C.K., they were not allowed to vote at them.[65]

Canon 59, re-enforced by individual prelates in their visitation articles, demanded that the young and servants be catechised regularly.[66] In most

---

[61] Gregory, *Restoration, reformation and reform*, pp. 235–81.
[62] Craig Rose, 'The origins and ideals of the S.P.C.K. 1699–1716' in *Toleration to Tractarianism*, pp. 173–7.
[63] Edmund McClure, *A chapter in English Church history being the minutes of the society for the Promoting of Christian Knowledge for the years 1698–1704; together with the abstracts of correspondents letters during the same period* (London, 1888), p. 81.
[64] Ibid., pp. 3, 6, 7.
[65] Lowther Clarke, *History of the S.P.C.K.* (London, 1959), pp. 22, 27, 89–90.
[66] W. M. Marshall, 'The diocese of Hereford and Oxford, 1660–1760' in Gregory and Chamberlain, *The national Church in local perspective*, p. 213.

parishes, however, this canonical standard was not achieved. This was less to do with a lack of will on the part of the parish clergy and more to do with the fact that they found it hard to persuade the laity to participate.[67] The teaching of the Anglican catechism to children was seen as the principal method by which the clergy could inculcate their congregations with an understanding of the basic precepts of the Christian faith, and their obligations to it.

Some clergymen, such as Hutchinson, believed that most adults could benefit from this type of instruction.[68] On 9 October 1700 he complained to the S.P.C.K. secretary that the poorer sort in his parish were especially 'ignorant, barborous, and without principles'.[69] He distributed printed catechisms among them, in an attempt to address this problem, but without much success. He attributed this failure to the fact that the poorer members of the parish could not read.[70] Gregory argues that eighteenth-century clerical reformers tried to develop Christian beliefs through reading skills because they associated religious commitment with understanding. It was thought that individuals gained a deeper understanding of Christianity if they read about it for themselves. Consequently, reform programmes like Hutchinson's often ran aground when it became apparent that a large proportion of the poor in their parish were illiterate.[71] His observations on literacy rates in his parish were largely accurate. In the early modern period, the vast majority of the labouring classes in the diocese of Norwich were unable to read or sign their name.[72]

If Hutchinson was anything, he was adaptable and after this initial failure he switched his tactics and began 'a course of catechishing at 5 in the evening on Sundayes' in his church. If the poorer sort could not read the catechism for themselves, he would read it to them. Unfortunately, for Hutchinson, this endeavour also failed to achieve the desired results. He noted in another letter to the S.P.C.K. that although a 'great number of the better sort came' to his lectures 'few or none' of 'the poor' followed their example.[73] Eighteen years later Hutchinson narrowed even

---

[67] Gregory and Chamberlain, 'National and local perspectives', p. 21.
[68] Gregory, 'Eighteenth-century reformation', pp. 71–5; John H. Pruett, *The parish clergy under the later Stuarts: the Leicestershire experience* (Illinois, 1978), pp. 116–18.
[69] Francis Hutchinson to John Chamberlayne, 9 Oct. 1700 (C.U.L., S.P.C.K. Correspondence, 1699–1701, p. 180).
[70] Ibid.
[71] Gregory, 'Eighteenth-century reformation', p. 79.
[72] David Cressy, 'Levels of illiteracy in England, 1530–1730' in *Historical Journal*, xx, no. 1 (1977), 8–9.
[73] Francis Hutchinson to John Chamberlayne, 9 Oct. 1700 (C.U.L., S.P.C.K., records, p. 180).

further his efforts to catechise adults by concentrating upon the aged poor, whom he coaxed into church with promises of food. In a letter to the society dated 6 April 1718, Samuel Knight noted that 'at Bury in Suffolk there is a catechetical lecture for old ignorant people, and every time they are to be examin'd they have a large loaf of bread, which charity was left some time ago by Mr Derby'.[74]

The S.P.C.K. not only printed and distributed religious materials but encouraged its members to set up parochial libraries for the edification of the laity and clergy alike. About 162 such libraries were founded between 1688 and 1750.[75] Hutchinson received many packages of books,[76] but fortunately did not have to set up a library himself since his parish, as he informed the S.P.C.K. secretary in 1701, already possessed a library 'of an ancient foundation'.[77] The glebe terriers of St James' parish state that in 1716 the church contained 'a large library with 2 large presses to contain the books'.[78]

The religious material of the S.P.C.K. was also used for proselytising. It may have been a non-partisan body, but it was strictly orthodox, and condemned Deism, Arianism and Socianism. It distributed anti-Catholic and anti-Presbyterian literature but only tried to proselytise the former. Surprisingly, it gave the conversion of Quakers a higher priority than that of Catholics, due in part to George Keith, a member who had been a Quaker; after his conversion he began to wage a proselytising campaign against his old religious denomination.[79] Hutchinson was obviously well aware of S.P.C.K. priorities: in October 1700 he proudly informed them that he intended 'to send the sheets to the Quakers'.[80] Four months later, he admitted to the S.P.C.K. secretary that the Quakers had been 'obstinat and disingenuous' and his proselytising campaign had ended abruptly, in acrimony, having converted just two

[74] Samuel Knight to [?], 6 Apr. 1718 (C.U.L., S.P.C.K. records, Abstract Letter Book [hereafter A.L.B.], no. 8 (1717–18), 5564).
[75] Jacob, *Lay people and religion*, pp. 174–5; W. O. B. Allen and Edmund McClure, *Two hundred years: the history of the Society for Promoting Christian Knowledge, 1698–1898* (London, 1898), pp. 125, 166; Rose, 'Origins and ideals', p. 181.
[76] Minute books, 9 May 1706 (C.U.L., S.P.C.K. records, MS A1/1, p. 385); Francis Hutchinson to [?], Sept. 1712 (C.U.L., S.P.C.K. records, A.L.B. no. 4 (1712–13), 3220); Francis Hutchinson to [?], 2 Nov. 1713 (Ibid., 3742); Francis Hutchinson to [?], 19 June 1717 (C.U.L., S.P.C.K. records, A.L.B. no. 7, (1716–17), 5254).
[77] Francis Hutchinson to John Chamberlayne, 25 Apr. 1701 (C.U.L., S.P.C.K. Correspondence (1699–1701), p. 286).
[78] Church terriers, St James' Parish, 1716 (S.R.O. (B), 806/1/30).
[79] Rose, 'Origins and ideals', pp. 186–90.
[80] Francis Hutchinson to John Chamberlayne, 22 Oct. 1700 (C.U.L., S.P.C.K. records, Correspondence (1699–1701), p. 193).

or three Quakers and 'none of note'.[81] He had little to say about Catholics, except that their numbers were 'almost one to forty' compared to Protestants.[82] However, the town had a substantial dissenting community: Presbyterian, Independent, Baptist and Quaker.[83] In common with most good Whigs in the aftermath of the 1715 Jacobite rebellion, Hutchinson's sense of the Catholic threat reached a new height. It was at this time that he began to use his pen in an effort to persuade the Catholic gentry of East Anglia to renounce recusancy and join the established Church.[84]

Another primary concern of the S.P.C.K. was to support the charity school system. Charity schools were set up in increasing numbers in the early eighteenth century to provide free primary education for the children of the poor. Although the S.P.C.K. did not set up charity schools, it encouraged and advised others to do so; it provided, on request, guidelines detailing how such schools could be founded, financed and run. Once schools were set up, the S.P.C.K. took no financial responsibility for them, and their governance was left in the hands of those responsible for founding them, the subscribers. At regular general meetings, these subscribers – the majority of whom came from the local gentry and clergy, and whose annual donations were most schools' main source of income – set the curriculum, appointed teachers and drafted the rules by which teachers and their pupils were to abide. They supervised and inspected the behaviour and work of both teachers and children, provided clothing for the children and listened to them recite the catechism. There was no standard age for entry to English charity schools but schooling time was restricted to four years.

Most schools possessed close links to parish incumbents, and teachers and stewards of the schools (chosen from among the school's subscribers) were expected to be communicating members of the Church of England. It was compulsory for charity school children to attend church and their curriculum was based on the Anglican catechism. The catechism was taught and tested by oral examination throughout their time at school. The gender intake of schools varied from school to school. It was normal practice for girls to be taught needlework and knitting rather than writing and arithmetic, because these skills were thought to better prepare them for their future lives as wives and mothers. Writing was

---

[81] Francis Hutchinson to John Chamberlayne, 25 Apr. 1701 (Ibid., p. 286).
[82] Ibid.
[83] Cruickshanks, Handley and Hayton, *The House of Commons, 1690–1715*, ii, 548.
[84] See p. 75 below.

taught only once reading had been mastered, as was common practice in most parts of Europe at that time.[85]

The enthusiasm for charity schools in eighteenth-century England, among laity and clergy alike, had one main source: the defence of the Church of England. Craig Rose argues that charity schools were advertised by their supporters as being an effective, relatively low-cost, practical way to 'evangelise their poor brethren, and combat the perceived rising tide of irreligion, heterodoxy, anti-clericism and Dissent'.[86] They argued that charity schools were able to achieve this goal for two main reasons. The schools were able to rear children who were devoted to the Church of England and its ministers. They also demonstrated, in a highly visible way, that to become an Anglican was the best way to achieve salvation. Charity schools demonstrated that Anglicans lived their lives in obedience to God's commands since charity was considered a central part of Christian piety. They also represented a supreme example of charity because they looked after both the spiritual and bodily needs of poor children. The 'better' and the 'middling' sorts in early eighteenth-century England gave generously to various good causes, especially charity schools, in order to fulfil this Christian obligation.[87] Charity schools were also seen by England's elite to perform a vital social function. They were widely perceived to instil social discipline into poor children by preparing them for their subordinate position in society and the workplace. They also taught them to be sober, industrious, honest, virtuous and deferential to established authority. Both Archbishop Moore and Bishop Stillingfleet supported the charity school movement, and their support was rooted in this perceived social function.[88]

---

[85] M. G. Jones, *The charity school movement: a study of eighteenth century Puritanism in action* (Cambridge, 1938), pp. 40–5, 81; Clarke, *History of the S.P.C.K.*, pp. 21, 42–6; Leonard W. Cowie, *Henry Newman: an American in London, 1708–43* (London, 1956), pp. 73, 75, 77–8, 81; Craig Rose, 'Evangelical philanthropy and Anglican revival: the charity schools of Augustan London, 1698–1740' in *London Journal*, xvi (1991), 36–48; Jacob, *Lay people and religion*, pp. 166–7.

[86] Rose 'Evangelical philanthropy', pp. 35, 35–6.

[87] Rose, 'Origins and ideals', pp. 177–81; idem, 'Seminary of faction and rebellion: Jacobite, Whigs and the London charity schools, 1716–1724' in *Historical Journal*, xxxiv (1991), 832–6; Rose, 'Evangelical philanthropy', pp. 35–6, 41–5.

[88] Rose 'Evangelical philanthropy', pp. 41–2; L. Davidson, T. Hitchcock, T. Keirn and R. B. Shoemaker, 'Introduction – the reactive state: English governance and society' in Davidson, Hitchcock, Keirn and Shoemaker (eds), *Stilling the grumbling hive*; Jones, *Charity school movement*, pp. xl, 28–35, 73–9; R. W. Unwin, 'Charity schools and the defence of Anglicanism: James Talbot, Rector of Spofforth, 1700–08' in *Borthwick Papers, University of York*, lxv (1984), 18–19, 26–7.

Given Hutchinson's commitment to the established Church, his membership of the S.P.C.K. and his veneration of the Whiggish ideal of a stable ordered society, it is no wonder Hutchinson was keen to set up charity schools in Bury St Edmunds.[89] On 9 May 1706, he wrote to the S.P.C.K. to inform them that he was starting 'a subscription ... for a charity school at Bury, towards which above £50 per. ann[um] is already subscribed' and to request advice about the practicalities of founding such an institution.[90] The S.P.C.K. acquiesced to this request and seven days later he was sent a 'printed account of the charity schools'.[91] The subscribers of the Bury St Edmunds charity schools held a general meeting on 29 July 1706 and promptly founded three single-sex charity schools, two for female children and one for males. The subscribers took upon themselves all of the responsibilities described above and the doors of their schools were officially opened on 31 August 1706.[92]

Hutchinson was one of these subscribers, contributing between 10s. and £1 every year between 1706 and 1720, except in 1719 when he contributed £7.[93] The day-to-day running of the Bury schools was handled by 11 stewards who were chosen every July at general meetings. The subscribers also agreed that the alderman of Bury St Edmund's, Thomas Macro, and the ministers of its two parishes of St James' and St Mary's (Hutchinson and Nicholas Clagett) were to be chosen as stewards every year they kept up their subscriptions.[94] Hutchinson acted as steward every year until 1721, when he left for Ireland, and diligently attended both ordinary and quarterly general subscriber meetings.[95] Thus he not only was the inspiration behind the Bury charity schools, but he helped to fund and run them.

II

Hutchinson's involvement in pastoral reform may have stemmed from a desire to work for the good of the established Church, but his interest between 1701 and 1710 in joining the Convocation of Canterbury was more politically motivated. It was his Latitudinarian Whig principles that fuelled his desire to help his fellow Low-Churchmen in their fight to prevent the High-Church majority in the lower house of Convocation

---

[89] See Chapter 4 below.
[90] Minute books, 9 May 1706 (C.U.L., S.P.C.K. records, MS A1/1, p. 385).
[91] Ibid., 16 May 1706 (C.U.L., S.P.C.K. records, MS A1/1, p. 387).
[92] Minutes and accounts, 1706–26 (S.R.O. (B), FL 545/11/11, pp. 210, 1–2, 4, 32).
[93] Ibid., pp. 14, 20, 31, 34, 37, 40, 43, 46, 49, 53, 61–3.
[94] Ibid., p. 210; Rose, 'Evangelical philanthropy', p. 38.
[95] Minutes and accounts, 1706–26 (S.R.O. (B), FL 545/11/11, pp. 1–70, 210–17).

from increasing its powers, attempting to quash Dissent and religious heterodoxy, and generally cause trouble for the Whig party. Hutchinson was first able to fulfil this desire in the 1701–2 session of Convocation, which ran from 30 December 1701 to 12 February 1702. Unfortunately for Hutchinson, a High-Churchman from his archdeaconry, Henry Halsted, was determined to have him removed and promptly protested against his election as diocesan proctor for the archdeaconry of Suffolk and Sudbury. A committee filled by High-Churchmen in the lower house immediately took up the case against Hutchinson. Although a judgment was not reached by Convocation itself, Halsted's protest made such an impression on the clerical voters in Suffolk that Hutchinson lost the next proctorial election, held in 1705. Hutchinson was so determined to get back into Convocation to support the Low-Church cause that in 1710 he embarked on a pamphlet campaign to persuade the Suffolk clergy to dismiss Halsted's protest and elect him instead. His campaign ended in failure.

In the first two convocations of the eighteenth century, the High-Church majority in the lower house aimed to appropriate from the archbishop his power to control the lower house of Convocation. The main battle of this war was fought over the issue of who had the right to control the date, place and time of the sessions of Convocation: on one side were the High-Church clergy of the lower house and the small number of High-Church bishops who sat in the upper house; on the other side were the Low-Church clergy of the lower house and their episcopal supporters in the upper house. In the 1701–2 session, Hutchinson supported the Low-Church episcopate and the Low-Church minority in this fight. This session was memorable for Hutchinson for another reason. The High-Church majority in the 1701–2 meeting of Convocation also began to use committees as a way to wrest control of the membership of the lower house from the archbishop. Hutchinson was dragged into this battle when Halsted lodged his protest with Convocation, immediately after the lower house had granted one of its committees the unprecedented right to make judgments in contested elections. In this way, then, Hutchinson's case can be seen to have been used by the High-Church majority to advertise their intent to use their new right to judge contested elections. The Low-Church majority, however, created such a furore over this issue that the committee spent most of its time justifying its assumption of the right to try elections rather than actually doing so. As a result, a decision was never reached in Hutchinson's case.

In the early eighteenth century there existed a mutual respect among clergy and a sense of professional identity, a situation created in part by the Church itself by a variety of social, educational and institutional means. This underlying unity was sporadically, sometimes fleetingly, shattered when specific issues or crises caused clergy to split into the two opposing factions of Low- and High-Church. Convocation created this type of situation nearly every time it sat between 1700 and 1717. William III had kept Convocation in perpetual prorogation since 1689, but High-Church Tory pressure made him reconvene it on 25 February 1701. The first session set the pattern for the conflict between the High- and Low-Church in all convocations until 1717. The convocations of Canterbury and York were split into two houses. The High-Church party dominated the lower house, where the deans, archdeacons, and chapter and diocesan proctors sat, whilst the Low-Church party dominated the upper house, where the archbishops and bishops met. The High-Church majority in the lower house were determined to use Convocation as a tool to solve the perceived problems of the Church. To do this, however, they first had to free the lower house from the autocratic rule of the president of both houses, the Latitudinarian Archbishop of Canterbury, Thomas Tenison. The High-Church Tory and future Jacobite, the Archdeacon of Exeter, Francis Atterbury, had provided the theoretical justification for this in two pamphlets he had written between 1697 and 1701. In them he argued that Convocation was a bicameral parliamentary assembly, whose purpose it was to advise the crown on ecclesiastical affairs. Consequently, the lower house had the right to control its own debates and to adjourn at the time and day of its choosing.[96]

The archbishop held firm to the, by now traditional, idea that Convocation was a completely ecclesiastical body and so was completely under his control. The majority of the episcopate in the upper house, who were Low-Church in their sympathies, and a minority of Low-Churchmen in the lower house, backed him fully in his assumption of this right. It was well understood by the Low-Church minority in Convocation that a lower house that was as constitutionally independent of the upper house as the House of Commons was of the House of Lords would become an unprecedented forum for causing trouble, both for the Whig government and for the Low-Church bishops. It would also align with the Tory party in an attempt to curb, by legislative means, the growth of Dissent and would condemn as heretical any book with which High-Churchmen did not, on theological grounds, agree. Therefore,

---

[96] Walsh and Taylor, 'Introduction', pp. 34–5, 45; Bennett, *Tory crisis*, pp. 44–62; G. V. Bennet, *White Kennet, 1660–1728, Bishop of Peterborough: a study in the political and ecclesiastical history of the early eighteenth century* (London, 1957), pp. 28–45; Every, *High-Church party*, pp. 83–103; Geoffrey Holmes, *British politics in the age of Anne* (2nd edn, London, 1987), p. 98; Sykes, *Church and state*, pp. 297–310; Gregory, *Restoration, reformation and reform*, pp. 69–99.

books which displayed a latitude on accepted Anglican doctrine would be condemned out of hand and their authors forced to recant their opinions.[97] To narrow the doctrinal standards of the established Church in this way was deemed completely unacceptable by Latitudinarians such as Hutchinson.[98]

The principal source of the archbishop's control over debate in the lower house was his ability to control the date, time and duration of meetings of both houses. He did this through the schedule of continuation: after the upper house had finished its business, this was handed to the lower house's president, the proculator, who was then supposed to read the schedule aloud to end debating there. The schedule of prorogation, on the other hand, allowed the king and the archbishop to silence the national synod permanently by keeping it in perpetual adjournment. The highest priority of the High-Church majority in the 1700–1 session of Convocation was therefore to oppose both schedules. In May 1701, Atterbury ousted the more moderate George Hooper as leader of the High-Church majority. Under his command the lower house repeatedly ignored the archbishop's schedule and began to meet, adjourn and debate without reference to the upper house.[99]

In the next meeting of Convocation, in 1701–2, the High-Church majority were not prepared to join Atterbury in re-enacting the open rebellion of the previous meeting. Faced with a reduced overall majority and a well organised Low-Church opposition, they opted instead for a policy of disobedience and obstructionism. This policy was executed in a number of ways. For example, the proculator deliberately delayed the entry to the lower house of the registrar when he had been sent from the upper house to deliver the schedule of prorogation. The schedule was then read to the house after debating had already finished. The Latin phrasing of the schedule was also changed in order to imply that the lower house was adjourning itself and not vice versa.[100] The Low-Church minority, on 9 February 1702, presented to the upper house a

---

[97] Every, *High-Church party*, pp. 86–7, 91–103; Bennet, *Tory crisis*, pp. 49–52, 56–62; idem, *White Kennet*, pp. 33–4, 58–64; Sykes, *Church and state*, p. 297; Speck, *Birth of Britain*, pp. 3–4.

[98] See pp. 79–80 below.

[99] Holmes, *British politics*, p. 98; Every, *High-Church party*, pp. 91–104; Bennet, *Tory crisis*, pp. 57–62; idem, *White Kennet*, pp. 42–5.

[100] Every, *High-Church party*, pp. 107–8; Bennet, *Tory crisis*, pp. 65–6; idem, *White Kennet*, pp. 58–64; White Kennet, *A reconciling letter, upon the late differences about convocational rights and proceedings as managed by those who have maintained the liberties of the lower clergy* (London, 1702), p. 5; idem, *The present state of Convocation in a letter giving the full relation of proceedings in several late sessions: beginning from Wednesday, January the 28th, and continued to Thursday, February the 19th, correcting the mistakes and*

formal protest against these tactics. The protest reads like a roll call of the leading Low-Churchmen, for it includes the names of William Sherlock (Dean of St Paul's), Trimnell (Dean of Peterborough), White Kennet and Stillingfleet. The still obscure name of Dr Francis Hutchinson was added to these.[101] Hutchinson's commitment to the Low-Church cause is also reflected by his maintenance of a 70 per cent attendance rate during this session of Convocation.[102]

The brevity and the relative calm of the 1701–2 meeting ensured that historians have viewed it as historically insignificant.[103] However, if one examines the role played by committees in this period it soon becomes apparent that this was far from the case. Committees were used as a means to wrest control of the membership and discipline of the representatives of the lower house from the hands of the archbishop. Hutchinson's election as diocesan proctor was used by the High-Church majority to test their new, self-appointed right to determine the outcome of contested elections. Committees were not used in this fashion in the previous session of 1700–1, and it is to that session which we now turn.

In the 1700–1 meeting, the committees given priority were those whose business related directly to the opposition of the schedule. The committee of 'custom and usages' was directed to search past books of Convocation to find precedents that proved that the lower house had the right to adjourn itself and meet on intermediate days. It sat from 6 March until at least 9 May and regularly delivered reports to the upper house.[104] Three more committees were set up between April and June

---

slanders of the pretended faithful accounts, Number, 1, 2 (1702), pp. 32, 20–7; Eyewitness account of proceedings in the lower house of Convocation in the hand of White Kennet, 13 Jan. 1702 (Lambeth Palace Library [hereafter L.P.L.], Gibson MS 934/5); Eyewitness account of proceedings in the lower house of Convocation in the hand of White Kennet, 20 Jan. 1702 (L.P.L., Gibson MS 934/8); Acts of the lower house of Convocation, 26 Jan. 1702 (L.P.L., Gibson MS 934/7); Eyewitness account of proceedings in the lower house of Convocation in the hand of White Kennet, 22 Jan. 1702 (L.P.L., Gibson MS 934/9); Eyewitness account [by White Kennet] of proceedings in the lower house of Convocation, 28 Jan. 1702 (L.P.L., Gibson MS 934/10, 67); Eyewitness account [by White Kennet] of proceedings in the lower house of Convocation, 3 Feb. 1702 (L.P.L., Gibson MS 934/11).

[101] Protest by nineteen members of the lower house of Convocation asserting the right of the Archbishop of Canterbury to prorogue both houses of Convocation by schedule, 9 Feb. 1702 (L.P.L., Gibson MS 934/13).

[102] Act books: lower house of Convocation, 1586–1727 (L.P.L., Convocation of Canterbury records, MS CONV I/2/6, fos. 4^v–12^v).

[103] Every, *High-Church party*, pp. 107–8, 103; Bennet, *Tory crisis*, pp. 65–6; idem, *White Kennet*, pp. 58–61.

[104] Act books: lower house of Convocation, 1596–1727 (L.P.L., Convocation of Canterbury records, MS CONV I/2/5, fos. 6^r–7^r, 9^v–12^v, 21^v, 23^r–27^r, 30^r–33^v, 45^v–46^r).

1701 to further this cause. The first was to inspect and examine the schedule of prorogation, whilst the second committee was charged with preparing, for propaganda purposes, the publication of a narrative of the proceedings of the present Convocation. The final committee was to prepare addresses to the upper house declaring that they possessed the right to adjourn themselves.[105] The controversy over the issue of adjournment reached a height in early April 1701 and as a consequence committees that were not directly related to this cause were suspended. Committees concerned with the promotion of the Anglican religion, with the initiation of the reform of Anglican doctrine and with the examination of the problem of the growth of dissenting academies were all adjourned.[106] There were exceptions, however, namely those committees regarded by the High-Church majority as a covert way of attacking Latitudinarian bishops of the upper house.

On 25 February 1701, the lower house appointed a committee to draw up a report condemning diocesans' right to try to influence proctorial elections by recommending certain candidates to their clergy. The report was a covert way of castigating Low-Church bishops who used their influence to get men of their own stamp into Convocation. The report was presented with the other grievances by Dr Birch to the upper house on 14 May. The bishops' reply to this report, delivered in June, was just as confrontational, for in it they claimed that it was their right to influence proctorial elections in order to keep fractious and troublesome high-flying clergy out of Convocation. In short, the committee of grievances was used to charge the Whigs, in conjunction with Low-Churchmen, with the ruination of the established Church.[107]

Similarly, the committee on heretical and scandalous books was allowed to sit well beyond the April 1701 deadline because it provided a perfect stick with which to beat the Latitudinarian bishops. It censured John Toland's *Christianity not mysterious* (1696) and Bishop Burnet's *An exposition of the thirty-nine articles* (1699).[108] Burnet's book offended High-Church sensibilities in two main ways. Firstly, High-Churchmen

---

[105] Ibid., fos. 41^r–41^v, 39^r, 40^v, 62^v, 52^r–52^v, 53^v, 55^v–56^v, 58^v–61^v; Every, *High-Church party*, pp. 98–102.

[106] Act books: lower house of Convocation, 1596–1727 (L.P.L., MS CONV I/2/5, fos. 13^v–14^v, 16^r–16^v, 18^r–18^v, 21^r, 34^v).

[107] Act books: lower house of Convocation, 1596–1727 (L.P.L., MS CONV I/2/5, fos. 6^v, 8^r, 47^r); Dr Birch's grievances and the answers given to them, n.d. (L.P.L., Gibson MS 934/33).

[108] Act books: lower house of Convocation, 1596–1727 (L.P.L., MS CONV I/2/5, fos. 19^r–19^v, 36^v–37^r, 49^r–49^v, 51^v–53^v, 55^v–56^r); The representation of the lower house of Convocation, 8 May 1701 (L.P.L., Gibson MS 934/22); Every, *High-Church party*, pp. 96–7; Bennet, *Tory crisis*, pp. 58–9.

claimed he misrepresented the Trinity and other Anglican doctrines by applying a Latitudinarian epistemology to them. Secondly, by virtue of his downplaying the differences between the Protestant denominations, they accused him of trying to lay the foundation for the future comprehension of Dissenters.[109] Toland's book was far more heterodox, going almost as far as was possible in the pursuit of reasonable religion.[110] The book, as Stephen Daniel points out, suggested 'that no tenets of true Christianity could be contrary to or above human reason, for if they were they would be unintelligible'.[111]

In the 1700–1 meeting, the lower house had also claimed other parliamentary rights: the right to appoint its own proxies for absent members; the right to control its own journals and act books; the right to give leave of absence to its own members; the right to punish its own members for misconduct and the right to appoint its own actuaries. The archbishop's determination not to relinquish his grip on these powers, combined with a reticence to challenge the archbishop's authority openly, forced the High-Church majority to switch tactics.[112] Committees, which had been used in the first session to attack the archbishop's right to adjourn the lower house, were now used to build cases that would justify their assumption of these other rights.

The fifth session of the 1701–2 Convocation, held on 28 January 1702, saw the majority set up three committees.[113] The first was the committee of rights and usages and it was filled with men of High-Church sympathies.[114] The main role of this committee was to decide whether or not the lower house had the right to appoint its own actuaries and control

---

[109] Martin Greig, 'Burnet, Gilbert (1643–1715)' in *OxDNB*.
[110] For a discussion of the Latitudinarian pursuit of reasonable religion, see pp. 23–5 above.
[111] Stephen H. Daniel, 'Toland, John (1670–1722)' in *OxDNB*.
[112] Act books: lower house of Convocation, 1596–1727 (L.P.L., MS CONV I/2/5, fos. 40^v, 44^v–45^r, 18^r); The representation of the lower house of Convocation, 8 May 1701 (L.P.L., Gibson MS 934/31); Committee appointed to search the act books of Convocation and papers relating to the disagreement between the two houses over the archbishops' power to prorogue Convocation, 1700–1701 (L.P.L., Convocation of Canterbury records, MS CONV IX/5/5); Every, *High-Church party*, p. 103.
[113] Act books: lower house of Convocation, 1596–1727 (L.P.L., Convocation of Canterbury records, MS CONV I/2/6, fos. 7^v–8^r).
[114] Eyewitness account, 28 Jan. 1702 (L.P.L., Gibson MS 934/10, 67); this committee had 13 members. These members backed the High-Church cause in the 1701/2 session: Archdeacon of Exeter, Francis Atterbury; Canon of Norwich, Dr Thomas Little; Dean of Litchfield, Dr William Binks; Prebendary of Flixton, Dr George Smalridge; Dean of Winchester, John Wickart; Dean of Gloucester, William Jane; Treasurer of Llandaff Cathedral, Dr Jonathan Edwards; Mr William Moore; Canon of Peterborough, Mr John Evans; Dr Robert Wyne; Canon of Exeter, Robert Burscough. Two members were on the opposing side: George Haley; Archdeacon of Norfolk, Dr Charles Trimnell.

its own journals. It was also to make judgments on the contested elections of members of the lower house.[115] With regard to the latter power, Kennet argued that only the archbishop had the right to judge in such matters and that the committee was thus 'taking in a subject of which we had no right to determine'.[116] The matter was put to the vote and Kennet's opposition was swiftly swept aside.[117]

Archdeacon Matthew Hutton, a leading member of the High-Church majority, then presented 'a petition directed to the proculator of the house from Mr Halsted and several others of the archdeaconry of Sudbury', claiming that 'Dr [Francis] Hutchinson was not duly elected'.[118] Henry Halsted was born in 1641 in Burnley, Lancashire, to a wealthy gentry family. He entered the clergy after attending Burnley Grammar School and Brasenose College, Oxford. His career was distinguished by a number of good livings: he was canon of St Paul's, rector of St Leonard, Eastcheap and rector of Stansfield, Suffolk. A bibliophile, he donated his massive library to his *alma mater* after his death in 1728.[119]

The Archdeacon of Suffolk, Dr Humphrey Prideaux, immediately requested that the petition be disregarded. The majority dismissed his motion and promptly agreed that the petition should be passed to the committee of rights and usages, which was to report its judgment back to the house.[120] Prideaux, in common with Hutchinson and most other representatives of the diocese of Norwich (Charles Trimnell, Nicholas Clagett, the Archdeacon of Sudbury and the other diocesan proctor of Norwich, John Whitefoot), was both a defender of the archbishop and a Low-Church Whig. It was precisely because Hutchinson was counted among this coterie of East Anglian Low-Churchmen that the committee showed such an interest in his case. Two sessions later, on 9 February, the report was presented to the house. The report clearly showed that the committee had been more concerned with asserting its right to judge contested elections than with exercising that right. In short, Hutchinson's case had been put on the back burner. It was then agreed that the

---

[115] Eyewitness account, 28 Jan. 1702 (L.P.L., Gibson MS 934/10, 67); idem, 26 Jan. 1702 (L.P.L., Gibson MS 934/7).
[116] Eyewitness account, 28 Jan. 1702 (L.P.L., Gibson MS 934/10, 67).
[117] Ibid.
[118] Ibid.
[119] Stuart Mews and Michael Mullet, 'Catholicism and the Church of England in a northern library: Henry Halsted and the Burnley Grammar School library' in Diana Wood (ed.), *Life and thought in the northern Church, c.1100–1700: essays in honour of Claire Cross* (Suffolk, 1999), pp. 533–4.
[120] Eyewitness account, 28 Jan. 1702 (L.P.L., Gibson MS 934/10, 67); Act books: lower house of Convocation, 1596–1727 (L.P.L., Convocation of Canterbury records, MS CONV I/2/6, fo. 8^r).

committee should expand on this report, much to the ire of the archbishop's supporters.[121] The untimely death of King William III a month later led to the dissolution of Convocation and a conclusion was never reached in the Hutchinson case.

Halsted's original protest is no longer extant and it is thus impossible to know for certain what motivated him to attack Hutchinson. It seems highly likely, however, it was for a mixture of political and personal reasons. Pride, for example, may have persuaded Halsted that Hutchinson was an upstart who had little right to challenge his privilege of serving as a proctor, a privilege justified by his being of the upper clergy, more senior in years and of higher birth. Party antipathy also played a major role. Halsted's protest did not relate specifically to Hutchinson, but also contained defamatory references to another key supporter of the archbishop: Nicholas Clagett, Archdeacon of Sudbury. If personal hatred of Hutchinson was the sole reason for Halsted's accusations, then why use the opportunity to attack another Low-Churchman? In the seventh session of Convocation, held on 9 February 1702, Clagett complained 'of his being aspersed in a protestation of Mr Halsted' and immediately 'desired a copy of that defamatory paper'.[122] After Clagett's plea was dismissed by the majority, he re-entered his plea. This second plea received exactly the same treatment from the High-Church majority as the first.[123]

Hutchinson's election also broke the monopoly which the High-Churchmen of the archdeaconry of Suffolk and Sudbury had enjoyed in electing diocesan proctors since the beginning of the eighteenth century. Norfolk, Norwich, Suffolk and Sudbury were the four archdeaconries that made up the diocese of Norwich and between them they returned two diocesan proctors to Convocation. It had become customary for Sudbury and Suffolk to alternate, election by election, in choosing a proctor to represent both.[124] In the 1700–1 and 1702 elections, the archdeaconry of Suffolk chose Peter Basford, rector of Blaxhall in Suffolk from 1680, as their proctor. On Basford's death, Samuel Crispe took over his role; he was first elected in 1708 and again in 1713.[125] Basford

---

[121] Act books: lower house of Convocation, 1596–1727 (L.P.L., Convocation of Canterbury records, MS CONV I/2/6, fo. 11ʳ); Eyewitness account, 9 Feb. 1702 (L.P.L., Gibson MS 934/12).

[122] Eyewitness account, 9 Feb. 1702 (L.P.L., Gibson MS 934/12).

[123] Ibid.

[124] Hutchinson, *Defence of the clergy's liberty*, p. 6.

[125] Act books: upper house of Convocation 1640–1727 (L.P.L., Convocation of Canterbury records, CONV I/1/10, fo. 2ᵛ); Returns of proctors 1640–1892, Norwich diocese, 1702, 1708 and 1713 (ibid., CONV V/1/1702, CONV V/1/1708 and CONV V/1/1713); *Alumni Cantabrigienses*, i, 102, 419.

and Crispe, during the reign of Anne, consistently voted for Tory candidates. Basford was also a committed High-Churchman: he regularly attended Convocation, signed his name to addresses presented to the archbishop pleading the High-Church case, and sat on numerous hand-picked High-Church committees. Unfortunately, it has been impossible to determine what brand of churchmanship Crispe subscribed to, but as a Tory supporter it is likely he was of the same stamp as Basford.[126]

In 1701–2, 1705, 1710 and 1715 it was Sudbury's chance to elect a proctor and the man they invariably chose was the High-Church Tory, Henry Halsted.[127] Halsted was virulently anti-Catholic and an opponent of Protestant Dissent in all its guises.[128] He attended Convocation only sporadically, but when he did he was counted among the High-Church majority. He denounced Erastianism (an ideology associated with Whigs, which in simple terms relates to those who maintain that in society the ecclesiastical should be subordinated to the secular) and voted for Tory candidates in parliamentary elections.[129] Halsted's election to Convocation was only upset once, in 1701–2, by a man of opposing principles, Hutchinson.[130]

The main concern of the second committee, set up on 3 February 1702, was to draw up an address condemning Gilbert Burnet's prosecution in the church courts of John Woodward for non-attendance of his visitation. Woodward was also the proculator for the lower house, and the majority saw the suit as an attempt to have their leader silenced. They

---

[126] *A true and exact list of the names of the gentlemen, and others, free holders, that voted for . . . the Earl of Dysart, Sir Robert Davers, Bart, Sir Dudley Cullum, Bart, and Samuel Barnardiston Esq; to be knights of the shire for the county of Suffolk . . . as the same was taken at Ipswich, the fifth day of August, 1702* . . . (London, 1702), pp. 7, 22; *A copy of the poll for the Knights of the shire for the county of Suffolk, taken at Ipswich, May 9th, 1705, Thomas Kerrage, Esq High Sherrif* (London, 1705), p. 24; *A copy of the poll for the Knights of the Shire for the county of Suffolk, taken at Ipswich, Oct. 18. anno dom. 1710. Stephen Bacon, Esq; High Sheriff. George Harrington, gent under sheriff. Candidates, Sir Thomas Hanmer, Sir Robert Davers, Barts. Sir Philip Parker, Baronet* (London, 1711), pp. 10, 22, 61; Act books: lower house of Convocation, 1596–1727 (L.P.L., Convocation of Canterbury records, MS CONV I/2/5, fos. 13^r, 34^r–36^r; CONV I/2/8, fos. 18^r–18^v, 37^r; CONV I/2/9, fos. 5^r, 22^v).

[127] Returns of proctors 1640–1892, Norwich diocese, 1705, 1710 and 1715 (L.P.L., Convocation of Canterbury records, CONV V/1/1705, CONV V/1/1710 and CONV V/1/1715).

[128] Mews and Mullet, 'Catholicism and the Church', pp. 533–4, 539–47.

[129] Henry Halsted to John Tillotson, 3 Aug. 1683 (Bodleian Library, Oxford, Tanner MS 34, fo. 101); Act books: lower house of Convocation 1596–1727 (L.P.L., Convocation of Canterbury records, CONV I/2/10, fo. 24^v); *A copy of the poll . . . 1705*, p. 24; *A copy of the poll . . . 1710*, p. 65.

[130] Returns of proctors 1640–1892, Norwich diocese, 1701 (L.P.L., Convocation of Canterbury records, CONV V/1/1701).

also saw it as a breach of the rights of members of the lower house. Members, they argued, had a constitutional right to attend their national synod and were immune from prosecution in ecclesiastical courts or in courts of law, whilst Convocation sat. In a futile attempt to have the issue sidelined, the archbishop issued a schedule of prorogation, which was promptly ignored. Meanwhile, in the lower house, Kennet tried to have the case referred back to the ecclesiastical courts. The majority finally referred the matter to the committee of grievances which, on 9 February, delivered a report heavily censuring Burnet. The archbishop defended Burnet in an address printed on 19 February. However, the controversy continued well after this date, as a result of the pamphlet debate carried on between Atterbury and Kennet. The committee of scandalous and heretical books was more concerned with establishing the rights of the members of the lower house than with attacking Bishop Burnet. Unfortunately for them, the committee did not have time to deliver their report to the house and had to rest content with delivering a report on a book written by a Quaker, which denounced the sacraments of baptism and communion.[131] It is unfortunately impossible to know what this Quaker book was.

Hutchinson was determined to sit again in Convocation and stood as a candidate in the next Convocation election in the archdeaconry of Subdury, that of 1705. When Hutchinson and Halsted drew an equal number of votes, Halsted entered, on 5 June 1705, in St Mary's Church, Bury St Edmunds, a verbal protest attacking the validity of Hutchinson's candidature.[132] Halsted argued that local custom allowed only rectors or vicars whose livings fell within the archdeaconry of Sudbury to stand as proctor. In contrast Hutchinson was a perpetual curate whose parish of St James' was 'peculiar' in that it fell under the jurisdiction of the Bishop of Norwich, but not that of the Archdeacon of Sudbury.[133] Therefore, stated Halsted, if Hutchinson was allowed to become proctor it would be to the 'ruin and destruction of the immemorial rights, ancient customs, and privileges of the . . . archdeaconry'.[134] The protest worked exactly according to plan, as Halsted was duly elected diocesan

---

[131] Act books: lower house of Convocation, 1596–1727 (L.P.L., Convocation of Canterbury records, MS CONV I/2/6, fo. 7ʳ); Eyewitness account, 28 Jan. 1702 (L.P.L., Gibson MS 934/10, 67); Eyewitness account, 9 Feb. 1702 (L.P.L., Gibson MS 934/12); Bennet, *Tory crisis*, pp. 65–6.

[132] The original manuscript protest is no longer extant but it was fortunately printed in full in Hutchinson's *Defence of the clergy's liberty*, pp. 3–4. On this printed copy are based the contentions in this chapter.

[133] Hutchinson, *Defence of the clergy's liberty*, pp. 1–4.

[134] Ibid., p. 4.

proctor.[135] Halsted was not content with victory in the 1705 election and promptly delivered this protest in writing to the actuary of the archdeaconry of Suffolk consistory court, Henry Goodwin, in order to act as a precedent in future Convocation election clashes.[136]

The High/Low-Church antipathy between Hutchinson and Halsted must have been heightened by party conflict, created by the issue of Church and Dissent, conflict that was unusually fierce in Suffolk and provoked agitation during the election campaign of 1705.[137] Convocation opened alongside Parliament on 25 October 1705, and the High-Church majority made it perfectly clear that they planned to use the meeting to prepare the way for Rochester to raise the 'Church in danger' debate in the House of Lords in December. This issue plagued Convocation until it was prorogued on 21 March 1706.[138] The 'Church in danger' debate reached a new height a few years later. Widespread rioting, involving an estimated crowd of 5,000 people, who represented all the social orders of London, bar the very poor, erupted during the nights of 1–2 March 1710. This rioting was a response to the Whig government's recent impeachment of the High-Church Tory firebrand, Dr Henry Sacheverell, for his incendiary sermon preached on 5 November 1709 at St Paul's Cathedral. The sermon, which was subsequently printed, attacked the Whig view of the Glorious Revolution (discussed in the next chapter) and branded Low-Churchmen and Whigs as 'false brethren' of the Church of England on account of their support of toleration, comprehension and occasional conformity. Occasional conformity was the practice whereby politically minded Protestant Dissenters qualified for municipal office by taking the Anglican sacrament once every twelve months in order to fulfil the requirement of the Corporation Act of 1661, while attending their own meeting houses for the rest of the year. Sacheverell was found guilty, but his sentence, imposed in late March 1710, was so lenient that it was regarded as a victory for the High Tories. The trial had a profound effect on the general public, who were now convinced that the Whig party was determined to ruin the established Church.[139]

This religious tension still hung heavy in the air when elections to Parliament and Convocation respectively were held in October and

[135] Returns of proctors 1640–1892, Norwich diocese, 1705 (L.P.L., CONV V/1/1705).
[136] Hutchinson, *Defence of the clergy's liberty*, pp. 3–4.
[137] See p. 57 below.
[138] Bennet, *White Kennet*, pp. 66–8; idem, *Tory crisis*, p. 82.
[139] Geoffrey Holmes, 'The Sacheverell riots: the crowd and the Church in early eighteenth-century London' in *Past and Present*, lxxii (August, 1972), 55–83; idem, *The making of a great power: late Stuart and early Georgian Britain, 1660–1722* (Harlow, 1993), pp. 354–5; Julian Hoppit, *A land of liberty? England 1689–1727* (Oxford, 2000), p. 234.

November 1710.[140] It was the turn of the archdeaconry of Sudbury to choose a proctor; given the political atmosphere at the time, it is unsurprising that the election contest between Hutchinson and Halsted reached a new level of intensity. In very late September 1710, on the eve of the elections to the Convocation, 230 copies of Hutchinson's pamphlet, *A defence of the liberty of the clergy in their choice of proctors for Convocation . . . in a letter to the Reverend clergy of the archdeaconry of Sudbury*, were published.[141] Shortly afterwards, Halsted noted that 'the protestation [made] . . . at an election about 5 years ago and being recorded sticks closely to the Dr, and which he endeavours to shake off'.[142]

Hutchinson knew that this was probably the last chance for himself, or indeed any Low-Churchman in his archdeaconry, to get into Convocation. He was thus determined to leave nothing to chance. He hoped his pamphlet would persuade those voters who had been swayed in the last election by Halsted's protest to reconsider. He implored the clergy to vote for him, even if they were unconvinced by his arguments, because then the matter could be fairly judged by Convocation itself.[143] He promised, if the decision went against him, he would give them 'no farther trouble'.[144] Contrariwise, if they did not vote for him, he would be without a defence for 'I cannot bring any petition against him [Halsted], because his capacity is unquestionable' since he was rector of a parish in the archdeaconry of Sudbury.[145] In order to accomplish this aim Hutchinson had studied the archbishop's mandate issued to the bishops telling them to inform their clergy that it was time to choose a proctor for the upcoming Convocation.[146] This mandate, argued Hutchinson, stipulated only that proctors should be 'Habilis & Idoneus' [sufficient and proper] and left it entirely up to the clergy to decide whether a proctor was a curate, vicar or rector.[147]

Hutchinson went on to argue that 'the books of Convocation, and precedents there' rather than the 'new customs' of Halsted were the only

---

[140] G. V. Bennett, 'The Convocation of 1710: an Anglican attempt at counter-revolution' in G. J. Cumming and Derek Baker (eds), *Councils and assemblies: papers read at the eighth summer and ninth winter meeting of the Ecclesiastical History Society* (Cambridge, 1971), p. 312.
[141] Hutchinson, *Defence of the clergy's liberty*, p. 12.
[142] Henry Halsted's manuscript animadversions on Dr Hutchinson's 'Defence of the clergy's liberty in their choice of Proctors', 1710 (Bodleian Library, Oxford, Tanner MS 138, fo. 69).
[143] Hutchinson, *Defence of the clergy's liberty*, pp. 6, 11.
[144] Ibid.
[145] Ibid., p. 12.
[146] Ibid., p. 5.
[147] Ibid.

things fit to decide whether a curate could become a proctor or not.[148] Hutchinson did not condemn the validity of *all* local customs (to do so would have drawn invective from his clerical readers for whom local custom was of the utmost importance), merely those 'new customs of our own devising'.[149] Halsted's local custom fell into this category because evidence of it rested on the testimony of living witnesses or, as Hutchinson put it, 'old men's memories'.[150] Hutchinson continued that such customs led only to continual disputes because there were always witnesses who interpreted local custom differently. In stark contrast, the books of Convocation were irrefutable records of the past.[151] Hutchinson, utilising the historical skills honed by his uncle Francis Tallents, mined these sources and found a plethora of examples (local and national, present and historical) of men who were not vicars or rectors but had, nonetheless, been elected to Convocation.[152] He then dealt with Halsted's other main argument succinctly by stating 'that although our two churches (St Mary's and St James') are not subject to the archdeacon, they are within the archdeaconry'.[153]

In his protest of 1705, Hutchinson also claimed that Halsted addressed him as a lecturer, rather than dignifying him with the title of a perpetual curate or minister, and he argued that this was a ploy to diminish the worth of his station.[154] Halsted used the term, argued Hutchinson, because the Church had 'once suffered' by the actions of an 'uncanonical sort of men', which had 'brought an odium upon' the position.[155] He then listed the virtues of a perpetual curate, in order to show that the holder of such a worthy position was indeed able to carry out the duties of a proctor with grace and ease. Firstly, he suggested that the pastoral duties of both vicar and curate were virtually the same. He went on to state that, since vicars and curates usually resided in the communities where they preached, this gave them a perfect understanding of the needs and aspirations of both the laity and the clergy. This meant that a vicar or curate could represent them better in Convocation. Secondly, he argued that the perpetual curacy of St James was more important than normal curacies: it had been occupied by famous churchmen, was subject to

---

[148] Ibid., pp. 6, 5, 3–5.
[149] Hutchinson, *Defence of the clergy's liberty*, p. 5; Douglas Hay and Nicholas Rogers, *Eighteenth-century English society: shuttles and swords* (Oxford, 1997), pp. 84–96.
[150] Hutchinson, *Defence of the clergy's liberty*, p. 6.
[151] Ibid., pp. 5–7.
[152] Ibid., pp. 5, 6, 7, 12.
[153] Ibid., p. 7.
[154] Ibid., p. 8.
[155] Ibid.

the bishop's visitation and licence, and had been established by the king's licence. In short, his living was in everything but name an ecclesiastical benefice. Finally, he argued that curacies were so badly paid that curates deserved to receive as compensation any other rights and privileges which could possibly be bestowed upon them.[156] Ironically, Hutchinson's perpetual curacy provided him with a relatively handsome salary.[157]

In the midst of the proctorial elections Halsted drafted a reply to Hutchinson's pamphlet. He distributed it among the clergy of his archdeaconry on 2 November 1710, nearly a month after the *Defence* was published. Hutchinson swiftly wrote a reply, which was distributed in the same manner. It is clear from the internal evidence of Hutchinson's pamphlet that it was written before Convocation opened on 25 November.[158] Both replies are handwritten, but neither is in the hand of Halsted or Hutchinson, suggesting that both men hired scribes to make multiple copies for them. These pamphlets are currently housed in the Tanner Collection in the Bodleian Library and are thus likely to have been in the possession of Thomas Tanner.[159] In 1710 Tanner was the commissary of the archdeaconry of Sudbury and would have received a copy of the pamphlets.[160]

The issue of whether or not it was a local custom to choose curates as proctors continued to be the main subject of debate. Hutchinson stuck to his original argument that it was not a local custom to choose only rectors and vicars as proctors, and not curates.[161] It was better, he suggested, to collect all the evidence from all of the parties involved and then pass it on to Convocation for it to judge the matter.[162] Halsted also stuck by his original argument, suggesting that it was 'indecent' of Hutchinson to make 'the Convocation entries and records ... the sole repositorys to prove all our locall customs by', without using 'evidence of the living and antient witnesses'.[163] Hutchinson had rejected the testimonies of Halsted's witnesses which, to Halsted, was tantamount to branding a section of the Suffolk community as unreliable.[164]

---

[156] Ibid., pp. 8, 9, 10–11.

[157] See p. 17 above.

[158] Francis Hutchinson's manuscript vindication of his 'Defence of the clergy's liberty in the choice of their proctors in a reply to Henry Halsted', 1710 (Bodleian Library, Oxford, Tanner MS 137, fo. 68); Bennett, *Tory crisis*, pp. 126–7.

[159] Hutchinson manuscript vindication, 1710 (Bodleian Library, Oxford, Tanner MS 137, fo. 68); Halsted manuscript animadversions, 1710 (Bodleian Library, Oxford, Tanner MS 138, fo. 69).

[160] Richard Sharp, 'Tanner, Thomas (1674–1735)' in *OxDNB*.

[161] Hutchinson manuscript vindication, 1710 (Bodleian Library, Oxford, Tanner MS 137, fo. 68).

[162] Ibid.

[163] Halsted manuscript animadversions, 1710 (Bodleian Library, Oxford, Tanner MS 138, fo. 69).

[164] Ibid.

Halsted's reply to the *Defence* shows clearly that his campaign was once more animated by High-Church antipathy. Halsted informed his readers that Hutchinson had let it slip that 'if he carried it at the election, it should not be in the power of the lower house of Convocation to throw him out' because he 'would appeal to the bishops in the upper house'.[165] Halsted was implying that Hutchinson was nothing more than a Low-Church lackey of the upper house and it was their duty, as High-Churchmen, to cast their vote elsewhere.[166] Hutchinson complained that he had been misquoted and that it was only Halsted's fear that the weakness of his case would be exposed if it went before Convocation which made him so anxious to avoid its interference. Hutchinson concluded that in any case elections were 'determined by the whole Convocation, (both houses together)'.[167]

In this new debate, rhetoric was complemented by personal insult. For example, Halsted in his reply denied that the station of perpetual curate even existed, arguing that ministers of 'appropriated churches' were merely 'voluntary and temporary curates', having neither been instituted nor inducted.[168] Hutchinson pedantically, but correctly, retorted that only ignorant people would deign to deny that such an office existed:

> The name of perpetuall curates, which is the first thing he objects against is not my devising, but is the usual term which I find learned men use to distinguish those that are the sole ministers in the appropriate churches, from those that are only assistants to other incumbents. They cannot be remov'd but by a due proof of a lawful cause; and as they enjoy this privilege of voting in other dioceses, I hope you still not think there is any reason to exclude them in this without having their case heard.[169]

Although a great collector, and possibly reader, of books, Halsted would have been seen by contemporaries as Hutchinson's intellectual inferior. He did not possess a DD and failed to publish even a single sermon. Hutchinson, by contrast, had obtained a DD in 1698, written a popular book on modern prophecy, published four sermons and was in touch with key scientific figures such as Sir Hans Sloane.[170] To Halsted, Hutchinson was merely an intellectual snob who unscrupulously used social connection and scholarly knowledge to try to worm his way into Convocation:

---

[165] Ibid.
[166] Ibid.
[167] Hutchinson manuscript vindication, 1710 (Bodleian Library, Oxford, Tanner MS 137, fo. 68).
[168] Halsted manuscript animadversions, 1710 (Bodleian Library, Oxford, Tanner MS 138, fo. 69).
[169] Hutchinson manuscript vindication, 1710 (Bodleian Library, Oxford, Tanner MS 137, fo. 68).
[170] See chapters 1, 3 and 5.

> He [has] taken great pains about it in advising with friends and collecting precedents far and near, new and old, and whether applicable or no, it matters not for this conqueror of all difficulties ... will make a beaten way to the Convocation house, through those devious and obscure passages.[171]

In the end Hutchinson's arguments were for nought. As the political tide in the country turned once again against Whigs and Low-Churchmen, Halsted was once more elected as diocesan proctor.[172]

In common with the majority of Anglican churchmen in the decades following the Glorious Revolution, Hutchinson was extremely partisan and his Latitudinarian Whiggism fuelled his repeated, often unsuccessful bids to play a part in successive Convocations. Dedicated to raising the status and authority of the established Church in an 'age of danger' and increased competition, he was convinced that this would be best achieved by voluntary means, by drawing moderate Protestant Dissenters back into the Anglican fold by means of comprehension and, more importantly, by increased pastoral effort on the part of the parish clergy. Hutchinson demonstrated his solidarity for the latter course by conducting a sustained programme of pastoral reform in his parish. This programme took two forms: he maintained a high standard of public worship by conducting regular services and Holy Communions and by providing frequent, high-quality sermons; and he employed a number of educational strategies designed to inculcate his parishioners with an understanding of their Anglican faith. He not only set up and helped finance and run three charity schools but he tried, on various occasions, to catechise the adult poor of his parish. He also distributed religious pamphlets and kept his parochial library well stocked with religious books. These activities were carried out in conjunction with the S.P.C.K, in his capacity as one of the corresponding members for the county of Suffolk. In short, the picture which emerges of Bury St Edmunds from an examination of Hutchinson's performance of his clerical duties is one that is similar to the one painted of the established Church as a whole in recent historiography, in that its people were provided with a relatively high standard of pastoral care by a well qualified, dedicated and competent clergyman.

---

[171] Halsted manuscript animadversions, 1710 (Bodleian Library, Oxford, Tanner MS 138, fo. 69).
[172] See Chapter 3 below (p. 58 relating to 1710 election) and this chapter, above (pp. 50–1 on Halsted's election in 1710 as diocesan proctor).

3

'A well affected man': Hutchinson and party politics, 1700–20

From 1689 to 1714, Tory and Whig was the standing political division in Parliament and in the political identities assumed by most MPs. From time to time this pattern was upset by coalitions between court and country members of both parties. These coalitions were more prominent in the 1690s than in the 1700s and the 1710s, when the Tory party increasingly became the natural home of the committed country supporter. The court *vs* country divide was characterised by the quest of country members to prevent any extension of the corrupting influence of the executive over Parliament that threatened the latter's independence and by consequence the liberty of English subjects.

The Tory/Whig divide was determined by their positions on the great events and issues of the day, grouped around concerns over the established Church and Protestant Dissent, the Protestant succession and the War of Spanish Succession between France and Britain and their allies – a prolonged, extremely expensive and expansive conflict, conducted on land and sea over a large part of the globe and involving forces of unprecedented scale and size. Underlying these divergent stances were ideological disagreements over what political position the established Church should have in society, the entitlement to and scope of the constitutional rights of Protestant Dissenters, what form monarchy should take and its relationship with the legislature, and how, and in what ways, the nation's interests in foreign lands should be increased and defended.[1] In this period, as a result of the increasing expense of fighting elections, especially in large constituencies such as Suffolk,

---

[1] Holmes, *Great power*, pp. 334–42, 346–8; idem, *British politics*, chapter 4; David Hayton, 'The "Country" interest and the party system, 1689–c.1720' in Clyve Jones (ed.), *Party management in parliament 1660–1784* (London, 1984), pp. 102–18; H. T. Dickinson, *Liberty and property: political ideology in eighteenth century Britain* (London, 1977), chapters 1 and 2; David Hayton, 'The politics of the house: introduction' in *The House of Commons, 1690–1715*, i, 434–44, 462–6.

polls were held only if the seat in question was not considered a 'safe seat'.[2]

Party conflict was not confined to Westminster, but reached deep into society and regularly determined some local government appointments and elections to borough common councils.[3] It even routinely permeated the private lives, work and leisure of the politically conscious classes.[4] Even those lower down the social ladder, if not on the bottom rung, could be moved by party issues, a prime example of which was the Sacherverell riots.[5] During the period 1701 to 1715 the English electorate also voted along party lines. Relatively autonomous, in that it could usually neither be bullied nor bought, and politically informed by virtue of the party propaganda (in the form of sermons, newspapers, broadsides and prints) which reported the great political issues of the day and the stance each party took on them, 'the rage of party' electorate voted largely as their conscience dictated in an unusually high number of general elections over an unusually high number of contested seats.[6] This electorate may have been growing steadily in the seventeenth and early eighteenth centuries, but it was still largely unrepresentative by modern standards, if not by those of the earlier seventeenth century or the later eighteenth century, of the English people at large. Nonetheless, the opinion this electorate expressed at the polls can be seen to have, broadly speaking, reflected public opinion, or less anachronistically, the political will of the nation, as in the Tory landslide victory in the 1710 general election.[7]

It was suggested in Chapter 1 that by the early 1690s (and probably even earlier) Hutchinson had aligned politically with the Whig party, an allegiance shared by members of his immediate family and which proved an invaluable asset during his slow ascent up the clerical ladder.[8]

---

[2] W. A. Speck, *Tory and Whig: the struggle in the constituencies, 1701–1715* (London, 1970), pp. 22–32, 33, 46, 74–5, 77–97, 120–1, 129; Murrel, 'Suffolk', pp. 101–2.

[3] Henry Horowitz, 'Party in a civic context: London from the Exclusion Crisis to the fall of Walpole' in Clyve Jones (ed.), *Britain in the first age of party 1684–1750* (London, 1987), pp. 173–93.

[4] Geoffrey Holmes and W. A. Speck, *The divided society: party conflict in England 1694–1716* (London, 1967), pp. 40–1.

[5] See p. 47 above.

[6] Speck, *Tory and Whig*; idem, 'Political propaganda in Augustan England' in *Transactions of the Royal Historical Society*, 5th series, xxii (1972), 27–8.

[7] J. H. Plumb, 'The growth of the electorate in England from 1600 to 1715' *Past and Present*, xlv (1969), 90–116; Geoffrey Holmes, 'The electorate and the national will in the first age of party' in idem (ed.), *Politics, religion and society in England, 1679–1742* (London, 1986), pp. 7–33.

[8] See chapters 2, 3 and 6.

However, it was not until Queen Anne's reign that he became heavily involved in national politics, albeit at a local level, through the production of political sermons and pamphlets.

I

In the later seventeenth and early eighteenth centuries it was still relatively rare for a parish priest to publish even a single sermon.[9] Hutchinson's two overtly political sermons, along with his voting behaviour, therefore give us a relatively rare insight into the political views of a parish minister in the reign of Queen Anne. Hutchinson used these sermons to voice support for the Whig party's stance on some of the great issues of the day: the 1707 Union with Scotland, the conduct of the War of the Spanish Succession and the toleration of Protestant Dissent. Despite their worth as a perfect piece of pulpit propaganda, they unfortunately shed only a little light on the precise nature of Hutchinson's political ideology in that period. An estimation of just how principled his Whiggery was is therefore impossible.

The late Geoffrey Holmes remarked that 'in the 172 years between the Restoration and the first Reform Act the representative system in England and Wales remained unchanged in its essential features: the two-member constituency norm, outside Wales; the universal forty-shilling freehold qualification for a voter in each of the 52 counties, yet the utterly fortuitous distribution of seats between counties; above all the bewildering variety of franchises in the 215 cities and parliamentary boroughs'.[10] In the early eighteenth century the county of Suffolk was divided into eight constituencies, seven borough and one county. In the borough of Bury St Edmunds the franchise was held by the town corporation, which numbered somewhere between 31 and 37 members. Hutchinson thus had to rest content with voting in county elections, where every freeholder was able to cast two votes each for the candidates of their choice. Between 4,500 and 6,000 people in Suffolk were enfranchised.[11]

In the Suffolk election held on 5 August 1702, Lionel Tollemache (the Earl of Dysart) and Sir Robert Davers stood for the Tories, Sir Samuel Barnardiston and Sir Dudley Cullum for the Whigs. Barnardiston represented the 'country' Whig interest, whereas Dysart and Davers were

---

[9] Pruett, *Parish clergy*, pp. 46–7.
[10] Holmes, 'Electorate and the national will', pp. 4–5.
[11] W. A. Speck, 'The electorate in the first age of party' in Clyve Jones (ed.), *Britain in the first age of party, 1684–1750: essays presented to Geoffrey Holmes* (London, 1987), p. 52; Murrel, 'Suffolk', pp. 8, 122, 164, 171; Cruickshanks, Handley and Hayton, *The House of Commons 1690–1715*, ii, 542, 547.

High-Church Tories who later became 'Tackers'.[12] The election campaign lasted over two months and generated a considerable amount of party heat, particularly over religious issues. The Tory Anglican revival generated by the accession of Queen Anne, who was a high Anglican and Tory sympathiser, augured ill for the Whig party in the forthcoming general election. Threatened by the possibility of a Tory landslide and a consequent Anglican backlash against Protestant Dissenters, Suffolk's large number of non-conformists rallied to the Whig cause. Consequently, for the first time in three general elections, a candidate who was unmistakably Whig in his party allegiance, Cullum, was returned to Parliament for Suffolk. Cullum was joined in the 1702 session of Parliament by Dysart. The defeated Barnardiston also represented the Whigs in this election. In previous elections, those of 10 August 1698, 22 January 1701 and 10 December 1701, Barnardiston had joined forces with Dysart to represent the 'country' interest. The situation at the Suffolk 1702 polls differed from that in the country as a whole, where a massive swing to the Tories enabled them to increase substantially their overall majority in Parliament.[13]

Unlike the majority of Church of England lower clergy, Hutchinson voted consistently for the Whig party in parliamentary elections.[14] In 1702 he was registered to vote in the parish of Hoxne where he was vicar. He subsequently cast only one vote, in favour of the Whig candidate Cullum. He abstained from using his other vote as this would have meant voting for either a Tory candidate or for Barnardiston.[15] The leading part Barnardiston played in the parliamentary opposition to the preparation for the war against Louis XIV's France and her allies made him politically repugnant to Hutchinson.[16] In common with most Whigs, Hutchinson saw the War of Spanish Succession as nothing less than a war of survival for the English nation.[17]

---

[12] Cruickshanks, Handley and Hayton, *The House of Commons 1690–1715*, ii, 543–4; ibid., iii, 141; ibid., v, 649. 'Tackers' were those high Tories who, in the 1704 session of Parliament, tried unsuccessfully to 'tack' an Occasional Conformity Bill onto a Land Tax Bill. More moderate Tories had voted against the tack, which led to deep divisions being formed within their ranks.

[13] Murrel, 'Suffolk', pp. 85–7; W. A. Speck, *The birth of Britain: new nation, 1700–1710* (Oxford, 1994), p. 39; Cruickshanks, Handley and Hayton, *History of Parliament, the House of Commons 1690–1715*, ii, 543–4.

[14] S. W. Baskerville, 'The political behaviour of the Cheshire clergy, 1705–1752' in *Northern History*, xxiii (1987), 74–5.

[15] *A true and exact list of the names ... that voted ... fifth day of August, 1702*, p. 24.

[16] Cruickshanks, Handley and Hayton, *History of Parliament, the House of Commons 1690–1715*, ii, 543–4; Ibid., iii, 141.

[17] For Hutchinson's views on the war, see pp. 60–4 below.

In the parliamentary session of 1704, eight out of the ten MPs who came from Suffolk had voted for the 'tack'. This had the immediate effect of re-igniting party tensions in Suffolk over the issue of Church and Dissent. This tension reached a height during the parliamentary campaign which began in February 1705. The election was finally held on 9 May 1705 and in the end the Whig candidates Barnardiston and Cullum were beaten by the high Tories Davers and Dysart. Once again the situation in Suffolk was slightly different from the rest of the country. In the Parliament that opened in September 1705 the Tories enjoyed an overall majority, but there were fewer 'Tackers' and more moderate Whigs and Tories than there had been in previous years.[18] The Tory victory had been created by the considerable electoral might of the Anglican clergy and by the tide of popular support for the idea, nurtured carefully by the Tory party, that the Whigs, by virtue of their attitude to Dissent and the practice of occasional conformity, had placed the 'Church in danger'.[19]

Hutchinson abstained from voting in this election, the reasons for which can only be guessed at. It may have been that Hutchinson chose not to vote because he believed that Barnardiston's and Cullum's election bid was doomed to failure and that his own time would be better spent trying to regain his seat as diocesan proctor in the forthcoming elections for the Convocation of Canterbury. In Convocation at least he could meet the High-Church menace head on.[20] In stark contrast to that of their Tory counterparts, the 1705 electoral campaign of the Suffolk Whigs was badly planned and poorly executed.[21]

In 1707, as a result of the Act of Union, Dysart was deprived of his Suffolk seat and made a peer of the British realm. He was replaced by local Tory, Leicester Martin, until the election on 5 May 1708,[22] when Sir Thomas Hanmer (a confirmed Tory, member of the landed gentry and relative newcomer to Suffolk) and Davers were returned to Parliament.[23] Barnardiston had died in November 1707 and Cullum had retired from political life.[24]

---

[18] Speck, *Tory and Whig*, pp. 98–9, 104–6; Murrel, 'Suffolk', pp. 89–97; Cruickshanks, Handley and Hayton, *History of Parliament, the House of Commons 1690–1715*, ii, 543.

[19] Holmes, *British Politics*, pp. 99–104; idem, *Dr Sacheverell*, pp. 41–6; Speck, *Birth of Britain*, pp. 76–89, 94–5; John P. Kenyon, *Revolution principles: the politics of party, 1689–1720* (Cambridge, 1982), pp. 96–100.

[20] See pp. 46–7 above.

[21] Murrel, 'Suffolk', pp. 392–5, 403–25.

[22] Cruickshanks, Handley and Hayton, *History of Parliament, the House of Commons 1690–1715*, ii, 543–4.

[23] Ibid., ii, 534; Ibid., iv, 187–90.

[24] Ibid., ii, 544.

In the next general election held in October 1710, the anti-Whig feeling in the country at large, produced by war-weariness and the fall-out from the impeachment of Dr Sacheverell gave the Tory party a landslide victory.[25] In the Suffolk county election Sir Philip Parker (the Whig candidate) was summarily beaten by the two Tory candidates, Sir Thomas Hanmer and Sir Robert Davers.[26] This election saw a higher level of split voting (the practice of using one vote for a Tory candidate and the other for a Whig candidate) among the clerical voters than had been witnessed in previous elections. Furthermore, of those clergy who split their votes, all but one split them between Hanmer and Parker. Pat Murrel argues that this pattern suggests that a number of the Whig clergy were tactically voting for Hanmer. There was only one Whig candidate standing for Parliament in 1710, which meant that whatever happened one of the two Tory candidates would be elected. It was Hanmer's views on the issue of Protestant Dissent that convinced those clergy of a Whiggish bent that it was best that he was returned to Parliament instead of the High-Church Tory Robert Davers. Hanmer had been a 'Tacker' in 1704, but in the following years he had shifted towards the Whigs on the question of Dissent. So much so, that by 1710 he had actively involved himself with a non-conformist body in Suffolk in a bid to secure their votes in the upcoming election. There had even been rumours spread during the run-up to the election that Hanmer was about to join with Parker to represent the Whigs.[27] Hutchinson was among the twelve clergymen in these elections who tactically split their votes between Hanmer and Parker.[28] Considering Hutchinson's view on Dissent, it is unsurprising that he would have favoured Hanmer over Davers, especially since the successful Tory candidate would take part in a parliamentary assembly where, owing to the High-Church revival caused by the Sacherverell affair, the issue of Dissent was bound to loom large.[29]

In the late seventeenth and early eighteenth centuries, clergymen often used the pulpit to dispense party propaganda. Sermons preached at assize court sessions were one of the ways in which central government, from 1700 onwards, disseminated party propaganda. It was thus those clergymen who possessed the right brand of party politics who were

---

[25] See p. 54 above.
[26] Speck, *Birth of Britain*, pp. 188–92; Murrel, 'Suffolk', pp. 491–2, 207, 109–10, 527, 517, 520.
[27] Murrel, 'Suffolk', pp. 425–8, 109.
[28] *A copy of the poll . . . 1710*, p. 19.
[29] See pp. 22–6 above.

chosen to preach on these occasions.[30] Hutchinson was selected to preach a sermon at the assize session at Bury St Edmunds on 25 March 1707 in support of the government and Whig-backed War of Spanish Succession, an honour which was to be repeated on several subsequent occasions:

> Under the greatest difficulty of our war and taxes ... I preached an assize sermon here at Bury to shew the peeple the necessity of patience under the burdens for the support of ourselves and our confederates ... besides three or four other sermons upon like occasions.[31]

It is obvious that the 1707 sermon performed the political function for which it was designed because, as Hutchinson went on to boast, 'the Judge and the two Grand juries unanimously desired and had it printed'.[32] The sermon formed a scathing attack on those criticisms raised, mainly by Tories, against the land war currently being conducted in the Low Countries under the auspices of John Churchill, 1st Duke of Marlborough. The sermon also demonstrates that underlying his unstinting support for the war was an attitude concerning Britain's natural relationship with Europe that was distinctly Whiggish.

Until 1710, and especially from 1705 onwards, Queen Anne and her government were completely committed to waging the war of Spanish Succession. During the parliamentary session that ran from December 1706 to April 1707 Queen Anne and her ministry, fronted by Marlborough, Sidney Godolphin and Robert Harley, was, as a result of Tory opposition, reliant on Whig support in the Commons to get money bills through Parliament.[33] Supplies were needed if Marlborough was to follow on from the gains made in 1706 by the allied victories at Ramillies and Turin. Combined, these victories had cleared French forces from the Spanish Netherlands and ended the war in Northern Italy. This left the Iberian Peninsula as the last bastion of Bourbon strength. Marlborough hoped to use this position as a springboard for a campaign to be undertaken the following year, which was designed to inflict the last great defeat on the Bourbon powers and secure peace on favourable terms.[34] The underlying ethos of Marlborough's military strategy was that the French war machine could be defeated via a land war, conducted as set-piece battles.[35]

---

[30] Pruett, *Parish clergy*, p. 155; G. Mischler, 'English political sermons, 1714–1742: a case study in the theory of "divine right of governors" and the ideology of order' in *Eighteenth-Century Studies*, xxiv, no. 1 (2001), 37.
[31] Hutchinson to Wake, 14 April 1720 (C. C., Wake Letters, vol. 21, no. 215).
[32] Ibid.
[33] Holmes, *Great power*, p. 424; Hoppit, *Land of liberty*, p. 295.
[34] Speck, *Birth of Britain*, p. 103; Hoppit, *Land of liberty*, pp. 117–21.
[35] Holmes, *Great power*, pp. 237, 238–40; Hoppit, *Land of liberty*, pp. 114–23.

From the beginning of the 1701 parliamentary session, the Whig party had been convinced of the need for a war with France. This commitment was the by-product of a distinctive Whig attitude as to what Britain's natural relationship with the rest of Europe should be. In their view, Britain had to have an active role in European affairs because her political security and economic prosperity and that of Europe were interdependent. This was none other than William III's concept of co-operative security and positive involvement, which the Whigs had warmed to during the Nine Years' War, when they became strong supporters of that monarch's land campaign. William's foreign policy, which subsequently became Whig foreign policy, centred on the protection of three main interests: the maintenance of the balance of power between the dynastic forces in Europe (a system of international politics becoming increasingly popular in Europe by the turn of the eighteenth century), which the growing military might of France clearly threatened; the protection of commercial interests, especially Britain's trade with continental Europe, which had been placed under threat by French expansionism after 1670; and the protection of England's Revolutionary settlement and her Protestant succession, which had been endangered by the fact that Louis XIV had recognised the Jacobite pretender, James III, as the true King of England after the death of James II in 1701.[36]

By contrast, the majority of the Tory party were at best fair-weather supporters of the way the Junto and the 'Duumvirs' (Marlborough and Godolphin) were conducting the war, and at worst vehement critics of it. Tory opposition to the conduct of the war took two main forms. First of all they complained that Britain was taking too great a part in a conflict fought essentially to protect the Portuguese, the Dutch and the Holy Roman Empire from French aggression.[37] Hutchinson answered this charge in his sermon, arguing that the French were bent on the appropriation and destruction of everything English, and thus to conduct the war as auxiliaries, rather than as principals, would be disastrous. He employed the allegory of a Biblical story in Judges 18 concerning the conflict between the people of Laish and the Danites, to demonstrate what would happen to Britain if she failed to face the threat of France head on. Hutchinson argued that the Danites, from the tribe of Canaan, had, for largely economic reasons, attacked the Laish who,

---

[36] Holmes, *Great power*, pp. 235–7; idem, *British politics*, pp. 64–5, 71–2; Hoppit, *Land of liberty*, pp. 111–14; William Roosen, 'The origins of the war of Spanish Succession' in Jeremy Black and John Donald (eds.), *The origins of war in early modern Europe* (Edinburgh, 1987), p. 165.

[37] Holmes, *British politics*, p. 72.

because they were a careless and unwarlike people, made an easy prey for their enemies.[38] The Danites had not only 'burnt up their city, put the people to the sword, and settled themselves'[39] in their place but had plundered their places of worship.[40] To spare the reader any confusion, Hutchinson stated, in no uncertain terms, who the Danite and Laish represented:

> Though we must not be a nation that delights in war, and is forward to disturb our neighbours: yet we must bear our several parts that are needful to carry on that war which our excellent government hath thought just and necessary ... to keep us from being served like *Laish*. We have a *Danite* near us, that without the pretence of poverty to excus him ... [and who] hath brought himself under high obligations, promises, and vows, to take the first time of doing that, which cannot be done without a sea of English blood.[41]

Secondly, during the War of the Spanish Succession, Tories were on the whole sceptical of the worth of military involvement in continental Europe, an outlook commonly referred to as the 'blue water strategy'. High and moderate Tories, respectively, provided consistent opposition to, and half-hearted support for, Marlborough's land war. Court Tories, on the other hand, between 1701–8 if not afterwards, toed the government line on the conduct of the war.[42] Unsurprisingly, Hutchinson was full of praise for Marlborough's land war and reasoned that, if the strategy of the war ministry had achieved such a 'wonderful success', why change it?[43]

Before 1707 some hotter Tories periodically went beyond merely criticising the government's conduct of the war and actually attacked the war itself. In the wake of the failure of the government to make peace after the battle of Ramillies in 1706, they claimed that the government was prolonging the war for their own advantage and that of the Whig 'monied interest' in the country.[44] Hutchinson, on the other hand, claimed that the British people possessed 'good magistrates' who were

---

[38] Hutchinson, *Sermon preached . . . 25 Mar. 1707*, pp. 1–9.
[39] Ibid., p. 1.
[40] Ibid., p. 4.
[41] Ibid., pp. 6–7.
[42] Holmes, *British politics*, pp. 71–9; Hoppit, *Land of liberty*, p. 113; Hayton, 'The "Country" interest', p. 59; Holmes, *Great power*, p. 240.
[43] Hutchinson, *Sermon preached . . . 25 Mar. 1707*, p. 14.
[44] Speck, *Birth of Britain*, p. 103; Hoppit, *A Land of liberty*, p. 122; Jonathan Swift, *The conduct of the allies and of the late ministry, in beginning and carrying on the war* (London, 1712, repr. 1888), pp. 421–2, 426; Holmes, *British politics*, pp. 64–71.

'often awake when their people sleep' in order 'to find out, meet with, and prevent all dangers at a distance'.[45] He also reminded them that nations, such as the Laish, who had lacked such good governors had been easily defeated by their enemies.[46] The British people, for their own safety, thus had to place their whole trust in their 'vigilant and wise government' until they had 'driven back' and 'shut up our Danite safe and quiet in his own tribe'.[47]

The Tory complaint that the war was being fought for the benefit of the Whig 'monied interest' was rooted in the social and economic changes Britain was undergoing at that time. It was a time of general economic hardship for the middling to the lesser landed gentry, as well as the bulk of the clergy, sections of society from which the core of the Tory party was formed. The land tax added to the strain because its burden fell principally upon their shoulders. On the other hand, the new 'monied interest', associated with the Whig party, remained relatively untaxed and, in some cases, made massive profits from the interest levied on loans given to the government to fund an expensive war. This fact led to Tory suspicion that Whig self-interest was the real motivation behind their vehement support for the war. The annoyance of the landed gentry with the 'monied men' was part of a general fear that their sudden rise in social and political prominence threatened their own social and political hegemony. In this way, social conflict added fuel to the fire of party conflict.[48]

The location of Hutchinson's parish made him acutely aware of these social tensions. East Anglia, like London, was particularly hard hit by the burden of the land tax, for the simple reason that the government's agents found it easier to collect taxes in these areas.[49] Hutchinson tried to allay these grievances in his sermon with the argument that their taxes were being used to stop an enemy bent on their annihilation:

> It is always acceptable and popular, to complain of the burdens, and call for peace and ease of taxes: but we must remember, that our taxes are not given for the invasion of our neighbours, but to keep us from being served like Laish.[50]

---

[45] Hutchinson, *Sermon preached . . . 25 Mar. 1707*, p. 2.
[46] Ibid.
[47] Ibid., p. 1.
[48] Horowitz, 'Party in a civic context', pp. 173–4; W. A. Speck, 'Conflict in society' in Geoffrey Holmes (ed.), *Britain after the Glorious Revolution, 1689–1714* (London, 1978), pp. 135–49; Holmes, *Great power*, chapters 17 and 18; idem, *British politics*, pp. 157–82.
[49] Holmes, *Great power*, pp. 360, 388; Baskerville, 'Political behaviour', p. 74.
[50] Hutchinson, *Sermon preached . . . 25 Mar. 1707*, pp. 6–7.

Thus, for their own sake, the landed gentry had to turn their back on 'ease, pleasure, and self-interest' and push themselves towards 'virtuous cares and publick spirit' in order to keep up the 'English warlike spirit' until France was defeated.[51] In short, though Hutchinson came from farming stock and was a member of the parish clergy, he shared none of their distrust for the new 'monied interest'. In fact, his support of this interest had grown stronger by the time he went to Ireland in 1720, where he not only dabbled in the stock market but became a vehement supporter of the foundation of an Irish national bank that was to be modelled on the Bank of England.[52]

The Tory critique of the war was also informed by a distinct view of what Britain's natural relationship with Europe and her allies should be. This view can be characterised as xenophobic and isolationist. Geoffrey Holmes argued that Tory country squires possessed an almost instinctive distrust of foreigners, born of a 'sheer ignorance' about foreign countries and their inhabitants, and nurtured by 'unabashed insularity'.[53] The antidote Hutchinson prescribed for this particular ideological ailment was an education in the ways of other nations and cultures: 'how dangerous and troublesome error, and ignorance, and superstition, often make men and nations to one another: and by consequence we learn that it is of great importance, that a people be well instructed in sound and true knowledge of things, and sober notions'.[54]

He also wished to change the attitudes of those Tories whose prejudice against Britain's European allies, especially the Dutch, was more principled. Many Tories had become convinced by the late 1690s that William III had fought the Nine Years' War mainly to line the pockets of the Whigs and to further the European influence of the Dutch. From this point on, they treated William's balance-of-power foreign policy with suspicion, resulting in their opposition to the partition treaties of 1698–1700.[55] This attitude to Europe once again manifested itself during the War of Spanish Succession among a large section of the Tory party. They believed the Dutch were prepared to let England bankrupt itself in order to protect their own interests and territories, whilst continually defaulting on their own promised quotas of men and money. These accusations were first raised in 1703 and again in 1705, before being quickly quietened by the historic victories at Blenheim (1704),

---

[51] Ibid., pp. 1, 7.
[52] See pp. 183–7 below.
[53] Holmes, *British politics*, p. 67.
[54] Hutchinson, *Sermon preached . . . 25 Mar. 1707*, p. 3; Holmes, *British politics*, p. 67.
[55] Holmes, *British politics*, pp. 64–9; Hoppit, *A Land of liberty*, pp. 111–14.

Ramillies and Turin (1706).[56] Hutchinson's reply to this criticism was characteristically Whiggish. He argued that Britain's only hope of survival against the French onslaught was the military help afforded by the Grand Alliance.[57] The Grand Alliance could achieve what Britain could not on her own, simply because two swords were better than one.[58] In any case, argued Hutchinson, Britain should willingly bear the disproportionate burden of war costs with honour because they had been given, by God's grace, the means to do so.[59]

Hutchinson's next opportunity to support the Whig party came on 1 May 1707, when he was asked to preach a sermon to celebrate, and of course vindicate, the newly forged Union between Scotland and England.[60] The monarchy was the first to come around to the idea of an incorporating parliamentary union when William III, on his death bed, finally realised that this was the only way he could prevent an increasingly uncontrollable Scottish Parliament from breaking away from the English Crown.[61] Since 1698 the country party in the Edinburgh Parliament had sought to curtail the English crown's grip on Scottish affairs and in particular to force a re-negotiation of the Anglo-Scottish economic relationship. Therefore, at this point in time, a union with England was the last thing on the minds of this section of Scottish MPs. Their relative parliamentary strength had allowed them to pass, in the 1703/4 sessions of Parliament, the Security Act, the Act anent Peace and War, and the Wines Act, which posed a very real threat to, respectively, the Hanoverian succession in Scotland, Scotland's continuation of the war and, less importantly, economic relations between the two countries.[62] The Scottish Parliament came around to the idea of Union between 1704 and 1706, though it remained unpopular in Scotland generally. The threat of English invasion or civil war, allied with that of an English economic embargo by virtue of the Aliens Act, persuaded many Scottish politicians to change their attitude to an incorporating union. The unexpected willingness of the English negotiators in 1706 to yield in a number of important points, such as securing the continuing independence of the Scottish legal and

---

[56] Holmes, *British politics*, pp. 64–71; J. R. Jones, *Marlborough* (Cambridge, 1993), pp. 90–8, 120–3, 129.
[57] Hutchinson, *Sermon preached . . . 25 Mar. 1707*, p. 2.
[58] Ibid., pp. 8–9; see also Holmes, *British politics*, p. 65.
[59] Hutchinson, *Sermon preached . . . 25 Mar. 1707*, p. 9.
[60] See Hutchinson, *Sermon preached . . . 1 May 1707*.
[61] Holmes, *Great power*, pp. 307–10; T. C. Smout, 'The road to Union' in Geoffrey Holmes (ed.), *Britain after the Glorious Revolution, 1689–1714* (London, 1978), pp. 179–80.
[62] Holmes, *Great power*, pp. 307, 309–10; Smout, *Road to Union*, pp. 181–2.

ecclesiastical establishments, finally persuaded the Scots Parliament to support the Union.[63]

In 1704 the English ministry, the Whig party and moderate Tories were indifferent to the idea of a union with Scotland, but by 1706 they were actively supporting it. This change of attitude was the principal factor that made the Union possible.[64] In the opinion of the late Geoffrey Holmes, 'Of the Union . . . the Whigs were the principal architects', and that 'without Whig initiative, wholehearted Whig co-operation, and in the final instance Whig votes it is virtually certain that the act of 1707 would never have been passed'.[65] The actions of the Scottish Parliament between 1703 and 1704 convinced the Junto and their supporters that Protestant succession in that country was now in extreme danger and that Union would remove this threat.[66] Owing to their disposition towards Dissent, Whigs did not balk at the prospect of joining themselves to a Presbyterian country.[67] Godolphin's court Tories (including Harley and his new Tory supporters) were also unwilling to sacrifice the prospect of success in war, or indeed the succession in Britain, on account of the trouble-making activities of the Edinburgh Parliament. Those Tories, like the war-party Whigs, had enjoyed substantial gains in the October election. Consequently, in complete contrast to the pre-1705 Parliament, where anti-Unionist Tories were in the majority, the pro-Unionist Tories and Whigs held a clear majority.[68] High Tories, lay and clerical, combined forces to prevent the Union Bill's having an otherwise easy journey through Parliament in February/March 1707. Their biggest fear was that union with a Presbyterian country would lead to pollution of the Church of England, thereby allowing a block Whig vote into Westminster, vitiating future attempts to pass an Occasional Conformity Bill.[69]

Since Hutchinson's stirring sermon at the end of March 1707, when his hopes for war had reached a zenith, the allied war cause had taken a turn for the worse. The rout by the French of the combined Dutch, Portuguese, and English army, at Almanza in Spain in April 1707, had

---

[63] John R. Young, 'The parliamentary incorporating Union of 1707: political management, anti-Unionism and foreign policy' in T. M. Devine and J. R. Young (eds), *Eighteenth-century Scotland: new perspectives* (East Linton, 1999), pp. 25–8, 40, 42–5; Smout, *Road to Union*, pp. 183–94.

[64] Young, 'Incorporating Union', p. 46; Holmes, *Great power*, p. 307.

[65] Holmes, *British politics*, pp. 84, 85.

[66] Holmes, *Great power*, pp. 312–14; idem, *British politics*, pp. 83–5; Young, 'Incorporating Union', pp. 40–2.

[67] Young, 'Incorporating Union', pp. 28–9.

[68] Holmes, *Great power*, p. 312.

[69] Ibid., pp. 310, 315; Speck, *Birth of Britain*, pp. 116–17; Every, *High-Church party*, pp. 112–13, 120–1.

ended all realistic hope of forcing Philip V off the throne of Spain. As a result, the primary war aim of both Tories and Whigs (at that time at least) had been dealt a punishing blow.[70] The Union, to Hutchinson, offered some compensation for this set-back because it offered increased national security. He was thus keen to guard the Union against any 'danger of miscarriage', being convinced that if the mass of people of Scotland and England did not immediately complement political Union with a social union, bound with cordial interpersonal relationships, then this 'miscarriage' would surely occur.[71] Hutchinson's fears were probably sparked by the anti-Union rioting in Scotland of the previous year and by the recent stream of anti-Union propaganda in England.[72]

Hutchinson used three main arguments in his bid to convince his readers that they should fully embrace the Union. His first argument was that the Union was part of God's providential plan and thus something that could not be disputed. He argued that God, after dividing the languages of mankind at Babel, had placed humankind 'into their appropriate places'.[73] God had 'reserved the land of *Cannan* for the children of *Israel*', just as he reserved the British Islands for one people.[74] Hutchinson went on to argue that a shared ethnicity between the Scottish and English people had also created the preconditions for Union. The 'nearness of this soil and climate forms them [the Scots] to a like temprament', he opined, and had made 'our blood . . . in great measures the same'.[75]

His second argument was more typically Whiggish: a Union was essential to England's national security. In common with many other Whigs, Hutchinson contended that it would provide a vital accretion of military strength in England's bitter struggle against the 'boundless ambition of France' because it secured, for the foreseeable future, Scotland's continued support for the War of Spanish Succession.[76] In 1703, Scotland had passed the Act anent Peace and War, which stated that the Scottish Parliament could, after the queen's death and even if the current war was still in progress, declare war and make peace at will. Beset as she was with numerous, serious health problems, it was obvious to many, even if the majority of the Tory party were loath to admit it, that it was

---

[70] Jones, *Marlborough*, pp. 121–9, 143–8; Speck, *Birth of Britain*, pp. 103, 123; Holmes, *Great power*, p. 203.
[71] Hutchinson, *Sermon preached . . . 1 May 1707*, p. 11.
[72] Speck, *Birth of Britain*, pp. 110–11.
[73] Hutchinson, *Sermon preached . . . 1 May 1707*, p. 4.
[74] Ibid., p. 4.
[75] Ibid., pp. 4, 12, 13.
[76] Ibid., pp. 12, 13, 9.

highly unlikely that the notoriously unhealthy, heirless Anne would reach old age.⁷⁷

Hutchinson's third and final argument was that the Union should be lauded because of its handling of the religious situation in Scotland. It not only recognised the Presbyterian Church in Scotland as Scotland's national Church, but also lent it legal protection for the first time.⁷⁸ By finally recognising the Presbyterian Church in Scotland as a 'true church', Anglicans were, in Hutchinson's view, finally giving it the 'respect and brotherly love' it deserved.⁷⁹ Hutchinson's views on Scottish Presbyterianism were unsurprisingly those of a Low-Church Whig. For obvious reasons, Low-Churchmen were much less likely than High-Churchmen to condemn other reformed churches on account of their Presbyterian structures.⁸⁰ It was after all only High-Churchmen who favoured the introduction of episcopacy to Switzerland, Prussia and Scotland.⁸¹ In typical Whig fashion, Hutchinson also took the opportunity to voice his support for the 'toleration that our government hath thought to give' to English Protestant Dissenters.⁸² Over a decade later, in 1717, Hutchinson was still convinced of the value of the Toleration Act:

> the powerful interest of the papists in the last reign [that of James II], had laid the poor non-conformist under the penalty of several severe laws, which were accounted no small dishonour to the Protestant name. But now these being suspended by an act of toleration, and a Christian liberty indulged.⁸³

Hutchinson found it expedient to neglect to point out that James II's pro-Catholic policy was complemented, albeit in the latter part of his short reign, with the religious toleration of Protestant Dissenters.⁸⁴

Hutchinson's sermon struck a particular chord with the Whig population of Bury St Edmunds. The minute book of Bury St Edmunds' Corporation recorded the following on 10 May 1707: that 'Dr Francis Hutchinson [be] requested to print the admirable sermon preached by him at St James' on 1 May upon the celebration of the happy union

---

⁷⁷ Holmes, *Great power*, p. 310.
⁷⁸ Every, *High-Church party*, pp. 120–4; William Gibson, *The Church of England 1688–1832: unity and accord* (London, 2001), pp. 184–93.
⁷⁹ Hutchinson, *Sermon preached . . . 1 May 1707*, p. 15.
⁸⁰ Every, *High-Church party*, pp. 120–4; Gibson, *Church of England*, pp. 184–93.
⁸¹ Every, *High-Church party*, p. 124.
⁸² Hutchinson, *Sermon preached . . . 1 May 1707*, p. 16.
⁸³ Hutchinson, *John Tillotson*, p. 30.
⁸⁴ John Spurr, 'Religion in Restoration England' in L. K. J. Glassey (ed.), *The reigns of Charles II and James VII and II* (Basingstoke, 1997), p. 96.

of England and Scotland, and thanks returned to him for his great labour therein'.⁸⁵ Susan, wife of Alderman Macro, even sent copies of the sermon to her friends, one of whom seemed particularly impressed with its contents:

> Madam, the favour of your ladyships I have the honour to receive together with Dr Hutchinson's sermon which I thereby most humbly acknowledge. If it were not too much trouble to your ladyship I should make bold, madam, to entreat you, you would give my thanks to the Dr for the sermon, which tho' it gave me a world of satisfaction when preach'd, I can but say it affords me a great deal more at its perusal.⁸⁶

II

The 'two-party system' of Anne's reign came to an end after her death when the new king, George I, began to purge the government, at local and national level, of Tory office holders. This Whig power base was complemented, after the parliamentary election of 1715, with a majority in the House of Commons. As a result, the Tories, along with the country Whigs, were to all intents and purposes, now excluded from place and power.⁸⁷ However, as Linda Colley points out, 'the Tory parliamentary party retained ideological identity, a capacity for concerted political action, and considerable economic power during its proscription'.⁸⁸

The court Whigs, headed by Sunderland and Stanhope prior to 1720, and then by Walpole from 1721 to 1742, subsequently developed an ideology of order (of which the Anglican clergy were the most vehement promulgators and which was dominated by the theory of the divine right of governors) to legitimise, and thus solidify, their new-found political power. This programme was born of the need to win the affections of a populace which had not taken to their new masters: the rioting that took place in all parts of Britain between 1714 and 1716 was less an expression of genuine popular Jacobitism and more an expression of an increasing dislike of the lower orders for the Whig oligarchy and the Hanoverian dynasty. This violence was taken extremely seriously by the English political elite. Popular rioting, endemic in eighteenth-century England, had long been seen as a prelude to popular revolt or even

---

⁸⁵ H.M.C., *14th Report, appendix, part viii*, p. 153.
⁸⁶ J. Slenbory to Susan Macro, 21 June 1707 (B.L., Add. MS 32556, fos. 51–2).
⁸⁷ W. A. Speck, 'The general election of 1715' in *English Historical Review*, xc, no. 356 (1975), 507.
⁸⁸ Linda Colley, *In defiance of oligarchy: the Tory party, 1714–60* (Cambridge, 1982), p. 7.

social anarchy. The worst-case scenario was, as far as the Hanoverian regime was concerned, that it might arise during a Jacobite invasion or rebellion.[89]

The theory of the divine right of governors differed from the traditional Tory doctrine of the divine right of kings in that it suggested that, although God ensured society possessed a government, he did not dictate what form it should take: it could be republican, monarchical or a limited, parliamentary monarchy. Furthermore, the governors of civil society at all levels, right down to the magistrates and parish officers, were owed complete obedience by the ruled because their authority was ultimately derived from God who had set them on earth to maintain peace and order. Obedience to them and their laws was equivalent to obedience to God.[90] More importantly, this ideology could be used to portray the Hanoverian state, the parliamentary monarchy that had evolved after the Glorious Revolution, and the new Whig administration, as divinely sanctioned and divinely ordained.[91] The theory of divine right of governors was almost certainly derived from what J. P. Kenyon named 'the standard Whig-Anglican view of the origins of political society: that the concept of government originated with God, but its operation depended on the sanction of human laws'.[92] Thus the construction of the ideology of order can be seen to have been part of the larger process whereby Whig ideology became more conservative after 1688.[93]

Doctrines similar to the old Tory staples of passive obedience also resurfaced in the Whig theory of the divine right of governors. In common with their moderate counterparts in the years between 1689 and 1714, court Whigs distanced themselves from the radical implications of Locke's political theory, of which his defence of the doctrine of the right of resistance of subjects against tyrannical rulers was the most disturbing. Resistance theory, establishment Whigs reasoned, could now be turned against their own regime just as their predecessors had used it against absolutism in the seventeenth century. They consequently argued

---

[89] H. T. Dickinson, *The politics of the people in eighteenth century Britain* (London, 1995), pp. 125, 147, 155–7; idem, 'Popular politics in the age of the Walpole', p. 61; idem, *Liberty and property*, pp. 121–7; Nicholas Rogers, *Crowds, culture, and politics in Georgian Britain* (Oxford, 1998), pp. 28–37; idem, 'Popular Jacobitism in a provincial context: eighteenth century Bristol and Norwich' in Eveline Cruickshanks and Jeremy Black (eds), *The Jacobite challenge* (Edinburgh, 1988), pp. 127, 129; Colin Haydon, *Anti-Catholicism in eighteenth century England, c.1714–80: a political and social study* (Manchester, 1993), pp. 82–3, 100–3; Mischler, 'Political sermons', pp. 36, 38–39; Black, *Robert Walpole*, pp. 33–51.
[90] Mischler, 'Political sermons', pp. 33–4, 35, 51, 39–40.
[91] Ibid., p. 38.
[92] Kenyon, *Revolution principles*, pp. 22–3.
[93] Dickinson, *Liberty and property*, p. 126.

that if government was derived from God, then its leaders could be resisted only if they undermined the constitution or the fundamental laws of God. Contrariwise, constant criticism of governors by the governed over 'trivial' matters was seen as unwarranted resistance. Establishment Whigs still had to justify the Glorious Revolution and the Hanoverian accession, as it was on these foundations that their regime rested. They thus maintained that James II, like all rulers, had been bound to the constitution and laws of his country, but had broken these bonds and had endangered the liberty and property of his subjects. Their subsequent resistance in 1688 was thus entirely justified. Many supporters of the new regime thus concentrated on justifying this clear-cut, yet unique, example of resistance rather than ruminating about when resistance of disgruntled subjects was permissible and when not.[94]

This continuity between pre- and post-Hanoverian Whig ideology is clearly illustrated in Hutchinson's sermons. In 1707 he presented an almost textbook example of Kenyon's standard 'Whig Anglican' theory of government. He argued that 'Patriarchal government' in the first civilised societies was 'the most common form of the first imperfect governments' until 'frequent encroachments, and robberies, and murders ... made it necessary for them ... to join together their several households into larger legal kingdoms and commonwealths'.[95] 'And upon that foot', Hutchinson continued, 'the mutual rights of Princes and people would be, by the eternal law and will of God, *Jure Divino*; not what they had been betwixt fathers and sons; not any one particular form of government; but what their several constitutions made them'.[96] Hutchinson, a decade later, was promulgating a full-blown version of the ideology of order. In a blaze of anti-Lockean contractualism, he argued that government was 'not meerly an arbitrary society, into which we have no obligation of entering unless we please' but a kingdom, 'fixed here among men by God'.[97]

Hutchinson may have condemned Locke, but he had no taste for Filmerian patriarchal theory either.[98] Sir Robert Filmer's *Patriachia*, written in the 1640s but not published until 1680, contained one of the

---

[94] Ibid., pp. 70–90, 130–1; Holmes, *British politics*, pp. 58–9; J. A. Downie, *To settle the succession of the state: literature and politics, 1678–1750* (London, 1994), pp. 24–6, 41–4; Mischler, 'Political sermons', pp. 42–4, 50.
[95] Hutchinson, *Sermon preached ... 25 Mar. 1707*, pp. 10–11.
[96] Ibid., p. 11.
[97] Francis Hutchinson, *A Sermon preach'd by the Right Reverend Father in God, Francis, Lord Bishop of Down and Connor, at his primary visitation, held at Lisburn, May 3rd, 1721, and published at the unanimous request of his clergy* (Dublin, 1721), p. 8.
[98] Hutchinson, *Sermon preached ... 25 Mar. 1707*, p. 10.

most convincing defences of the theories of divine right, passive obedience and non-resistance of the seventeenth century. 'Publick government', Hutchinson opined, was divinely ordained and therefore it was the duty of every subject to 'acquiesce in the judgement of those that God and nature have appointed to judge for us'.[99] Hutchinson did not claim that human laws should have the force of divine laws, as some less moderate promulgators of the ideology of order were wont to do.[100] He did, however, advise that human laws should be followed like 'divine guides',[101] because 'law makers' had had 'God's blessing to assist and help them in their great work'.[102] This added 'a sacred weight to every ordinance of man' whereby increasing the reverence with which humankind was to regard them.[103] Subjects were thus expected to stand 'fast like rocks in defence of right, and our constitution', without 'being eternally troublesome to just princes with frights and fears where no evil is intended'.[104] Redress of a perceived grievance through legal means was to be the first, and in most cases, the only recourse of the aggrieved subject.[105] Resistance to established authority was justifiable only as a very last resort after a ruler had threatened the ancient constitution of the country.[106] In common with other promulgators of the ideology of order, Hutchinson held up the Revolution as a unique example of justified resistance, describing William and Mary as the 'princes, who so happily preserved our endangered religion'.[107] William III was painted, in true Whig fashion, as the Protestant deliverer who had 'knockt off the fetters of our bondage'.[108] Hutchinson was also not above employing the

---

[99] Francis Hutchinson, *A sermon preached in Christ-Church, Dublin, on Friday, November 5th 1731. Being the anniversary ... of ... the gun-powder plot: ... before His Grace Lionel Duke of Dorset, Lord Lieutenant of Ireland, and the Lords Spiritual and Temporal in Parliament assembled. By Francis, Lord Bishop of Down and Connor. Published by command of his Grace the Lord Lieutenant, and by order of the House of Lords* (3rd edn, Dublin, 1731), p. 10.

[100] Mischler, 'Political sermons', p. 43.

[101] Francis Hutchinson, *A sermon preached in Christ's Church, Dublin, on the first of August, 1721. Being the anniversary of His Majesty's happy accession to the throne* (Dublin, 1721), p. 16.

[102] Hutchinson, *Sermon preached ... 1 Aug. 1721*, p. 15.

[103] Ibid., p. 15.

[104] Francis Hutchinson, *A sermon preached in Christ-church Dublin, on Thursday the 30th day of January, 1723. Being the anniversary fast for the martyrdom of King Charles the First, before ... Charles Duke of Grafton ... And the Lords spiritual and temporal ... By Francis Lord Bishop of Down and Connor ...* (Dublin, 1723), p. 5.

[105] Ibid., p. 6.

[106] Hutchinson, *John Tillotson*, p. 21.

[107] Ibid., p. 30.

[108] Hutchinson, *Sermon preached ... 1 Aug. 1721*, p. 4.

common Anglican shibboleth that William's bloodless Revolution succeeded only because it was a work of divine providence.[109]

In conjunction with the ideology of order, anti-Catholic propaganda was regarded as being of paramount importance by the Whig administration in helping to forge popular support for the new Hanoverian and Whig regime. This propaganda came in various forms, each drawing upon a different strand of anti-Catholic belief. Hutchinson added to this growing body of Whig propaganda with his books, *A compassionate address to those Papists* (1716) and *A defence of the compassionate address to Papists* (1718). The anti-Catholicism contained in Hutchinson's books can be seen as a synthesis of that contained in three other main types of Whig propaganda issued between 1714 and 1716: sermons, almanacs, government proclamations and loyal addresses.

Colin Haydon argues that in the period immediately following the Hanoverian accession the Whig administration and its supporters tried to 'whip up anti-Catholicism in the country at large' because they 'conceived anti-papist propaganda as of the utmost value in helping to unite the population behind the new Hanoverian dynasty'.[110] The Whigs aimed to exploit the anti-Catholic prejudices and fears of the British people in order to convince them that the irrefutably Protestant Whig and Hanoverian regime was the only viable alternative to the popery and absolutism offered by Tories and the House of Stuart.[111] The loyal addresses and official proclamations issued by the government industriously promoted the view that English Catholics were, by virtue of their allegiance to the pope, inherently disloyal to Protestant monarchs, and that a Stuart Restoration would mean that England would once again become Catholic. At the same time, the ever-popular almanacs of the period contained lurid accounts of the cruelty of foreign Catholics towards their Protestant countrymen. The sermons of Whiggish Anglican ministers tended to inform their audience of the consequences of a successful Stuart rebellion in England: an immediate return to absolutism and Catholicism, combined with organised persecutions of Protestants.[112]

These propagandists drew mainly on political and popular anti-Catholic beliefs, which by the reign of George I were well defined and deeply

---

[109] Hutchinson, *Sermon preached . . . 5 Nov. 1731*, p. 26; Kenyon, *Revolution principles*, pp. 24–9.

[110] Haydon, *Anti-Catholicism*, p. 91.

[111] Bruce P. Lenman, *The Jacobite risings in Britain, 1689–1746* (London, 1980), pp. 119, 155.

[112] Haydon, *Anti-Catholicism*, pp. 92–5.

entrenched in English society. The popular belief was that Catholics saw it as their religious duty to extirpate heretics, including Protestants, in order to make the world Catholic. Political anti-Catholicism was built around the belief that Catholics were by definition disloyal to Protestant monarchs. Catholics were required to give their primary allegiance, both temporal and spiritual, to a pope whose professed mission it was to extirpate all heretics. The pope also laid claim to two other medieval doctrines which made this temporal allegiance particularly frightening: dispensing and deposing powers. Firstly, Catholics were not expected to keep any obligation or oath to 'heretic' monarchs and could be commanded by the pope at any time to dispense with any oaths already taken. Secondly, Catholic subjects were allowed to murder and depose monarchs who had been excommunicated by the pope. Political anti-Catholic dogma also asserted that if England was made Catholic, an absolute form of government would be imposed on the people. Catholics were also regarded as un-English because popery was regarded as an international system of religion and politics.[113]

In his two books, Hutchinson echoed the anti-Catholicism of the 'Whiggish' sermons and almanacs, by warning of the terrors that would accompany a Stuart Restoration. He argued that if the Jacobite rebellion had not been defeated in England in 1715, then the British people would surely have had the pope's 'halters' around their necks.[114] He also took time to blacken the name of the exiled House of Stuart. He referred to the Old Pretender, James III, as an 'unfortunate man' who only masqueraded as the son of the exiled James II. This was an unashamed allusion to the old Whig myth that the newborn Pretender had been smuggled into the bedchamber of the king's consort, Mary of Modena, in a warming pan in 1688 to ensure a Catholic succession. Hutchinson also cast James III's 'pretended father', James II, in the role of the ape of both the pope and Rome. James II, Hutchinson contended, had 'suffer'd himself to be made as arrant a sacrifice to their interests, as any that ever fell in their cause'.[115] Hutchinson further suggested that if the old Pretender regained the throne he would carry out an even

---

[113] R. Blackey, 'A war of words: the significance of the propaganda conflict between Catholics and Protestants, 1713–1743' in *Catholic Historical Review*, iv (1973), 545–6; Haydon, *Anti-Catholicism*, pp. 3–4, 22, 77; Eamon Duffy, 'Englishmen in vaine: Roman Catholic allegiance to George I' in *Studies in Church History*, xviii (1982), 345; Marianne Elliott, *The Catholics of Ulster: a history* (London, 2000), p. 169.

[114] Hutchinson, *Compassionate address*, p. 8.

[115] Ibid., p. 172.

bloodier persecution of English Protestants than that carried out by Catholic Queen Mary after her accession to the English throne in the mid-sixteenth century.[116] He contended that all of that religion, not just those of the House of Stuart, were compelled by their religion to burn Protestants,[117] the result of their having 'bound themselves under an oath' to the pope 'to destroy that holy religion, which they call heresy'.[118] Thus, in his opinion, the ritual pope burnings that had been sporadically organised by Whig grandees in the past were completely justified, being but 'a small return for the real fires' that the pope 'lights of the bodies of our Protestant brethren'.[119]

In common with the authors of government proclamations and loyal addresses, Hutchinson too argued that Catholics were inherently disloyal to Protestant monarchs. In doing so, he gave an almost textbook rendition of political anti-Catholic ideology: English Catholics not only kept a fanciful union with the irreconcilable enemy of the British nation, the pope in Rome, but would willingly dispense with their oaths to their Protestant monarch if ever there arose a chance to depose him.[120] Hutchinson was convinced that a Stuart monarch, once he gained the throne, would not waste any time in overturning the Revolution Settlement of 1689, as all Catholic monarchs were by definition absolutist and tyrannical, and thus would never share power with the English Parliament. In his opinion this would be particularly lamentable in Britain's case because it was Britain's Parliament that had facilitated the growth in its wealth, population, knowledge and learning during the previous thirty years.[121]

The 1715 Jacobite rebellion offered to Hutchinson definitive evidence of the disloyalty of English Catholics to the Hanoverian regime, and their determination to impose 'a foreign yoke upon their own nation'.[122] The Jacobite army in the 1715 rebellion contained a majority of Catholics, as had indeed every Jacobite uprising and plot since the Glorious Revolution, both in the ranks and in positions of command. Most of these soldiers hailed from the north of England, especially Lancashire. The rebellion failed as a result of the incompetence of its commanders and

---

[116] Francis Hutchinson, *A defence of the Compassionate address to papists. Being an answer to the queries of a papist, relating to that address. In a sixth letter*... (London, 1718), pp. 39–41.

[117] Hutchinson, *Compassionate address*, pp. 17, 99.

[118] Ibid., p. 22.

[119] Ibid., p. 86.

[120] Ibid., pp. 9–10, 99–100, 158, 167, 175; idem, *Defence of the compassionate address*, p. 41.

[121] Hutchinson, *Sermon preached... 30 January 1723*, pp. 4–5; idem, *Sermon preached ... 5 Nov. 1731*, p. 26.

[122] Hutchinson, *Compassionate address*, p. 100.

a lack of support, both from abroad and from the mass of the English people. It nonetheless represented the most serious revolt ever launched by the Jacobites.[123]

In the aftermath of this rebellion the Whig administration had made moves to tighten its grip on the Catholic community by a renewed effort to make Catholics take an oath of allegiance to George I and by increased penal taxation.[124] Hutchinson not only dedicated the *Compassionate address* to an unnamed Whig peer but also thanked the Whig government for the 'necessary laws' which they had been 'forc'd to make for guarding of the nation against the power of papists'.[125] Hutchinson was convinced that penal legislation of this type, if combined with the proselytising efforts of Anglican ministers, would persuade recusants to renounce their allegiance to Rome and the pope, whereby removing the threat they posed to Protestant rule and religion forever.[126] In short, in true Low-Church style, he believed that coercion had its limits when bringing apostates back into the Anglican fold.[127]

Hutchinson's own proselytising efforts in were concentrated on the Catholic gentry of Suffolk who made up most of the extremely small Catholic population who lived there.[128] This explains why a large portion of the *Compassionate address*[129] is addressed to 'a popish gentleman in the author's parish' and his 'lady'.[130] In these sections of his book, Hutchinson beseeched the unnamed pair to join the established Church: only then would they become true Englishmen and women. Furthermore, he argued, they could do so without necessarily compromising their Catholic religious beliefs and practices.[131] This was achievable, Hutchinson maintained, because the Church of England shared much of its liturgy with the Roman Catholic Church. Furthermore, those beliefs and practices that did clash with Protestant orthodoxy, such as purgatory, transubstantiation, modern miracles and worship of saints

---

[123] Haydon, *Anti-Catholicism*, pp. 49–50, 78, 81–3, 98; idem, 'Samuel Peploe and Catholicism in Preston' in *Recusant History*, xx (1990), 76–7; Geoffrey Holmes and Daniel Szechi, *The age of oligarchy: pre-industrial Britain, 1722–1783* (London, 1993), p. 100; Speck, *Stability and strife*, pp. 179–80; M. D. R. Leys, *Catholics in England, 1559–1829: a social history* (London, 1961), p. 116; Daniel Szechi, *The Jacobites: Britain and Europe, 1688–1788* (Manchester, 1994), pp. 18–19.
[124] Haydon, *Anti-Catholicism*, pp. 104–14.
[125] Hutchinson, *Compassionate address*, p. 22.
[126] Ibid.
[127] See p. 22 above.
[128] See p. 34 above.
[129] See Hutchinson, *Compassionate address*, pp. 25–102.
[130] Ibid., p. 25.
[131] Ibid., p. 58.

and images,[132] could be conducted by the convert in private, if not in public. After all, the Anglican Church did not 'require her common communicants to make any declarations' about such things.[133] Hutchinson's overlooking of these private beliefs and practices should not be taken to mean that he did not find them superstitious and idolatrous, and thus perversions of true Christianity.[134] These views, which Colin Haydon has recently termed theological anti-Catholicism, were as much a part of English Protestant culture in the early eighteenth century as popular and political anti-Catholicism.[135]

In Anne's reign Hutchinson consistently voted for Whig candidates in parliamentary elections and, from the pulpit, defended the Toleration Act, the War of Spanish Succession and the 1707 Union against Tory criticism. After 1714, he joined the Whig administration in its effort to drum up support for a rather unpopular Whig and Hanoverian regime, both through the issue of anti-Catholic propaganda and the promulgation of the new Whig 'ideology of order'. His spirited defence of the Whiggish ideology of 'politeness' throughout the first two decades of the eighteenth century would not have gone unnoticed among England's Whig and Latitudinarian elite, nor would his defence of the Low-Church position on religious politics in the party-fuelled Convocation of 1701/2.[136] As we saw in the last chapter, Hutchinson's Whig credentials secured him the patronage of the Whiggish Maynard family during the reign of William III. Similarly his unabashed and public defence of the Whig party during the 'rage of party' and the early years of the Hanoverian dynasty was rewarded by George I and his Whig ministers and ecclesiastical advisers with a royal chaplaincy in 1715 and a bishopric in Ireland in 1720.[137]

---

[132] Ibid., pp. 58–64, 110; for Hutchinson's view of modern miracles, see next chapter.
[133] Hutchinson, *Compassionate address*, p. 61.
[134] Ibid., pp. 61, 64.
[135] Haydon, *Anti-Catholicism*, pp. 5–7.
[136] See Chapters 2, 4 and 5.
[137] See Chapter 6.

4

Angels and demons: the mental world of an eighteenth-century Anglican pastor

Examinations of Hutchinson's life and *oeuvre* have veered more towards the perfunctory than the systematic.[1] This approach has ensured that Hutchinson's intellectual, political and religious views have been sketched out only in broad brush strokes by historians. Part of this lacuna in the historiography has been filled in previous chapters by examining Hutchinson's particular brand of churchmanship and party politics. This chapter will continue in this vein by examining his view on those subjects considered unorthodox, vulgar or enthusiastic by his contemporaries, such as astrology, modern miracles and divine inspiration. In doing so, it will provide a background and a context on which to build an extended discussion of Hutchinson's witchcraft theory in the next chapter. It will also provide a more complete picture of the cultural and social aspects of Hutchinson's Latitudinarian-Whig ideology.

I

The late seventeenth and early eighteenth centuries witnessed a rise in the prestige and application of the new science, especially in its Newtonian variant. Newtonian natural philosophy was born with the publication of Sir Isaac Newton's *Philosophiae naturalis principia mathematica* in 1687 and soon became ensconced in elite culture, primarily as a result of the popularising efforts of his followers.[2] Latitudinarians, for example, used the Newtonian conception of the natural order in their sermons,

---

[1] See pp. 1–3 above.
[2] Larry Stewart, *The rise of public science, rhetoric, technology and natural philosophy in Newtonian Britain, 1660–1750* (Cambridge, 1992), pp. 119, 154, 146; Steven Shapin, *The Scientific Revolution* (Chicago, 1996), pp. 115, 117–22; John Gascoigne, 'Politics, patronage and Newtonianism: the Cambridge example' in *Historical Journal*, xxvii (1984), 1–24.

lectures and published work to justify their Whiggish notion of a modern, stable, urban and commercial society: if the natural world was stable and ordered, then it was man's duty to God to ensure that the social order was similar. Newtonian science after all portrayed a mechanistic universe, composed of a myriad of atoms, all of which were organised by God in a harmonious fashion according to natural laws, chief among which was Newton's universal law of gravitation.[3] To justify their adoption of the new science, Latitudinarians often invoked theories of natural theology. Natural theologians stated that the glory of God was revealed not only through the study of his word, as laid down in the Scriptures, but also by the scientific study of his works in creation, because such an impressive, beautiful and well-planned universe clearly reflected the magnificence of its creator.[4] The rise of natural theology can be seen as symptomatic of a larger theological shift towards a more rational religion, as Latitudinarians, among others, sought to ensure that faith was underpinned by reason as well as revelation.[5]

Theories of politeness venerated agreeable social behaviour and conversation, as well as the mutual pleasures occasioned by such activities, and blossomed in all sections of eighteenth-century elite society. This was especially true of urban Whig circles where it was used, along with Newtonian natural philosophy, to vindicate their social and cultural ideology.[6] The ideology of improvement was also a dominant feature of English elite culture in this period, not least because it held human betterment as its core concept without actually delineating exactly what form this should take. This characteristic allowed it to change its external shape, in order to accommodate changing cultural fashions and their accompanying ideologies, without compromising its internal coherence. By virtue of its concern to promote personal development, achieved through the cultivation of polite conduct, manners and taste, politeness became closely associated with improvement ideology.[7] Furthermore, as Larry Stewart points out, ' "promoting the publick good"

---

[3] Margaret C. Jacob, *The Newtonians and the English Revolution, 1689–1720* (Hassocks, 1976), pp. 18, 20, 163–200, 271; Gascoigne, *Cambridge in the age of the Enlightenment*, pp. 4–6.

[4] Peter Harrison, *The Bible, Protestantism, and the rise of natural science* (Cambridge, 1998), pp. 193–204.

[5] Roy Porter, *Enlightenment, Britain and the creation of the modern world* (London, 2000), pp. 99–128.

[6] Markku Peltonen, 'Politeness and Whiggism, 1688–1732' in *Historical Journal*, xlviii, no. 2 (2005), 391–413.

[7] Peter Borsay, 'The culture of improvement' in Paul Langford (ed.), *The eighteenth century* (Oxford, 2002), pp. 183–4, 189.

became part of the enduring rhetoric of the rise of science in the seventeenth and eighteenth centuries' and 'assertions of the need for improvement were intimately related to the justification for the Royal Society'.[8]

Hutchinson's Anglicanism was that of a moderate Latitudinarian, in that he contended that, though religion should as much as possible be placed on a reasonable basis, it was only the unwise or deliberately heterodox who were willing to challenge core Anglican doctrines in the pursuit of rational religion.[9] And in common with many Latitudinarians, Hutchinson was also a Newtonian. Fully conversant with the Newtonian inductive/deductive method of scientific reasoning,[10] Hutchinson waxed lyrical about the universe in mechanistic, Newtonian terms:

> the vast stretch of space ... is fill'd with sun, and moon, and [a] thousand stars. Think of their mystick dance, so just, so strange. Their motions swifter than bullets fly, yet punctual to their time and their place: their magnitudes above what thought can reach, yet steady, and even in their violent career: all things vast, every thing rapid, yet beautiful, and unconfused, and regular as an army marches.[11]

All 'matter' in the universe, he continued, was 'dead and passive'[12] and its motion could be explained only by reference to Newton's 'wonderful law of attraction'.[13] Natural laws, like matter itself, he contended, had been 'dispos'd and laid in order by the wise creator'.[14] Hutchinson also possessed more than a passing acquaintance with the rhetoric of natural theology. The majesty of the heavens, he stated in his 1718 sermon *The Christian religion demonstrated*, declared 'the glory of God'.[15] 'It is plain, that matter must be not only created, but created with great contrivance', he went on, 'because the marks of the Creator's infinite wisdom and power are upon the first principles of it, as plainly as upon the finish'd works that are produced from it'.[16]

Hutchinson's support of the new science was intimately related to his defence of theories of improvement, politeness and sociability. He lauded the achievements of the Royal Society by listing the ways its encouragement of scientific discovery had improved England, cultural, socially and

---

[8] Stewart, *Public science*, p. 16.
[9] See Chapter 2 above.
[10] See p. 109 below.
[11] Hutchinson, *Sermon preached ... 3 July 1698*, pp. 11–12.
[12] Hutchinson, *Historical essay*, p. 258.
[13] Hutchinson, *Sermon preached ... 5 November 1731*, p. 22.
[14] Hutchinson, *Historical essay*, Sermon II: Concerning angels, p. 257.
[15] Hutchinson, *Historical essay*, Sermon I: The Christian religion demonstrated, p. 232.
[16] Hutchinson, *Historical essay*, Sermon II: Concerning angels, p. 257.

economically.[17] He admitted that his own contribution to this programme had been more rhetorical than tangible, admitting that his 'maggotty projecting brain'[18] had been put 'to little purpose' while living in England.[19] New-found wealth and comparatively light episcopal duties, combined with the fact that Ireland was a country almost constantly in the grip of economic crisis and thus more than any other warranted the interference of projectors, provided Hutchinson with both the spur and resources to reverse this behaviour pattern.[20]

He was also convinced of the virtues of polite society: 'I would ask an objector, whether the calm and serene pleasure of society, be not the highest and noblest pleasure, that we know of in rational beings?'[21] He defended this ideal in two main ways. Firstly, he denounced its anti-type: vulgar, socially disturbing, unsociable (or enthusiastic) forms of religious practice and belief, such as modern miracles and prophecy, astrology and those aspects of angelology that smacked of non-conformity. Among the heterodox, he counted witchcraft belief. In fact, it was in attacking witchcraft that he made an overt connection between Whig social and cultural ideology and Newtonian science, of which more will be said in the next chapter. Secondly, he lauded sociable forms of religion, exemplified for Hutchinson in Anglicanism. An examination of these beliefs, with the exception of witchcraft, will be carried out below through a study of Hutchinson's attack on the French millenarian group, the French Prophets, in his book *A short view of the pretended spirit of prophecy, taken from its first rise in the year 1688, to its present state among us*. The *Pretended spirit of prophecy* was first published in London in 1708 and reprinted in Edinburgh a year later.

II

The Huguenots were those Protestant communities who lived in the Dauphiné and Languedoc regions of Catholic France. The religious persecution they suffered at the hands of the French authorities became worse after the legal status they had enjoyed for three generations came to an end with the revocation of the Edict of Nantes on 17 October 1685. It was at this time that they found solace in millenarian speculation and rejoiced when, in 1688, prophets began to appear amongst

[17] Hutchinson, *Historical essay*, p. 134.
[18] Francis Hutchinson to Cox Macro, 12 Nov. 1722 (B.L., Add. MS 32556, fo. 151).
[19] Francis Hutchinson to Sir Hans Sloane, 12 Oct. 1723 (B.L., Sloane MS 4047, fos. 67–8).
[20] See Chapter 8 below.
[21] Hutchinson, *Certainty of Protestants*, p. 17.

them. This was regarded as a sure sign that the millennium that would end their persecution was fast approaching. In the winter of 1688–9, French royal officials hunted down, imprisoned, executed or banished the various Prophets. Less than two years later, more prophets began to appear among them. In 1702, three of them, 'Colonel' Jean Cavalier, Abraham Mazel and Elie Marion, led armed bands (afterwards known as the Camisards) in a revolt against the troops of Louis XIV, whom they regarded as the enemy of God. By 1704, the rebellion had been bloodily quashed and many of the Camisards fled to other Protestant European countries, including England, where Marion, Durand Fage and Jean Cavalier (nephew to 'Colonel' Cavalier) landed in 1706. Camisard rebels continued to wage a guerrilla war against the French authorities until 1710.[22]

The Prophets did not restrict their preaching to the exiled Huguenot communities in London, but actively sought out and subsequently found English converts. Despite initial high expectations, by March 1707 they had converted only 24 people. Exiled Huguenot ministers and their congregations had begun to denounce them as frauds, and public clashes between the two groups ensued. This reflected the cold reception Camisard refugees received on the continent, especially in Switzerland and Germany, from the Huguenot populations living there. Recruitment numbers only began to increase in England in the summer of 1707, when the Prophets began to capture the popular imagination with increasingly spectacular prophecies, miracles and demonstrations of divine possession, such as heaving chests, gasping, trances, fits and the emission of strange humming noises. The Prophets claimed their coming was evidence of God's providence in the world, prophesied that the millennium was on its way and stated that all who ignored their pronouncements would incur the wrath of God. This message was a departure from that which they had promulgated on the continent, where the twin emphasis had been on highlighting how Catholicism had subverted true religion and recruiting military support to liberate France from the clutches of Louis XIV. By the end of 1708, 15 Huguenot Prophets and 22 English Prophets commanded between them over 400 followers from London and provincial towns such as Birmingham and Bristol. The followers of the Prophets were overwhelmingly English, attached

---

[22] Hillel Schwartz, *Knaves, fools, madmen and that subtile effluvium: a study of the opposition to the French Prophets in England, 1706–1710* (Gainesville, 1978), pp. 5–15; Ruth Whelan, 'Reading the bible in early eighteenth-century Dublin: the Huguenot pastor Henri de Rocheblave (1665–1709)' in *Eighteenth-Century Ireland*, xxi (2006), 9–13; Clarke Garrett, *Spirit possession and popular religion: from the Camisards to the Shakers* (Baltimore, 1997), pp. 11, 15, 22, 26–35, 42.

to various religious denominations (Quaker, Philadelphian, Presbyterian and Anglican), usually under 30 years old and just as likely to be male as female. John Lacy, a prosperous English Presbyterian justice of the peace, and Sir Richard Bulkeley, of Irish landed gentry stock, were two of the most prominent English Prophets.[23]

In early modern England, the term 'enthusiast' was used to describe anyone who claimed to be blessed with direct divine inspiration, but it was most frequently applied to zealous sectarians. In mid-seventeenth-century England the Fifth Monarchy Men and the Quakers were regarded as prominent enthusiasts, whereas in the early eighteenth century it was the French Prophets.[24] All critics of enthusiasts shared the same basic reason for their opposition: enthusiasts were seen to challenge established authority, whether political, social, religious, or intellectual.[25] In the late seventeenth and early eighteenth centuries, Church of England clerics opposed religious enthusiasm because they believed it posed a direct threat to the established Church and the status quo. The religious threat from enthusiasm stemmed from the fact that enthusiasts claimed to have experienced direct divine inspiration: if it were admitted that the Holy Spirit worked directly through ordinary people, there would be little need for an organised clergy to act as mediators between man and God.[26] Margaret Jacob argues that the French Prophets posed a particular threat to the established Church because they 'preached against the power of the clergy' and 'criticised the entire clerical structure of the English Church'.[27] The threat that the French Prophets supposedly posed to the status quo stemmed from the widespread belief that they used miracles and prophecies to capture the imaginations of the lower orders, in an attempt to lead them in a crusade against the established political and social order.[28]

---

[23] Schwartz, *Knaves, fools, madmen*, pp. 1–26; R. A. Knox, *Enthusiasm: a chapter in the history of religion, with special reference to the 17th and 18th centuries* (Oxford, 1950), pp. 359–60, 365–7; Sharpe, *Instruments of darkness*, pp. 252–3; Garrett, *Spirit possession*, pp. 35, 40–51, 54.

[24] Michael Heyd, *'Be sober and reasonable': the critique of enthusiasm in the seventeenth and early eighteenth centuries* (New York, 1995), pp. 2–5; J. G. A. Pocock, 'Enthusiasm: the anti-self of the Enlightenment' in Lawrence E. Klein and Anthony J. Vopa (eds), *Enthusiasm and the Enlightenment* (San Marino, CA, 1998), pp. 9–11.

[25] Heyd, *'Be sober and reasonable'*, p. 8.

[26] Jacob, *The Newtonians*, pp. 259–69; Heyd, *'Be sober and reasonable'*, pp. 165–72; Lawrence E. Klein, 'Sociability, solitude and enthusiasm' in *Enthusiasm and the Enlightenment*, pp. 161–2.

[27] Jacob, *The Newtonians*, pp. 262, 259.

[28] Schwartz, *Knaves, fools, madmen*, pp. 55–63, 69–70; Jacob, *The Newtonians*, pp. 251–63.

From the summer of 1707 onwards a flood of pamphlets appeared attacking the French Prophets, the vast majority of which were written by Anglican clergy. It had become, by the late seventeenth century, the standard practice of clerical critics of enthusiasm to use Scripture and reason as the main two criteria by which to judge the validity of particular claims to divine inspiration. However, on occasion, the ability to perform miracles was used as a third arbiter. Given the fact that the French Prophets claimed the ability to work miracles, it is no surprise that the majority of their critics used all three, including Hutchinson in his *Pretended spirit of prophecy*.[29]

Although Anglican orthodoxy accepted that the Scriptures verified the fact that God had used miracles in Biblical times to demonstrate to unbelievers his divine power, it also contended that to search continually for new wonders or miracles was a sign of non-conformity and enthusiasm: the Scriptures provided sufficient proof of the truth of Christianity and so modern man did not need constant signs from God, in the form of miracles, to give him faith.[30] In the *Pretended spirit of prophecy*, Hutchinson also maintained that miracles had ceased in Apostolic times. He argued that the 'blessed saviour hath not promised us any new prophets and miracles' after he had 'put his seal to the inspired books [the Scriptures]'.[31] Hutchinson, a man convinced that a 'sober belief of good and bad spirits' was an 'essential part of every good Christian's faith',[32] nonetheless contended that most 'signs and wonders' were 'the feats of evil spirits' whom God had 'been permitted to delude those, who are not content to depend upon God's providence, but seek after signs'.[33]

A Protestant religious context with little room for modern miracles left little logical place for angelic intervention. By the eighteenth century, the majority of Protestant commentators would have regarded it as a scriptural fundamental to accept both the existence of angels and the fact that they worked tirelessly for the good of humankind by guarding and protecting nations, if not individuals. It was not expected that humans could or would see angels at work or would be able to communicate

---

[29] Heyd, *'Be sober and reasonable'*, pp. 173–90.

[30] Peter Marshall and Alexandra Walsham, 'Migrations of angels in the early modern world' in eidem (eds), *Angels in the early modern world* (Cambridge, 2006), p. 17; Sharpe, *Instruments of darkness*, pp. 247–50.

[31] Hutchinson, *A short view of the pretended spirit of prophecy, taken from its first rise in the year 1688: to its present state among us . . .* (London, 1708; repr. Edinburgh, 1709), p. 25.

[32] Hutchinson, *Historical essay*, p. vi.

[33] Hutchinson, *Compassionate address*, p. 106.

with them. In fact the invocation of angels was commonly regarded as an idolatrous practice redolent of Catholicism. The Scriptures, however, failed to provide such a clear-cut guide to what angels looked like and thus there was much disagreement among writers on the subject.[34]

Hutchinson's view of angels was as orthodox as his view of modern miracles. It was illogical and irrational for humans to think that they were the only thinking beings in his stable, ordered, providential universe:

> is it not irrational to imagine, that we poor worms of the earth should be the head of the creation? Can we once think, that the Almighty spirit should have no creatures more excellent that we are, to admire his works, and know and worship him? When we see our own changeable, infected, disordered region full of creatures with life, sense and reason, can we believe that the immense, and pure, and celestial places above, are without any?[35]

In any case, he added, the Scriptures not only provided proof of their existence but the only reliable description of their myriad characteristics.[36] Angels had not only been created by God at the same time as the earth,[37] they were 'immaterial and immortal', moved with 'great swiftness', and were in possession of 'great force and power',[38] and 'wisdom and knowledge'.[39] The latter attribute was regarded as a consequence of their 'easy motion, and capacious faculties, and long duration'.[40] In other words, their swiftness of movement, high intellect and longevity. Since man could not see angels, and the Scriptures provided little information on the matter, Hutchinson refused to comment on what they looked like or indeed what their names were.[41] In his schema, angels had many purposes. First and foremost, because they constantly worked for the good of humankind, they helped to increase man's faith in God and his providence.[42] Angels, Hutchinson opined, 'encamp about our dwellings to do us good; they catch us from dangers; prosper our ways; rejoice at our conversion; and when we die, they carry our souls, if good, to the place of happiness'.[43] Despite these good works, he warned, men were

---

[34] Marshall and Walsham, 'Migrations of angels', pp. 17–18; Owen Davies, 'Angels in elite and popular magic, 1650–1790' in Marshall and Walsham, *Angels in the early modern world*, pp. 299–301, 303–4.
[35] Hutchinson, *Historical essay*, p. 10.
[36] Ibid., Sermon II: Concerning angels, p. 251.
[37] Ibid., pp. 258–9.
[38] Ibid., p. 261.
[39] Ibid., p. 262.
[40] Ibid.
[41] Ibid., pp. 251, 262.
[42] Ibid., pp. 263–5.
[43] Ibid., p. 265.

not to pray to them or worship them: to do so was to place oneself in the realms of popery and idolatry.[44] Similarly, those who harked after more knowledge than the Bible relayed about the natures of angels were to be considered both dangerous and enthusiastic.[45]

The second arbiter Hutchinson employed in the *Pretended spirit of prophecy* to combat the French Prophets' claim to divine inspiration was Scripture, which, he was at lengths to point out, did not promise man any new prophets:

> But by what authority of Scripture, or reason, doth any man now presume to pray, or even desire to be made a prophet in our age, when we have neither promise, nor want of prophets, and when God have been pleased to preserve his church so long without them?[46]

Although it was a recognised Biblical necessity to accept the possibility that the creator might send new prophets to earth it was also believed that if he did so they would bring new instructions to humankind from their creator. The French Prophets, on the other hand, preached nothing original and did not lay claim to any new doctrines.[47] They did, however, introduce their own sacraments towards the end of 1707, such as a new form of communion, which was held on Christmas Day in the form of a dinner party (called a 'Love feast') in which sacramental bread and wine were distributed on the command of the Holy Spirit.[48] Hutchinson summarily pointed out this fact in his book: 'I know not whether they have many false doctrines; for they have hardly any doctrines at all'.[49] The doctrines they did possess, he added, were not only blasphemous but 'an offence to any sober person'.[50] Furthermore, although the 'blessed saviour and his apostles'[51] had not foretold the coming of any new prophets, they had warned of the arrival of 'false Christs and false prophets'.[52] These false prophets, Hutchinson maintained, would 'both try the faith of Christians, and exercise the courage and vigilance of magistrates and ministers, both in Church and state'.[53]

---

[44] Ibid., p. 266; Davies, 'Angels in elite and popular magic', pp. 303–4.
[45] Hutchinson, *Historical essay*, Sermon II: Concerning angels, pp. 250–1.
[46] Hutchinson, *Pretended spirit of prophecy*, p. 49.
[47] Schwartz, *Knaves, fools, madmen*, pp. 25, 65; Heyd, 'Be sober and reasonable', pp. 175–6.
[48] Garrett, *Spirit possession*, p. 55.
[49] Hutchinson, *Pretended spirit of prophecy*, p. 54.
[50] Ibid., p. 57.
[51] Ibid., p. 1.
[52] Ibid., p. 2.
[53] Ibid.

The Scriptures also provided clerical opponents of enthusiasm with a true model of prophecy against which they could compare any new claims to divine inspiration. This model was the biblical apostles, in comparison with whom new prophets always seemed barely credible.[54] Hutchinson argued that he had 'examined these pretenders by the marks of true prophets, and found them wanting in every particular'.[55] First of all, unlike the French Prophets, scriptural prophets did not go into convulsions, fits or trances when they were divinely inspired. They did not need such tricks because their prophecies, doctrines and miracles were awe-inspiring enough on their own.[56] Secondly, how could the French Prophets claim to be blessed with the gift of foresight if they consistently got their predictions wrong?[57] Thirdly, was it not ridiculous that men with characters as bad as Cavalier, Fage and Marion would be sent by God to prepare the way for the millennium?[58] To dispel any doubts about the veracity of this contention, Hutchinson detailed Cavalier's cursing, his use of prostitutes and his singing of bawdy verse and song, as well as Fage's public drunkenness.[59]

The clerical critics of the French Prophets not only used the Scriptures and the cessation of miracles to deny that the Prophets were divinely inspired, but they also provided reasonable, alternative explanations for the symptoms of such inspiration. They argued that it was more plausible that the outward signs of divine inspiration were caused by one or more of the following: disease (mental illness), delusion, demonic possession, deliberate deception or imposture.[60] Hillel Schwartz argues that Hutchinson attributed the inspiration of the French Prophets to delusion and disease.[61] In reality, although Hutchinson was convinced that some of the Prophets were indeed deluded, possessed by the devil or mentally diseased, he nonetheless argued that most of them had purposely faked their miracles, prophecies and signs of divine possession. The deception theory proved attractive to Hutchinson because it vindicated his belief that the French Prophets were trying to subvert the social and political order.

In the eighteenth century, when clerics explained away symptoms of divine inspiration in medical terms, they shunned the Galenic conception

---

[54] Heyd, *'Be sober and reasonable'*, p. 176.
[55] Hutchinson, *Pretended spirit of prophecy*, pp. 56–7.
[56] Ibid., pp. 39–41.
[57] Ibid., pp. 62–4.
[58] Ibid., pp. 17–18.
[59] Ibid., pp. 15, 16, 17.
[60] Schwartz, *Knaves, fools, madmen*, p. 31.
[61] Ibid., p. 83.

of melancholy, highly influential in the sixteenth and seventeenth centuries, in favour of more mechanistic explanations of melancholy, which attributed inspiration to irregular motions of the blood, turbulent animal spirits and vapours arising from the stomach.[62] Critics of the Prophets relied almost solely upon the notion of animal spirits (the medium by which the mind or the soul affected the body and in turn caused madness, vapours, hypochondria and hysteria) when using medical explanations.[63] Critics who employed the deception thesis usually denied the validity of the medical explanation, because it implied that the Prophets were not fully responsible for their actions. The deception thesis was not, however, incompatible with the medical explanation because it could be used to account for the success of certain impostures.[64] Hutchinson argued that, though John Lacy's speaking in tongues was undoubtedly a deliberate imposture,[65] his other, more impressive feat of sliding 3 ft across a room was probably caused by madness: 'when persons are fallen into a state of madness, their strength, at some critical times, is much greater than it is in its usual course; and ... the person may very well slide cross a floor with motion unusual'.[66] Hutchinson was not comfortable with the medical explanation. He used it only once and even then only in conjunction with the deception theory.

Demonic possession and delusion were Hutchinson's second and third explanatory mechanisms. The possession thesis was for the most part employed by older, High-Church critics who felt threatened by the new scientific disposition and equated naturalism with materialism and scepticism. On the other hand, younger clerics and advocates of the new experimental philosophy usually shunned the demonic explanation.[67] Although Hutchinson was around 48 years of age at the time of publication and a Latitudinarian-Newtonian, he mooted that it was a possibility that some of the Prophets were possessed:

> The behaviour in their inspirations, is not like that of men moved by the Holy Ghost: whistling, singing, drumming, and laughing ... are usual signs of madness or possession; but no ways agreeable to divine inspiration.[68]

The third explanation for the symptoms of enthusiasm was thought to be delusion, caused by mental disorder or demonic intervention, or

---

[62] Heyd, 'Be sober and reasonable', pp. 191–8.
[63] Schwartz, Knaves, fools, madmen, pp. 31, 35.
[64] Ibid., pp. 63, 54–6; Heyd, 'Be sober and reasonable', pp. 207–8.
[65] Hutchinson, Pretended spirit of prophecy, pp. 30–2.
[66] Ibid., p. 33.
[67] Schwartz, Knaves, fools, madmen, pp. 42–3, 47.
[68] Hutchinson, Pretended spirit of prophecy, p. 57.

sometimes both together.[69] Hutchinson avoided the medical explanation, regarding the delusion to be caused solely by demonic intervention. He maintained that the French Prophets were merely victims of those 'lying spirits' which had been the 'most mischievous instruments that ever the Devil had made use of for the deceiving the nations'.[70] The 'priests' and 'worshippers of Bacchus' in classical times were prominent examples of this type of deception.[71] Hutchinson's unusual willingness to afford such a large role to demonic agency in his critique can be explained by the fact that, unlike the majority of his contemporaries, he maintained Satan and evil spirits played a very active role in the temporal world, constantly possessing, tricking and deluding humankind.[72]

The final and by far the most important explanation used by Hutchinson was that the Prophets had deliberately faked their symptoms of divine inspiration. The deception thesis was favoured by those opponents particularly convinced of the social and political threat posed by the Prophets.[73] Hutchinson argued that not only was the conduct of the Prophets suspicious, but so were the miracles that they claimed to have performed. For example, he argued that in France one of their number had been able to walk through a fire and emerge unscathed because his clothes were damp and the fire had been made with straw rather than with wood, straw being a fuel that produces more light than heat.[74] Similarly, argued Hutchinson, 'forty cunning fellows' could imitate the female prophet Betty Gray's episode of divine intervention that had been characterised by her 'not seeing for one hour, and looking black in the face for two'.[75] Gray, he concluded, was one who had 'conversed so much with the play-house' that it was much more likely that she was 'an actress than a prophetess'.[76] He also noted that William Somers had worked exactly the same imposture in order to accuse a woman of witchcraft in the sixteenth century.[77]

Advocates of the deception thesis highlighted the political radicalism of the French Prophets by accusing them of possessing 'levelling principles'. These critics made this accusation on the basis of two assertions. First of all, the new heaven and new earth that the Prophets spoke of

---

[69] Schwartz, *Knaves, fools, madmen*, pp. 43–5, 47–8.
[70] Hutchinson, *Pretended spirit of prophecy*, pp. 38–9.
[71] Ibid., p. 43.
[72] See pp. 83, 103, 108–9.
[73] Schwartz, *Knaves, fools, madmen*, pp. 55–63, 69–70.
[74] Hutchinson, *Pretended spirit of prophecy*, pp. 27–8.
[75] Ibid., p. 33.
[76] Ibid., pp. 34–5.
[77] Ibid., pp. 36–7.

in their millennial visions was one where the material needs and wants of all individuals would be met.[78] Secondly, the Prophet Abraham Whitrow claimed that the rich could only enter heaven if they became poor and advocated a charity dispersal policy so widespread as to resemble a programme of social levelling. Most Prophets distanced themselves from Whitrow, including Lacy, but a prominent English convert, Sir Richard Bulkley, not only lent him his support but accompanied him on a tour of England and Ireland to disseminate his prophecies. In the summer of 1708, Bulkley gave Whitrow's charity scheme practical application, using funds from his own estate.[79] 'Levelling' principles directly challenged the legitimacy of the social order which benefited England's elite, but that was not the only reason such principles were abhorrent to them. Eighteenth-century Englishmen, irrespective of their station in life, accepted the social structure and their allotted position in it. This was a social order dominated by a social hierarchy whose relations were determined in the main by considerations of dependence and deference.[80] Hutchinson was particularly concerned with the fact that the 'levelling principle[s]' purportedly espoused by the French Prophets were eagerly imbibed by the poorer members of society 'with little examination'.[81] This was a frightening prospect for a man who possessed a strict reverence for the social order and who lent credence to the widely held assumption that the English social hierarchy was an earthly manifestation of the great chain of being that stretched downwards from God to the angels, and thence to humankind and flora and fauna.[82]

The Prophets' penchant for egalitarianism was bad enough, but Hutchinson was also convinced they were virulently anti-clerical and committed to 'overturning of states'.[83] Their 'continual railing against us ministers', he suggested, proved that they lacked any regard for 'our Saviour's institution',[84] a consequence of their being supplied 'with money,

---

[78] Schwartz, *Knaves, fools, madmen*, pp. 59–61; Jacob, *The Newtonians*, pp. 261–6.
[79] Schwartz, *Knaves, fools, madmen*, pp. 60–1; Garrett, *Spirit Possession*, p. 56.
[80] J. C. D. Clark, *English society, 1660–1832: religion, ideology and politics during the ancien regime* (Cambridge, 2000), pp. 53–4, 162–200; J. H. Plumb, *The first four Georges* (Glasgow, 1985), pp. 23–7.
[81] Hutchinson, *Pretended spirit of prophecy*, p. 68.
[82] Hutchinson, *Sermon preached... 1 Aug. 1721*, pp. 19–20; idem, *Historical essay*, Sermon II: Concerning angels, pp. 268–9; Hay and Rogers, *Eighteenth-century English society*, p. 17.
[83] Hutchinson, *Pretended spirit of prophecy*, p. 38.
[84] Ibid., p. 66; Heyd, *'Be sober and reasonable'*, p. 168; idem, 'The reaction to enthusiasm in the seventeenth century: towards an integrative approach' in *Journal of Modern History*, liii (1981), 276.

and manage[d]' by atheists.⁸⁵ He also argued that if 'ever their numbers or opportunities' gave 'them the occasion', the French Prophets would engulf England with 'massacres' and 'carnage', and cause blood to run 'down the streets'.⁸⁶ Hutchinson proffered three main reasons why the Prophets would sooner or later find the opportunity and numbers to effect such a revolt. First of all, the country had just experienced a period of general instability and there was no indication that things were about to improve. The rise to prominence of the Prophets in the summer of 1707 coincided with heavy defeats for the allies at Almanza and Stolhofen, the threat of conflict disturbing trade in the Baltic region and a mild financial panic. By the time Hutchinson put pen to paper in early 1708, the Allied war effort might have taken a slight turn for the better, but Britain's vulnerability had just been exposed by an, albeit unsuccessful, French-backed Jacobite invasion. Hutchinson wrote later that, 'when the French Prophets both disturbed and dishonored our nation in an unsettled time, I traced them from the beginning, and wrote a short history of them from their first rise in France'.⁸⁷

Secondly, the Prophets seemed to possess an almost mesmeric influence over the lower orders. Hutchinson argued that, having already seduced some of the weaker members of the lower orders, it was only a matter of time before the majority were led in armed revolt against the establishment.⁸⁸ Hillel Schwartz argues that 'critics who incorrectly emphasised the plebeian circumstances and revolutionary tendencies of most French Prophets were . . . simply making connections, by now traditional, among irrationality, enthusiasm, and the lower classes'.⁸⁹ It is certainly true that the main reason why Hutchinson believed that the lower ranks were so receptive to the influence of religious enthusiasts was because they possessed weak, superstitious natures, which predisposed them to belief in ill-founded notions.⁹⁰ Finally, the possibility of crowd action became almost synonymous with the name of the French Prophets after a reported 20,000-strong crowd, the majority of whom were of low social status, turned out on 25 May 1708 to see the promised, but unsuccessful, resurrection of the recently deceased, leading English Prophet, Dr Thomas Emes.⁹¹

---

⁸⁵ Hutchinson, *Pretended spirit of prophecy*, p. 67.
⁸⁶ Ibid., p. 59.
⁸⁷ Hutchinson to Wake, 14 Apr. 1720 (C.C., Wake Letters, vol. 21, no. 215).
⁸⁸ Hutchinson, *Pretended spirit of prophecy*, pp. 24, 22, 23, 68.
⁸⁹ Schwartz, *Knaves, fools, madmen*, pp. 60–1.
⁹⁰ Bostridge, *Witchcraft and its transformations*, pp. 147–50.
⁹¹ Jacob, *The Newtonians*, pp. 261, 263–4; Schwartz, *Knaves, fools, madmen*, pp. 22–4; Garret, *Spirit possession*, pp. 52–4.

III

For Hutchinson the religious experience offered by the French Prophets constituted an indisputable instance of unsociable religion, because it encouraged adherents to challenge the established social, political and religious order. In common with the majority of clerical opponents of religious enthusiasts, however, he did not attack the theology of the French Prophets, but rather their claim to have experienced direct divine inspiration. Clerical critics in the seventeenth and eighteenth centuries used three main arbiters to test claims of divine inspiration: reason, Scripture and the ability to perform real miracles. Hutchinson used all three arbiters and concluded that the source of the prophecies, miracles and convulsions of the French Prophets did not lie with God.

Hutchinson maintained that the anti-type of unsociable religion was sociable religion, as it complemented rather than challenged the Whig order of things. The Anglican faith exemplified this latter type of religious experience as it encouraged submissive and deferential behaviour in its followers, and it possessed a 'settled order of teachers' who strove to instruct 'every rising generation, in sober notions of true piety, virtue, and humble submission to government'.[92] In this way, ministers such as he helped to 'calm and soften the roughness of men's passions'.[93]

Hutchinson's book was generally well received and stood out from the flood of anti-Prophet literature that engulfed the English book market at that time. *The Pretended Spirit of Prophecy* sold enough copies to warrant a Scottish reprint. It also struck a chord with the English Whig elite. Hutchinson bragged of this success to Archbishop William Wake, when chasing promotion in 1720:

> your Lordships Predecessor [Thomas Tenison] did it the honor to say it was the best answer that had been given to them [the French Prophets], the Attorney-general that then was (Sir James Mountagu) gave me thanks for it, and said I had strengthened their hand in the execution of the law.[94]

IV

As we have seen in previous chapters, in the generation after the Glorious Revolution, Hutchinson moved from being the second son of an obscure yeoman farmer to become a relatively well-off clerical pluralist and an

---

[92] Hutchinson, *Pretended spirit of prophecy*, p. 67; Bostridge, *Witchcraft and its transformations*, pp. 147–8, 151.
[93] Hutchinson, *Compassionate address*, p. 20.
[94] Hutchinson to Wake, 14 Apr. 1720 (C.C., Wake Letters, vol. 21, no. 215); for Hutchinson's promotion to the Irish episcopacy, see pp. 131–5 below.

active and vocal member of a small band of Latitudinarian-Whig clerical reformers. This outlook not only shaped his view of the political issues of the day, dictated his voting behaviour, determined his theology and formed his attitude to Catholicism and Protestant Dissent, it also informed his social and cultural ideology. Like many Latitudinarian-Whigs, he envisaged an improved, polite, ordered, civil society – an ideal he believed was at particular threat from lower-class enthusiasm, at a time of almost total war with France and the continued threat of Jacobite revolt or invasion. What Hutchinson regarded as enthusiastic was almost always that which Anglican orthodoxy – in particular the orthodoxy of its adherents of a Whiggish disposition – held to be socially dangerous, vulgar or enthusiastic.

Although Hutchinson's Newtonian universe was populated with good and evil spirits, and human affairs were seen to be guided by divine providence, he considered it non-conformist and enthusiastic to continually look for signs of this providence, whether by worshipping angels (or prying too deeply into their natures) or searching for instances of modern miracles and divine inspiration. Related beliefs, such as astrology and witchcraft, he also condemned as enthusiastic. However, lest we paint Hutchinson too much as a paragon of enlightened, Whig sociability, we would do well to remember that to Hutchinson evil spirits and Satan constantly wreaked havoc among the living and punished the departed in hell; an outlook that many of those who considered themselves cultured, orthodox or polite would have baulked at.[95]

---

[95] See chapters 5 and 7 below.

5

Hutchinson and witchcraft: *An historical essay concerning witchcraft* (1718)

Hutchinson's famously sceptical witchcraft text, the *Historical essay* (1718), has long enjoyed an intimate connection with the historiography of the decline of educated belief in witchcraft. This connection has been renewed in recent years, in particular by the work of James Sharpe and Ian Bostridge.[1] Bostridge contends that by the end of the second decade of the eighteenth century, witchcraft became a marginal concern for mainstream educated culture because it was no longer needed, or able, to perform its original ideological function of forging Christian unity by bolstering the ideal of a confessional state: firstly, it was revealing itself to be more capable of fostering disunity and discord than forging religious and political concord; and secondly, the idea of a confessional state was increasingly regarded as either unattainable or intellectually unattractive, especially after the trial in 1712 of an elderly woman named Jane Wenham from Walkern, Hertfordshire. Wenham's trial saw witchcraft belief become embroiled in the party conflict of Anne's reign. As a result, credulity and incredulity became polarised across Tory and Whig lines so that, by the latter half of the 1710s, those who continued to be credulous in such matters were largely political marginals, in particular high-flying Tories or country Whigs, dissatisfied with the new Whig and Hanoverian regime.[2]

James Sharpe, on the other hand, propounds that by the eighteenth century witchcraft belief was becoming an increasingly marginal concern within elite culture due to a series of gradual mental shifts that 'challenged the broader belief system which provided the context within which an educated acceptance of witchcraft could exist'.[3] This *mentalitie*,

---

[1] See pp. 1–3 above.
[2] Bostridge, *Witchcraft and its transformations*, pp. 107–63.
[3] Sharpe, *Instruments of darkness*, p. 270.

and thus incredulity in matters of witchcraft, was more likely to affect those in contact with the latest ideas and modes of thought, the provincial and metropolitan gentry and the higher clergy, rather than the rural parsons and gentry.[4] The later seventeenth and early eighteenth centuries in England, argues Sharpe, witnessed a move towards a more moderate religious experience. One element of this was the gradual shift away from the idea that divine providence often directly interfered in everyday human affairs towards one that accepted the reality of God's ability to direct human affairs but was unwilling to see his hand in apparently miraculous occurrences, natural disasters, monstrous births or apparitions. Furthermore, it was generally accepted by many theologians that in contemporary society miracles no longer operated as a proof of the veracity of revealed religion. A literal belief in Satan also lost much of its cultural currency. In such a religious context, the belief that people existed (witches) who used Satan's power to inflict harm on their fellow humans (witchcraft) was unlikely to thrive. Sharpe further states that this period witnessed the educated elite's rejection of astrology, a quasi-scientific, 'occult' belief that inhabited the same mental landscape as witchcraft and magic, on the grounds that it was vulgar and enthusiastic, and thus more suited to the lower orders. Even traditional aspects of witch belief, in particular the 'proofs' of witchcraft, had fallen prey to this sort of thinking by the early eighteenth century. These attitudinal shifts formed part of a broader process, of the elite distancing themselves from popular culture, during the later seventeenth and early eighteenth centuries.[5]

Sharpe also suggests that – though there was no straightforward triumph by the rationalists, armed with the weapons of the new science, over spiritual and occult forces – certain intellectual changes did take place which helped to chip away at the credibility of witchcraft belief:

> there was a slow process taking place in which old ways of categorizing and compartmentalising knowledge (this was essentially the polymathic age) were changing. The old system (perhaps demonstrated at its clearest in neoplatonism) of correspondences, of the interplay between the microcosm and the macrocosm, of sympathetic actions and hence sympathetic magic, was becoming less tenable. Newly located and more definite wedges were being driven between the scientific and the occult, between the natural and the spiritual, and hence magic and witchcraft were becoming marginalized.[6]

---

[4] Ibid., pp. 286–7.
[5] Sharpe, *Instruments of darkness*, pp. 235–54, 270–1; idem, *Witchcraft in early modern England*, pp. 82, 84–5; for a description of these proofs, see pp. 118–21 below.
[6] Sharpe, *Witchcraft in early modern England*, p. 79.

Both Bostridge and Sharpe's view of decline shape their view of Hutchinson's scepticism. Sharpe regards Hutchinson as a man who 'was willing to nod at the impact of the new science and the Royal Society, but was unable or unwilling to follow this line of approach through'.[7] He consequently locates his scepticism in two main outlooks: his embracing of a more moderate religious experience, for which the idea of a moral universe, in which God and Satan and other immaterial essences constantly intervened, held little weight; and his belief that credulity in matters of witchcraft was more suited to the vulgar lower orders than to polite society, of which he regarded himself a member.[8]

Bostridge, on the other hand, locates Hutchinson's rejection of witchcraft in his politics. To Bostridge, Hutchinson is a typical Latitudinarian-Whig who not only favoured religious pluralism over the idea of a confessional state, but used Newtonian reasoning to bolster the Whiggish notion of a polite, ordered, civil society. He did this by attacking what he believed threatened it, religious enthusiasm, of which witchcraft was a salient example, as it encouraged the lower orders to act in ways that threatened public, and thus social, order.[9] Bostridge further argues that Hutchinson, panicked by the credulity of the Scottish elite in matters of witchcraft and by the conviction of Wenham, made plans to publish the *Historical essay* first in 1707 and then again in 1712, but decided against publication on both occasions. In 1707, two Low-Church Whig prelates – the Bishop of Norwich, John Moore, and the Archbishop of Canterbury, Thomas Tenison – advised Hutchinson not to publish the *Historical essay*, lest he upset the still credulous godly elite in Scotland and make the upcoming Whig-backed, incorporating Union more difficult than it would be otherwise. In 1712, his acquaintance, Sir Hans Sloane, advised him to shelve his publishing plans again because the Wenham trial had made witchcraft too politically controversial for a respectable cleric, with aspirations to high preferment, to write upon.[10] According to Bostridge, Hutchinson had to wait until 1718 to publish the *Historical essay*, when witchcraft had become a marginal concern to mainstream, educated culture.[11]

So far we have focused on the decline theories of Bostridge and Sharpe, and how these have shaped their view of Hutchinson's scepticism. However, they are not the only historians in the past two decades to have

---

[7] Sharpe, *Instruments of darkness*, p. 273.
[8] Sharpe, *Witchcraft in early modern England*, pp. 81–2, 85; idem, *Instruments of darkness*, p. 285.
[9] Bostridge, *Witchcraft and its transformations*, pp. 143–53.
[10] Ibid., pp. 34–5, 143–4.
[11] For a discussion of this see pp. 121–5 below.

pondered the problem of decline. The late Roy Porter, in his recent book on the English Enlightenment, took Sharpe's decline theory to its logical conclusion by arguing that 'the discrediting of witchcraft belief' in the late seventeenth and early eighteenth centuries was 'perhaps the most telling instance of the rejection of traditional Christian dogmas in favour of new secular models', a shift that 'occurred against a backdrop of controversy regarding the reality and agency of spirits in general.'[12] Porter regarded Hutchinson, by virtue of his *Historical essay*, as personifying this new, secular-minded, progressive, enlightened mental world.[13] In *Witchcraft, magic and culture, 1736–1951*, Owen Davies contends that although many of the educated had, by the mid-eighteenth century, come to consider 'witchcraft to be a vulgar notion bred of ignorance and credulity',[14] many others 'continued to believe that witchcraft had existed and could exist, but ceased to believe that it continued in their own times'.[15] This ambivalence, Owen notes, did not exist for the vast majority of those placed lower down the social ladder, especially those living in rural areas, who continued to regard the existence of the malefic witch as a threat to their property and persons.[16] Malcom Gaskill goes even further in questioning the validity of the old historiography of decline. He argues that 'witchcraft was still very much alive as a subject in the eighteenth century, but that its meaning could vary according to context'.[17] Thus, he suggests, 'to characterise the history of witchcraft in terms of simple models – whether of the dynamics of accusation, or the decline in beliefs – is to overlook the variety, subtlety and contingency of how attitudes, ideas, perceptions and behaviour were deployed in practice and changed over time' and that 'even sensitive attempts to identify distinctions between popular culture and the culture of the elite tend to narrow the issues at stake'.[18]

Historians are just as divided over how far elite belief in witchcraft was connected with witch hunting and witchcraft trials. Bostridge suggests that 'the numbers of executions for witchcraft, and the virulency, currency, or significance of witchcraft belief are two different things ... a decline in prosecutions cannot be equated with a weakening of belief'.[19]

---

[12] Porter, *Enlightenment*, p. 219.
[13] Ibid., pp. 220–2.
[14] Owen Davies, *Witchcraft, magic and culture, 1736–1951* (Manchester, 1999), p. 7.
[15] Ibid., p. 8.
[16] Ibid., pp. 79–166.
[17] Malcolm Gaskill, *Crime and mentalities in early modern England* (Cambridge, 2000), p. 107.
[18] Ibid., p. 118.
[19] Bostridge, *Witchcraft and its transformations*, p. 36.

Stuart Clark advises against making any simple correlation between witchcraft beliefs and witchcraft trials: 'it is simply not the case that witchcraft theory caused "witch hunts" or that its incidence influenced theirs; indeed, the reverse is much more likely to have been true.'[20] Malcolm Gaskill maintains that 'successful witchcraft prosecutions declined regardless of changes in belief', but this decline 'did not necessarily reflect scepticism',[21] for the judiciary and juries could 'believe in witchcraft and yet be sceptical of any means of proving it; or, conversely ... be sceptical of witchcraft but ready to compromise personal belief in the interests of legal utilitarianism'.[22]

Sharpe, on the other hand, suggests that the process of cultural distancing that saw the increasing polarisation of patrician and plebeian cultures helped bring about a drop in prosecution rates before it helped to marginalise witchcraft belief for educated culture. He argues that the decline of witchcraft trials occurred decades before that of belief because the judiciary, who for the most part still believed in witchcraft, became even more reluctant than they had been earlier to convict on the proofs or evidences of witchcraft brought before them by members of the lower orders. They regarded these proofs as part of the superstitious belief system of the lower classes, which was not to be trusted by those of their own social group, the educated elite. In seventeenth-century witchcraft trials, the presiding judge (usually an assize court judge in witchcraft trials) could influence the outcome of the case through his direction to the jury, his method of summing up and his overall attitude to the evidence put before him. The attitude of the magistrate (justice of the peace) who prepared evidence for the assize court could prove equally decisive. If both men were against the witchcraft accusation, the chances of acquittal were dramatically increased.[23]

In arguing this point, Sharpe creates a relationship between decline in belief and decline in trials because, as we have seen, one of the factors he highlighted as contributing to the mental context in which witchcraft belief became marginalised decades later was the cultural distancing from certain types of witchcraft belief now considered vulgar. Peter Elmer goes even further than Sharpe by arguing that high prosecution rates for witchcraft were reliant on a high intensity of belief. In common with Sharpe, he contends that although accusations of witchcraft remained steady during the sixteenth and seventeenth centuries, they only resulted

---

[20] Clark, *Thinking with demons*, p. vii.
[21] Gaskill, *Crime and mentalities*, p. 93.
[22] Ibid., p. 118.
[23] Sharpe, *Instruments of darkness*, pp. 213–34.

in a trial if judges and magistrates took their accounts seriously. However, he goes on to argue, they were more likely to do this at times when their sense of belief in witchcraft was high, namely at times when the established religious or political order was under threat. This, he contends, accounts for the uneven geographical and temporal patterns of witchcraft trials during the sixteenth and seventeenth centuries in England.[24]

It is generally agreed by historians of the subject that witchcraft trials in England were, for most the part, sporadic, trying the crimes of individuals or very small groups, and very likely to end in acquittal.[25] This last point is borne out by some of the figures that exist for the number of indictments at assize courts between 1560 and 1700 that ended in execution: in Kent 17.5 per cent, in Surrey 9.2 per cent and in Essex 27 per cent.[26] It is also clear that, even though accusations remained steady at a high level, indictments and successful prosecutions became rarer as the seventeenth century wore on, especially after the Restoration of Charles II in 1660. The last trial in England for witchcraft was at Leicester in 1717,[27] the last conviction was at Hertford in 1712 (the Wenham trial), and the last person executed was at Exeter in 1685. In the century before that date, about five hundred people, mainly women, had been executed for witchcraft. Those 500 represent just over 1 per cent of the estimated 40,000 witches put to death in western Europe between 1400 and 1800, when England held 5 per cent of the total European population.[28]

Taking into consideration what has been argued in previous chapters about Hutchinson's political, religious and intellectual outlook, as well as the reasons given by historians for his scepticism, this chapter will reconsider the reasons why Hutchinson condemned witchcraft trials in the *Historical essay*. In particular, did his personal experience of witchcraft trials do anything to shape his antipathy to witchcraft? This chapter will also provide a literary critique of the *Historical essay*, ascertaining how it was constructed and how it works as a text. Finally, its

---

[24] Peter Elmer, 'Towards a politics of witchcraft in early modern England' in Stuart Clark (ed.), *Languages of witchcraft: narrative, ideology and meaning in early modern culture* (Basingstoke and New York, 2001), pp. 101–18.

[25] James Sharpe, 'Introduction: the Lancashire witches in historical context' in Robert Poole (ed.), *The Lancashire witches: histories and stories* (Manchester, 2002), p. 3; George Durston, *Witchcraft and witch trials: a history of English witchcraft and its legal perspectives, 1542 to 1736* (Chichester, 2000), pp. 348–9.

[26] Davies, *Witchcraft, magic and culture*, p. 83.

[27] Gaskill, *Crime and mentalities*, pp. 79n, 80–3; Sharpe, *Witchcraft in early modern England*, pp. 24–5, 33–4.

[28] William Monter, 'Re-contextualizing British witchcraft' in *Journal of Interdisciplinary History*, xxxv, no. 1 (September, 2004), 106; Gaskill, *Crime and mentalities*, p. 79n.

reception by the English educated public will be studied: did the *Historical essay* actually pass into the educated mainstream as quickly and quietly as has been suggested in the past?

I

As has been argued, Hutchinson was a Newtonian, a committed Whig and a Low-Church, Latitudinarian activist. He defended the Whiggish social and cultural ideology of politeness against its anti-type, religious enthusiasm, in all its myriad forms, and it is certain that Hutchinson regarded witchcraft as a salient example of religious enthusiasm. The 'vulgar opinions of witchcraft', Hutchinson contended in the *Historical essay*, should be 'combatted, oppos'd, and kept down' because the 'credulous multitude' will always 'have a bias towards the belief of them; and ... will be frighted into actions that disturb the places where they shall be', leaving 'no man's life safe in his own house'.[29] The 'tryals of witches', Hutchinson stated in 1712, immediately after attending the Wenham trial, 'never fail'd to bring great trouble and disturbance, not only to the poor old creatures, but to all timerous persons, and the whole neighbourhoods where they are, and which, if it once gets head, our learned Judges will find hard to suppress'.[30] 'Polite men, and great lovers of ease' were thus to 'turn away their thoughts from it [witchcraft] with disdain'.[31] Bostridge's contention that Hutchinson rejected witchcraft for political reasons thus fits more closely with the available evidence than Sharpe's thesis (and Porter's), which regards Hutchinson's scepticism as a result of his embracing the religious, cultural and intellectual values of his social class, the urban, educated elite. However, it is also clear, contrary to what Bostridge argues about the relationship between belief and trials, that the experience of witchcraft trials, whether direct or indirect, focused and deepened Hutchinson's ideological distaste for witchcraft belief.

England may have escaped the worst ravages of the 'witch-craze' of the early modern period, but Hutchinson was a resident of Suffolk from 1690 to 1720 (first in Hoxne and then Bury St Edmunds), a county that, more than most, had witnessed at first hand the social and human cost of witch-hunting. Suffolk bore a large part of the brunt of England's only clear-cut example of a European-style witch panic, the mass witch-hunts conducted in East Anglia between 1645 and 1647 by Matthew Hopkins and his cohort, John Stearne. Of the 250 or so suspected witches brought

---

[29] Hutchinson, *Historical essay*, pp. vj, xiv, viij, vj.
[30] Francis Hutchinson to Sir Hans Sloane, 3 Apr. 1712 (B.L., Sloane MS 4043, fo. 38).
[31] Hutchinson, *Historical essay*, sig. A4ʳ.

before the authorities, 117 were from Suffolk. It is estimated that about 100 of these 250 suspects were executed.[32] This episode in witchcraft history held a special attraction for Hutchinson, who detailed it in the *Historical essay*. Hutchinson conjectured that the whole episode claimed 40 Suffolk lives, including some residents of Bury St Edmunds and Hoxne. Hutchinson's knowledge of these cases came from reading relevant literature (including Hopkins' own book about the episode) and by asking Hoxne residents alive in 1645 to recount their experiences.[33]

Furthermore, after Margaret Elmore was tried and acquitted at Ipswich assizes by Lord Chief Justice Holt in 1694 for bewitching a Mrs Rudge, Hutchinson by his own admission made a 'particular enquiry' into the case. This enquiry further convinced him of Margaret's innocence, as he discovered that after her death Mrs Rudge once again fell ill and died of the 'same distemper' once attributed to Elmore's witchcraft.[34] Furthermore, Hutchinson had been moved to try to publish the *Historical essay* by the belief that Scottish credulity would spread south after the union between Scotland and England, igniting a new spate of English witch-hunting.[35]

The trial of Jane Wenham also had a profound effect on Hutchinson. In March 1712, Wenham was found guilty as charged by a jury and was sentenced to death by hanging. She was saved from the gallows by the intervention of the sceptical presiding judge, Sir John Powell, who ordered her to be reprieved before securing her a royal pardon from Queen Anne on 22 July 1712. The experience of attending her trial not only persuaded Hutchinson to re-draft the *Historical essay* in preparation for publication, but to visit Wenham after her acquittal in a house provided for her own safety at Gilston, Hertfordshire, by a Whig landowner, Colonel Plummer.[36] After the trial, Hutchinson wrote to Sir Hans Sloane to ask him to approach Judge John Powell to see whether Powell would mind the *Historical essay* being dedicated to him. Hutchinson believed he could not do so himself because this would have overstepped his station as both 'a perfect stranger' to Powell and 'an obscure country parson'.[37]

---

[32] Sharpe, *Instruments of darkness*, pp. 128–9.

[33] Hutchinson, *Historical essay*, pp. 59–72; Matthew Hopkins, *The discovery of witches: in answer to severall queries, lately delivered to the judges of assize for the county of Norfolk . . . by Matthew Hopkins, witch-finder . . .* (London, 1647); Sharpe, *Instruments of darkness*, p. 129; Malcolm Gaskill, *Witchfinders: a seventeenth-century English tragedy* (London, 2006), p. 281.

[34] Hutchinson, *Historical essay*, p. 44.

[35] Francis Hutchinson to Sir Hans Sloane, 4 Feb. 1707 (B.L., Sloane MS, 4040, fo. 302); see p. 95 above.

[36] Francis Hutchinson to Sir Hans Sloane, 3 Apr. 1712 (B.L., Sloane MS 4043, fo. 38); Hutchinson, *Historical essay*, pp. 130–1; P. J. Guskin, 'The context of witchcraft: the case of Jane Wenham (1712)' in *Eighteenth-Century Studies*, xv, no. 1 (1981), 48, 53, 68–9.

[37] Francis Hutchinson to Sir Hans Sloane, 3 Apr. 1712 (B.L., Sloane MS 4043, fo. 38).

Hutchinson was convinced Powell's approbation would act as some sort of protection against the 'censure as I should meet with from some', namely those still credulous in matters of witchcraft.[38] Hutchinson also probably admired the way in which the sceptical Powell had handled the Wenham trial, doing everything in his power to persuade the jury to bring in an innocent verdict. Powell even stated, after a witness had accused Wenham of flying, that 'there is no law against flying'.[39] Hutchinson took Sloane's advice and decided against publishing his book at that time.[40]

II

In *Thinking with demons*, Stuart Clark points out that the majority of sceptical texts could not damage the coherence of traditional witchcraft beliefs because mainstream sceptical and demonological theorists alike wrote within the confines of traditional demonology. Consequently, consensus was reached between the two groups of thinkers on many fundamental issues. For example, all writers on witchcraft, irrespective of what side of the divide they stood upon, stuck to the golden rule that Satan worked his evil using natural means: only God could overturn the natural laws by which the universe ran, using miracles (*miracula*). Most sceptics, no matter how zealous or well constructed their attack on traditional witchcraft belief was, failed to argue it out of existence because they left intact the central idea which maintained its intellectual coherence as a belief system, Satan's ability to intervene in the temporal world. It was this debt to traditional demonology that made most sceptical works concern themselves with refuting specific instances of witchcraft or with the legal or scriptural bases of witchcraft belief. Only two writers broke free of these intellectual constraints, and for their trouble were regarded by their contemporaries as extremists: Reginald Scot, who challenged the prevailing patterns of the sceptical tradition by depriving the devil of the ability to influence the workings of the temporal world; and Jean Bodin, who believed in witchcraft but asserted that the devil was not constrained by natural laws and thus could perform not only *mira* (lesser wonders) but also, like the creator himself, *miracula*.[41]

---

[38] Ibid.
[39] Cited in *OldDNB*, xlvi, 244–5; see also Guskin, 'Jane Wenham', p. 53.
[40] Hutchinson to Sloane, 3 Apr. 1712 (B.L., Sloane MS 4043, fo. 38).
[41] Clark, *Thinking with demons*, pp. 161–8, 190–214; this view of Scot's witchcraft scepticism as iconoclastic is also voiced in David Wootton, 'Reginald Scot/Abraham Fleming/The Family of Love' in *Languages of witchcraft*, p. 120, and Sydney Anglo, 'Reginald Scot's *Discoverie of Witchcraft*: scepticism and sadduceeism' in idem (ed.), *The damned art: essays in the literature of witchcraft* (London, 1977), pp. 108–10.

Hutchinson might have regarded witchcraft as a form of religious enthusiasm, but the structure of his book owes rather more to the work of sceptical witchcraft theorists than to critics of enthusiasm.[42] The *Historical essay* is a typical sceptical witchcraft text, as delineated by Clark, because it fails to attack the core doctrine of traditional witchcraft belief and rests content with disputing witchcraft theory on biblical and legal grounds and with arguing away specific instances. Furthermore, even when tailoring the *Historical essay* so as to appeal to a specific audience – the literate lower orders and the legal profession – Hutchinson dug deep into the bank of arguments and narrative devices held in other sceptical witchcraft tracts.

By the late seventeenth century, the English educated elite were beginning to believe that Satan's powers were rarely felt on earth; they were particularly sceptical of the reality of demonic possession and his ability to assume bodily form. The belief that the age of miracles had passed bolstered educated scepticism about the possibility of possession and exorcism. Possession was after all a form of miracle in which the natural workings of the universe ceased in order to allow Satan or an evil spirit to enter a human body.[43] Hutchinson, eager to define the boundaries of polite, orthodox belief in the spirit world, frowned upon the image of Satan portrayed in the popular witchcraft pamphlets and books so eagerly consumed by the lower orders: 'for the vulgar opinion is, that the Devil is something like a man, but with tail, and claws, and horns, and cloven foot . . . but the holy Scriptures tell us no such tales as these'.[44] He also condemned those who were in 'over-great dread or terror' of bad spirits or devils, especially those who believed 'heathenish stories, that the holy Scriptures never taught them',[45] such as that 'when the sun goes down, and the wild beasts come out of their dens, evil spirits . . . come out at the same time from their hidden places, and roam about the dark, to fright those they meet with'.[46] He even warned against taking the Scriptures too literally in matters of demonology,

---

[42] The sceptical tradition of witchcraft theory comprised men such as Reginald Scot, George Gifford, Samuel Harsnett, John Cotta, John Gaule, Nathaniel Holmes, Sir Robert Filmer, Thomas Ady, John Wagestaffe and John Webster. For a list of their written works, see Sharpe, *Witchcraft in early modern England*, pp. 132–7.

[43] Thomas, *Religion and the decline of magic*, pp. 570–2; Kathleen R. Sands, 'The doctrine of transubstantiation and the English Protestant dispossession of demons' in *History*, lxxxv, no. 279 (2000), 458–62; Clark, *Thinking with demons*, pp. 161–8, 190–214; Sharpe, *Instruments of darkness*, pp. 250–1; Phillip C. Almond, *Demonic possession and exorcism in early modern England* (Cambridge, 2004), pp. 8–9.

[44] Hutchinson, *Historical essay*, p. 10.

[45] Ibid., Sermon II: Concerning angels, p. 266.

[46] Ibid., pp. 266–7.

suggesting that mention of an evil spirit or Satan often actually referred to a 'bad man', or a 'remarkable miraculous token of God's presence', or 'some prophet or minister acting in his name'.[47]

Despite these words of caution and his belief that the age of miracles was past, Hutchinson nonetheless took a view of Satan, his demons and his works that had more in common with the views of demonologists and sceptics, and consequently sixteenth- and early seventeenth-century theological orthodoxy, than with educated, eighteenth-century Britain – a stance especially surprising in a Latitudinarian-Whig. According to Hutchinson, the 'holy prophets' taught that evil spirits or demons were 'executioners of some of the greater acts of God's justice ... so they also, when he sees fit, are instruments in his hand to fulfill his will'.[48] He believed that God used Satan and evil spirits to test, delude, deceive, punish and possess innocents, sinners and unbelievers alike.[49] In common with all those who worked within the confines of traditional demonology, Hutchinson placed clear limits on Satan's power, denouncing those free-thinkers, whether of ancient or contemporaneous origin, who claimed that the devil's existence was 'natural, eternal, independent, and even divine', and of 'as long continuance ... as the supreme being'.[50] Hutchinson argued that this stance was both unreasonable and un-scriptural, as God was the supreme power in the universe and even the devil was under his command.[51] He further noted that the devil was not capable of performing *miracula*, only *mira*.[52]

Hutchinson matched his unfashionable belief in a very active Satan and evil spirits with traditional, High-Church notions of eternal torment in hell. As if almost to inform the reader of the limits of his willingness to place religion on a reasonable footing, he insisted, in a sermon preached at the commencement of his DD at Cambridge, that the Scriptures provided ample proof of the immortality of the soul and the existence of eternal punishments and rewards. These doctrinal essentials, he continued, should be accepted as a matter of faith whether they proved to be 'reasonable' or not.[53] Hutchinson, however, was unwilling to get bogged down in a discussion over what the precise nature of hell was. He thus refused to give 'any determination' of how 'much of the descriptions

---

[47] Ibid., p. 252.
[48] Ibid., p. 267.
[49] See pp. 83, 87 above and pp. 108–9 below.
[50] Hutchinson, *Historical essay*, Sermon II: Concerning angels, pp. 256, 257, 259; see also ibid., Sermon I: The Christian religion demonstrated, pp. 245, 247.
[51] Hutchinson, *Historical essay*, Sermon II: Concerning angels, pp. 267–8.
[52] Ibid., Sermon I: The Christian religion demonstrated, p. 245.
[53] Hutchinson, *Sermon preached ... 3 July 1698*, pp. 5–10, 11–13, 13–20.

we have of them is literal, and how much metaphorical, and popular'.[54] Instead, he condemned one of the main arguments used by those sceptical of the existence of afterlife punishment: that it was inconsistent with the idea of a just and compassionate God.[55] Although God undoubtedly loved mankind, his love was 'not so great, as his love of true Excellency and virtue . . . and hatred of base qualities'. Furthermore, God had 'given us abundant proof, that his indulgence of our persons is not so infinite but he can very easily make us miserable and shamefull, if we make ourselves deserving to be so'.[56]

The doctrine of eternal punishment in hell remained part of Anglican orthodoxy up until the middle decades of the eighteenth century, largely because denial of these doctrines was associated with the radical sectarians of the Civil War period.[57] It was almost universally believed that moral anarchy would ensue if men and women did not have the fear of hell to restrain their appetites.[58] High-Churchmen, however, were more likely to support the Anglican orthodox opinion on the matter of eternal rewards and punishments, as these notions fitted perfectly with their wider ideology, which decreed that authority, dogma and tradition were the best guides for human beings in all matters. In their view, human nature was so corrupt and man, since the Fall, so prone to sin that reason could not provide enough restraint for his appetites; only the allure of eternal rewards and the threat of eternal punishment could do this.[59]

However, as Philip Almond points out, there were 'from the time of the Restoration . . . a small number by whom it was privately disbelieved, publicly, although discreetly questioned, or anonymously challenged, in the name of the conviction that all would ultimately be saved, or the belief that the wicked would be annihilated after a period of punishment appropriate to their wickedness'.[60] Arians, Socinians and Neo-Platonists were all characteristically convinced of this fact this, but it was Latitudinarians, albeit to varying degrees, such as Simon Patrick and Archbishop John Tillotson, who did most to carry on this process of dulcification.[61]

---

[54] Ibid., p. 13.
[55] Philip C. Almond, *Heaven and hell in Enlightenment England* (Cambridge, 1994), p. 149; Paul C. Davies, 'The debate on eternal punishment in late seventeenth- and eighteenth-century English literature' in *Eighteenth-Century Studies*, vii (1973), 260–2, 275.
[56] Hutchinson, *Sermon preached . . . 3 July 1698*, p. 15; see also idem, pp. 19–20.
[57] Almond, *Heaven and hell*, p. 144.
[58] D. P. Walker, *The decline of hell: seventeenth-century discussions of eternal torment* (London, 1964), pp. 4–7.
[59] Davies, 'Eternal punishment', pp. 261–2; Kenyon, *Revolution principles*, p. 92.
[60] Almond, *Heaven and hell*, p. 145.
[61] Walker, *The decline of hell*, pp. 8–11; Davies, 'Eternal punishment', pp. 275, 257–69, 259; Almond, *Heaven and hell*, pp. 156–7.

It is unsurprising that Hutchinson's demonology was similar to that of continental sceptics and demonologists. He possessed an in-depth knowledge of their writings[62] and built up a large library of them during his lifetime. Sometime during the 1730s, Hutchinson catalogued the books in his library. His catalogue contained over 707 books in 712 volumes, of which 92 titles were dedicated to 'witches, conjuror's, devils, [and] oracles'.[63] These books were auctioned in 1756 by his widow Anne.[64] His library included John Webster's *Displaying of suppos'd witchcraft* ... (1677), Reginald Scot's *Discouerie of witchcraft* ... (1584), Meric Casaubon's *Of incredulity and credulity in things natural, civil, and divine* ... (1668), Jean Bodin's *De la demonomanie des sorciers* ... (1580) and Richard Baxter's *The certainty of the world of spirits and consequently, of the immortality of souls* (1691).[65]

Unable, or unwilling, to attack witchcraft on demonological grounds, mainstream sceptics, such as Hutchinson, concentrated their efforts on undermining traditional beliefs in three other ways. Firstly, they argued that traditional witchcraft beliefs had no scriptural foundation. Hutchinson expended a whole chapter of the *Historical essay* in deliberating over whether the popular image of the demonic witch contained in witchcraft pamphlets had any biblical foundation, before concluding that 'the holy Scriptures tell us no such tales as these, nor any thing like them'.[66] He went on to argue that the scriptural text in Exodus 22: 18, 'thou shalt not suffer a witch to live', had been mistranslated and misinterpreted. The term 'witch' in the Bible did not relate to the demonic witch of contemporaneous culture but only to the false prophets, wizards and diviners of biblical times.[67] This argument was one that was repeated time and time again in the books of witchcraft sceptics.[68]

Secondly, most sceptics expressed legal misgivings both about the way witchcraft accusations were investigated and the way in which witchcraft trials were conducted.[69] The nature of the witch's crime, inflicting harm by invisible means, made it an extremely hard crime to prove in court.

---

[62] Hutchinson, *Historical essay*, pp. xiij–xiv, 56.
[63] Hutchinson's commonplace book, 1731–9 (Down and Connor Diocesan Registry, Belfast [hereafter D.R.] unpressmarked, pp. 553–6).
[64] *A catalogue of books: being in the library of the Right Rev. Dr Francis Hutchinson, late Bishop of Down and Connor. To be sold by auction, by William Ross, at the coffee house ... the House of Lords, on Monday, the twenty-sixth of April 1756* ... (London, 1756).
[65] Bishop Hutchinson's account book, 1731–9 (D.R., pp. 553–6).
[66] Hutchinson, *Historical essay*, p. 11.
[67] Ibid., pp. 144–57.
[68] Thomas, *Religion and the decline of magic*, pp. 570–1; Russell Hope Robbins (ed.), *The encyclopaedia of witchcraft and demonology* (New York, 1959), p. 167; Anglo, 'Scepticism', pp. 109, 111, 115–16, 118; Davies, *Witchcraft, magic and culture*, p. 3.
[69] Clark, *Thinking with demons*, p. 203.

The English criminal system therefore found it necessary to use evidence and ways of dealing with witness testimonies that were peculiar to witchcraft trials.[70] Hutchinson examined a sample of the types of 'proofs' that had been used in past witchcraft trials to prove that a particular person was a witch or to tie a particular witch to a particular crime. He concluded that these proofs were not sound grounds on which to take a person's life. For example, the devil's mark could simply be a mole or a spot; the adverse reaction of a victim to the touch of a witch could be faked by the victim; and the fact that a person was unable to recite the Lord's Prayer was probably due to ill-education rather than the fact that they had sold their soul to the devil. Spectral evidence, he continued, (when the guilt of a person is established by the victim's sight of the ghost of the accused) was also untrustworthy because the devil could have created the spectral illusion in order to implicate an innocent person. He also argued that if a suspected witch floated when swum in a river or stream, this was not a sufficient proof of guilt, nor was a failure to produce tears or possessing areas on the body insensible to pain.[71]

Hutchinson went on to argue that accusers and their supporters were often on a criminal par with demonic witches because they used supernatural charms, magical rituals and herbal medicines provided by cunning-folk to cure bewitchment, detect witches and protect against future witchcraft attacks. Hutchinson proposed that these charms and rituals, if indeed they possessed any power at all, derived it from Satan. Therefore, it was only partiality on the part of the judiciary that determined that demonic witches, and not their accusers, or the cunning-folk they employed, were guilty of the type of sorcery and conjuration banned by the witchcraft acts of 1563 and 1604. The argument that cunning-folk were as bad as demonic witches was one that was used repeatedly by learned demonologists and sceptical authors alike, both in England and in continental Europe. Cunning-folk, or white witches, were a common element in early modern villages, towns and cities, and, after the late seventeenth century, became the principal providers of witchcraft cure and detection, when orthodox medical practitioners ceased providing such services.[72] Hutchinson, as we shall see later in this chapter, codified these unsatisfactory 'proofs' so that the judiciary had a practical guide to help them prevent guilty verdicts being brought in witchcraft trials.

[70] Thomas, *Religion and the decline of magic*, pp. 442–9.
[71] Hutchinson, *Historical essay*, pp. 140–1, 117–18, 74–5, 130, 4–5, 120, 99, 136–8, 65–6, 139, 132.
[72] Hutchinson, *Historical essay*, pp. 132, 109–19; Owen Davies, *Popular magic in English history* (2003, repr. Cornwall, 2007), pp. 6–8, 29–33, 40–1, 67–9, 103–11; Geoffrey Scarre, *Witchcraft and magic in 16th and 17th century Europe* (London, 1987), p. 31.

Thirdly, witchcraft sceptics concerned themselves with arguing away specific instances of witchcraft. Clark argues that they did this in four main ways. The first was to blame acts of witchcraft on the devil directly. Satan wreaked havoc, caused human illness, and possessed people without the agency of witches. The other three explanatory mechanisms attributed supposed acts of witchcraft to natural causes. The first of these aimed to show that certain phenomena – the witch's ability to change shape or fly – were in fact illusions wrought by the devil. Satan used such illusions to trick humankind into believing that he had the same power as God when in reality he acted under God's licence. The second explanatory mechanism was that nature itself could trick humans into believing almost anything, for example by hallucinations, sensory malfunctions or the misreading of natural events. The third explanation was that certain phenomena were true natural wonders, wrought either by nature itself or by natural magicians who knew about the secret workings of nature. This third explanatory mechanism was slightly different from the other two categories, in that it dealt with real phenomena. Clark asserts that it was in these three areas that believers in witchcraft exercised as much scepticism as any 'sceptic'. Demonologists, who were also wont to attribute certain instances of supposed witchcraft to one of these three explanations, on many occasions anticipated the arguments of the sceptics.[73]

Hutchinson may have, like most sceptics, dedicated a large portion of his book to explaining away famous instances of witchcraft, either in demonic or natural terms, but the actual explanatory mechanisms he used bore a greater resemblance to those he had employed in the *Pretended spirit of prophecy*, where he had used this method with great success to argue against the enthusiasm of prophecy. Thus it must have seemed appropriate to use it to argue against enthusiastic witchcraft beliefs. He wrote, but did not publish, a version of the *Historical essay* in 1707, nearly a year before he published the *Pretended spirit of prophecy*. However, in 1712 he admitted to having made some 'little improvements' to the 1707 manuscript. Although it is impossible to state with any degree of certainty what exactly these 'improvements' were, it is highly likely that, after the success of the *Pretended spirit of prophecy*, Hutchinson began to believe that his book on witchcraft could be improved by employing the same sort of explanatory mechanisms to explain away instances of witchcraft that he had used to such great effect when proffering alternative explanations for divine inspiration of the French Prophets.[74]

---

[73] Clark, *Thinking with demons*, pp. 203–13, 190–4.
[74] Hutchinson to Sloane, 3 April 1712 (B.L., Sloane MS 4043, fo. 38).

Hutchinson explained away famous witchcraft cases by attributing suspected witchcraft to disease, imposture, demonic delusion or possession.[75] He first of all argued that the fits which afflicted the bewitched were better explained by attributing them to much more mundane natural causes than witchcraft:

> some sort of fits which are undoubtedly natural, continue . . . [and] alter the habit of the body: whence many times there grows a lurking intermitting fever, and delirium, or particular madness.[76]

He went on to say:

> In deep melancholy, they shall think themselves glass, or a rotten stick, or kings or queens, or even God himself . . . [thus] why may they not think themselves bewitch'd by those they hear of, or believe that they are witches themselves?[77]

Secondly, he laid the possibility before the reader that the victim had lied in his or her testimony, or had used one of the 'multitude of tricks that may be done by slight of hand' in order to fake the symptoms of witchcraft.[78] He pointed out, for example, that the chief witness in the Wenham trial, a young woman named Ann Thorn, had deliberately faked the symptoms of her supposed bewitchment.[79] In order to remind the reader that this was far from an isolated incident, he dedicated two chapters to the subject of the discovery of notorious witchcraft impostures.[80] He concluded that if all witchcraft accusations had undergone such a strict examination as these, even more frauds would have been detected.[81] Hutchinson also stated that Satan often used his vast knowledge of nature to work illusions in order to deceive the gullible and superstitious, to set up the innocent in false witchcraft accusations, and to tempt the weak and sinful.[82] He lamented:

> How many righteous Abels fall every day by men that are as cruel and as ungodly as wicked Cain? And how do we know but that some may fall also by the craft of evil spirits deluding majistrates that take not due care to prevent them?[83]

---

[75] For instances of Hutchinson doing precisely this, see *Historical essay*, pp. 59–136, 144.
[76] Ibid., p. 4.
[77] Ibid., p. 5.
[78] Ibid., p. 9.
[79] Ibid., p. 130.
[80] Ibid., chapters 9 and 15.
[81] Ibid., pp. 47, 131, 120.
[82] Ibid., pp. 50–2, 72–6, 90–3, 112–15.
[83] Ibid., p. 91.

Finally, he argued that 'those afflicted persons that have been the accusers, have often had great appearance of being daemoniacs... and the Devil by their mouths hath carried on his great work of false accusing and murdering innocent people'.[84]

Hutchinson may have used the arguments and methodology of witchcraft sceptics and opponents of enthusiasm in the *Historical essay*, but he nonetheless made deliberate parallels between his book and Newton's *Principia Mathematica*. It was typical of Newtonian Latudinarians to try to bolster Whig social and cultural ideology by reference to Newtonian science. Hutchinson was after all attacking witchcraft belief because it was inimical to his Whiggish view of the social order.[85] As Ian Bostridge first pointed out, Hutchinson in the *Historical essay* claimed to have used the Newtonian rational-cum-empirical style of reasoning to prove that witchcraft was neither a rational nor a worthy system of belief,

> for rational arguments without facts can never decide this case. A man may as well compose a true system of natural philosophy, without experiments, as state the case of witchcraft, without careful enquiry into those appearances of it, that have made so many wise men believe it.[86]

Hutchinson argued that witchcraft should be rejected because it relied upon unconvincing, empirical evidence: the facts or reported instances of witchcraft. Having rejected the old system of witchcraft belief, he then presented the reader with a new, rational witchcraft theory. He argued that the number of witches in any society was not determined by the devil, but by the principles held by that society in relation to witchcraft at the time. Hutchinson elaborated on this point by presenting a set of negative principles which operated in times when witches abounded, along with a set of positive principles which operated in times when there were few witches. Therefore, just as Newton created a new law of motion through a re-examination of the available facts, Hutchinson claimed to have created a new law of witchcraft.[87] The idea of constructing a law of witchcraft might have been particularly Newtonian, but upon examination, the two sets of principles reveal themselves to be, for the most part, lists of the types of proofs and legal procedures that witchcraft sceptics had long regarded as insufficient grounds on which to convict suspected witches.[88]

---

[84] Ibid., p. 52.
[85] See Chapter 4 above.
[86] Hutchinson, *Historical essay*, p. 12.
[87] Ibid., pp. 12, 50, 150–160; Bostridge, *Witchcraft and its transformations*, pp. 145–7.
[88] See pp. 118–21 below.

III

Hutchinson hoped that his deployment of the old wine of the sceptics' arguments in the new bottles of the 'new science' would provoke, or harden, witchcraft scepticism among England's educated elite. He nonetheless crafted his book to appeal to the two sectors of society who he believed played a pivotal role in the creation and conduct of witchcraft trials. Firstly, he wanted to change the views of those who made witchcraft accusations, the lower classes. Secondly, he wanted to provide judges and justices of the peace – who, along with grand juries, represented, in the eighteenth century legal system, the final barrier against successful prosecution – with a practical guide to enable them to continue to keep the prosecution rate as low as it had been since the early 1680s and until such time as the witchcraft statutes were repealed. Hutchinson had to wait until 1736 for the repeal of the 1604 witchcraft statute (9 Geo. II, c.5).[89]

Hutchinson aimed to influence the opinion of the credulous masses, who he stated were ever 'ready to try their tricks, and swim the old women, and wonder at and magnify every unaccountable symptom and odd accident.'[90] Hutchinson first of all appropriated the narrative structure of George Gifford's *A dialogue concerning witches and witchcraft* (1593) for the *Historical essay*, in the belief that it would lend his book more popular appeal. Gifford, a puritan, believed that those afflicted by supposed witchcraft should examine their lives to identify the sins that had provoked God to use the devil to punish them in the first place. This would stimulate a process of re-education that would, in turn, increase the individual's piety and reduce the likelihood of further demonic attacks. Gifford wrote his book in the form of a dialogue to make his arguments more accessible to the common people, whom he believed to be largely impervious to normal intellectual reasoning and debate.[91]

Similarly, the main narrative structure of the *Historical essay* takes the form of a dialogue between a Scottish advocate, a clergyman and a juryman. The juryman is said to have come to the clergyman for advice on a witchcraft trial that he has to attend. In the discussion that ensues

---

[89] For a discussion of the repeal of the witchcraft statutes, see Ian Bostridge, 'Witchcraft repealed' in J. Barry, M. Hester and G. Roberts (eds), *Witchcraft in early modern Europe: studies in culture and belief* (Cambridge, 1996), pp. 309–34, and Davies, *Witchcraft, magic and culture*, pp. 1–3.

[90] Hutchinson, *Historical essay*, p. viij.

[91] George Gifford, *A dialogue concerning witches and witchcraft* (London, 1593, repr. 1931), pp. 84–8; Alan Macfarlane, 'A Tudor anthropologist: George Gifford's *Discourse and dialogue*' in *The damned art*, p. 148; James Hitchcock, 'George Gifford and Puritan witch beliefs' in *Archiv für Reformationsgeschichte*, lviii (1967), 90–9.

the advocate takes up the case for active belief in witchcraft, while the clergyman argues for caution in such matters.[92] Hutchinson even tailored the language of the *Historical essay* to suit the less educated by including translations of the Latin texts from which he quoted.[93] Similarly, when he wanted his sermons to be understood by the most uneducated person in his parish he avoided the use of Latin.[94] In contrast, the *Defence of the clergy's liberty* . . . , written for the exclusive consumption of the classically educated clergy of his archdeaconry, is peppered with un-translated Latin and Greek quotations.[95]

Hutchinson hoped that his explosions of famous English cases of witchcraft would help to weaken popular belief in witchcraft, believing that 'with the generality of mankind a frightful story weigh[ed] more than the clearest reason'.[96] Conversely, he believed that the pamphlets which detailed famous witchcraft trials,[97] of which he had an admirable personal collection,[98] encouraged plebeian belief because they provided the reader with an abundance of witchcraft 'stories':

> These books and narratives are in tradesmen's shops, and farmer's houses, and are read with great eagerness, and are continually levening the minds of the youth, who delight in such subjects: and considering what sore evils these notions bring where they prevail, I hope that no man will think but that they must still be combatted, oppos'd, and kept down.[99]

One of Hutchinson's witchcraft pamphlets, Zachary Taylor's *The Surey imposter: being an answer to a late fanatical pamphlet entituled the Surey demoniack* (1697), later became part of the library of the early

---

[92] See Hutchinson, *Historical essay*, pp. 1–230.
[93] Ibid., pp. 164–5.
[94] See pp. 27–8 above.
[95] Hutchinson, *Defence of the clergy's liberty*, pp. 3, 5, 6, 8, 10.
[96] Hutchinson, *Historical essay*, p. 184.
[97] A famous example of which details the trial and execution of ten witches in Lancaster in 1612, namely Thomas Potts, *The wonderfull discoverie of witches in the countie of Lancaster. With the arraignement and triall of nineteene notorious witches, at the assizes and general gaole deliverie, holden at the castle of Lancaster, upon Munday, the seventeenth of August last, 1612. Before Sir James Altham, and Sir Edward Bromley, Knights; barons of his Maiesties Court of Exchequer: and justices of assize, oyer and terminor, and generall gaole deliverie in the circuit of the north parts. Together with the arraignement and triall of Jennet Preston, at the assizes holden at the castle of Yorke, the seven and twentieth day of Julie last past, with her execution for the murther of Master Lister by witchcraft. Published and set forth by commandement of his Majesties justices of assize in the north parts* (London, 1613). This trial has recently been studied in detail in a collection of essays: Poole, *The Lancashire witches* (see n.25, above).
[98] Hutchinson's commonplace book, 1731–9 (D.R., pp. 533–6).
[99] Hutchinson, *Historical essay*, p. xiv.

twentieth-century writer, occult book collector and psychical researcher, Harry Price.[100]

Hutchinson mooted that plebeian witchcraft beliefs possessed a definite theoretical basis and he believed that witchcraft pamphlets perpetuated these beliefs. However, before examining his view of popular witchcraft belief, it is first necessary to categorise the different types of witchcraft belief that existed in England in the early modern period. Learned demonologists were, from about 1550 to 1700, mainly concerned with the theoretical problems of witchcraft and emphasised the fact that both cunning-folk and witches derived their power from the devil.[101] The witchcraft theory of continental authors, though it varied greatly in detail, had three main elements: the demonic pact, the sabbat, and the allied beliefs of night-flying and the witch's ability to change from human to animal form.[102] There existed a substantial array of printed demonological works in England by the 1620s, some of which were penned by English demonologists, such as William Perkins. English authors were particularly concerned with the way a witch performed her role as demonic agent and with the Satanic pact. They also argued that witchcraft needed three things in order to operate: divine permission, Satanic power and human agency.[103] In Elizabethan and Jacobean England, the educated elite generally held a very different view of witchcraft. As Sharpe points out, most people were 'willing to accept witchcraft as a possibility, able to recognise or suspect it when they thought it was harming them or people they knew, yet seeing it only as one of the many hazards that life might throw at them, loathe to believe in the cosmic danger posed by a sect of Satanic witches, and unlikely to respond to a suspicion of witchcraft in an unthinking or hasty fashion'.[104]

It has long been argued that the common people were more concerned with the tangible effects of witchcraft – the effects of a cunning-man or – woman, or the harm done by a malefic witch – rather than with the theory of learned demonologists.[105] It has recently been suggested, however, that popular witchcraft belief was not homogenous and even experienced change over time. For example, the idea of the witches' sabbat and the demonic pact slowly filtered down to popular level

[100] This pamphlet is held in the University of London Library special collections department.
[101] Sharpe, *Instruments of darkness*, p. 70.
[102] Brian Levack, *The witch-hunt in early modern Europe* (2nd edn, London, 1995), pp. 35–50.
[103] Sharpe, *Instruments of darkness*, pp. 82–94.
[104] Ibid., p. 57.
[105] Thomas, *Decline of magic*, p. 448.

during the course of the seventeenth century.[106] The witchcraft beliefs presented in popular pamphlets and books, on the other hand, lay somewhere between plebeian and learned witchcraft belief. Although the demonic element was not as great as it was in the learned tomes, the witches described in pamphlets were still seen to be more than just purveyors of *maleficium*: they were agents of the devil who had lost their souls through a secret pact and were now eager to cause harm to the good and the godly. This struggle was placed within the context of an eternal cosmic war between good and evil, God and Satan. The idea that witches attended sabbats or copulated with Satan, however, was as conspicuously absent from these pamphlets as it was present in demonological works.[107]

In the *Historical essay*, Hutchinson made the distinction between the vulgar, popular notions of witchcraft and the demonological beliefs of the educated:

> for if any wicked person affirms, or any cracked brain girl imagines, or any lying spirit makes her believe, that she sees any old woman, or other person pursuing her in her visions, the defenders of the vulgar witchcraft tack an imaginary, unproved compact to the deposition, and hang the accused parties for things that were doing, when they were perhaps, asleep upon their beds, or saying their prayers; or, perhaps, in the accusers own possession, with double irons upon them.[108]

His main concern was with vulgar notions of witchcraft, which he defined in the following terms:

> The narratives, tell us, that he [Satan] makes compacts with the witches, and lies with them, and sucks their blood: and that at their bidding, he kills children and cattel, and sinks ships by sea, and carries them to foreign meetings, where they revel with other witches, and drink up the wine in Princes cellars.

He added to this description an integral part of all types of English witchcraft belief, the notion that witches owned familiars.[109] The familiar was given to the witch by Satan upon completion of the demonic pact and was in actuality an evil demon who had taken the shape of an animal or an insect. The familiar was the source of the witch's power and at her bidding destroyed crops, men, butter and beasts. Blood, sucked

---

[106] Sharpe, *Instruments of darkness*, pp. 60–79; Barry Reay, *Popular cultures in England* (London, 1998), pp. 117–19.
[107] Sharpe, *Instruments of darkness*, pp. 94–102.
[108] Hutchinson, *Historical essay*, p. vij.
[109] Ibid., pp. 11, 69–71, 9–10.

from the witch at a site on her body called the devil's mark, was given as payment for such actions.[110] In short, the witchcraft beliefs that Hutchinson referred to as vulgar, popular notions were in fact those disseminated through popular pamphlets and books.

Hutchinson's hostility to Richard Boulton's book, *A compleat history of magick, sorcery, and witchcraft*, which was published in two volumes in 1716, stemmed from the fact that he regarded it as nothing more than a longer, more elaborate witchcraft pamphlet. It poisoned the minds of the common people with its detailed descriptions of witchcraft cases, thus encouraging their credulity. This in its turn paved the way for future witchcraft accusations and trials.[111] Thus, just as the Wenham trial had convinced him of the need to see the *Historical essay* in print in 1712, Boulton's work persuaded him in 1718 to try, for the third and final time, to have the work published:

> I humbly take leave to present your lordships with the following historical collections and observations, which have lain by me several years; and, it may be, had still slept in obscurity, if a new book which very likely may do some mischief, had not lately come forth in two volumes, under the pompous title of A Compleat History, Magick, Sorcery, and Witchcraft.[112]

Boulton's *Compleat history* was presented in the same format as books published by Joseph Glanvill and Henry More in the preceding century. It consisted of a collection of case histories, or narratives, which the respective authors presented as empirical, 'scientific' evidence of the reality of the activity of spiritual essences in the temporal world.[113] Boulton, in his introduction, congratulated himself on his selection of only well-verified case histories:

> And for as much as several tracts have been published upon these subjects, several of which are too prolix, and intermix'd with long and tedious relations, which are less worthy our notice, as they are less authentick and not so well attested . . . in this work we have taken notice only of such as appear to be of undoubted credit and authority.[114]

Glanvill in the introduction to his book *A Blow at modern sadducism* . . . (1668) gave almost the same argument:

---

[110] Thomas, *Religion and the decline of magic*, pp. 445–6.
[111] Hutchinson, *Historical essay*, p. 94.
[112] Ibid., p. vj.
[113] Bostridge, *Witchcraft and its transformations*, p. 142; Alan C. Kors and Edward Peters, *Witchcraft in Europe, 1100–1700: a documentary history* (London, 1972), p. 293; Brian P. Levack, *The witch-hunt in early modern Europe* (3rd edn, Edinburgh, 2006), p. 266.
[114] Richard Boulton, *A compleat history of magick, sorcery, and witchcraft* (2 vols, London, 1715–16), i, sig. A3ᵛ.

> I have no humour nor delight in telling stories, and do not publish these, for the gratification of those that have; but I record them as arguments for the confirmation of a truth, which hath indeed been attested by multitudes of the like evidences in all places, and times: but things remote, or long past, are either not believed, or forgotten: whereas these being fresh, and near, and attended with all the circumstances of credibility, it may be expected, they should have the more success upon the obstinacy of unbelievers.[115]

In his book, Boulton examined a variety of famous sixteenth- and seventeenth-century trials and possessions, for example the possession cases of William Somers and 'the Surrey Daemoniack' Richard Dugdale, the Salem witch trials of 1692, and the trial of Rose Cullender and Amy Denny at Bury St Edmunds in Suffolk in 1662.[116] It was no coincidence that the cases that Hutchinson chose to examine and explain away in the *Historical essay* were the same cases detailed by Boulton. Hutchinson believed that by contesting Boulton's empirical evidence he had undermined his argument.[117] The fact that Hutchinson was particularly affected by, and interested in, Suffolk witchcraft may have contributed to his decision to include the Bury St Edmunds case. However, unlike his other examinations of Suffolk witchcraft cases, Hutchinson's knowledge of it seemed to come entirely from printed material rather than personal investigation.[118]

Boulton saw theorising on the matter of witchcraft as largely superfluous, because the instances of witchcraft, the 'facts' of witchcraft, spoke for themselves:

> since then the truth of such things [witchcraft and sorcery] is indisputable, being confirmed by the testimony of eye-witnesses, and the undoubted authority of both ancient and modern authors, we shall not here trouble the reader with tedious recital of arguments, to prove the possibility of such things.[119]

---

[115] Joseph Glanville, *A blow at modern sadducism in some philosophical considerations about witchcraft. To which is added, the relation of the fam'd disburbance by the drummer in the house of Mr John Mompesson: with some reflections on drollery and atheisme* (London, 1668), sig. B3v.
[116] Boulton, *Compleat history*, i, 49–150, 152–168; ibid., ii, 166–235, 255–62.
[117] Hutchinson, *Historical essay*, pp. 101–8, 193–209, 72–94, 124–8, 109–24; Davies, *Popular magic*, p. 39.
[118] Hutchinson, *Historical essay*, pp. 109–24. For a detailed examination of the trial and execution of Amy Denny and Rose Cullender, see Gilbert Geis and Ivan Bunn, *A trial of witches: a seventeenth century witchcraft prosecution* (London, 1997).
[119] Boulton, *Compleat history*, i, 2.

He dedicated 414 pages of the book's 433 pages to witchcraft narratives, with only 19 pages given over to theoretical exposition. This exposition formed the first chapter to the first volume,[120] which Boulton argued was necessary to enable the reader to have a 'clearer apprehension of the manner and method of such unlawful practices', namely witchcraft.[121] It was added to introduce and complement the narratives which formed the core of the book and it demonstrates that Boulton's witchcraft theory was, more than Hutchinson gave credit for, shaped by traditional demonology. For instance, he deliberated upon the witches' sabbat, the validity of swimming as a test for witchcraft, the Satanic pact, the devil's mark, the nature of familiars, the extent of the Scriptural evidence for demonic witchcraft and the machinations of incubi and succubi.[122] An incubus was the male form that Satan took to have sexual intercourse with a female human; a succubus was its female counterpart.[123]

IV

Hutchinson also crafted the *Historical essay* to appeal to the legal establishment, men long cautious of the legal difficulty of proving the crime of witchcraft and who could do most to prevent witchcraft accusation being turned into prosecution. He was not the first witchcraft sceptic to do so. Thomas Ady's *Candle in the dark, or a treatise concerning the nature of witches and witchcraft* . . . (1665), for example, was subtitled 'being advice to judges, sheriffes, justices of the peace and Grand Jury men, what to do, before they passe sentence on such as are arraigned for the lives, as witches'.[124] In common with justices of the peace and judges, grand juries also played a part in turning accusations into prosecutions, because at preliminary hearings they decided whether or not the bills of indictment brought before them by magistrates were to be upheld and the case proceed to trial.[125]

Hutchinson was all too aware of the power of judges to prevent guilty verdicts in witchcraft cases. Judge Powell's behaviour at the Wenham trial served as a potent reminder of this fact. The narrative device used

---

[120] Ibid., i, 5–23.
[121] Ibid., i, 3.
[122] Ibid., i, 14–15, 23, 9, 23, 5–6, 21.
[123] Hugh Trevor-Roper, *The European witch-craze of the 16th and 17th centuries* (Harmondsworth, 1978), pp. 17–18.
[124] Hutchinson owned Thomas Ady's *Candle in the dark, or a treatise concerning the nature of witches and witchcraft* . . . (1665); see, Hutchinson's commonplace book, 1731–9 (D.R., p. 536).
[125] Gaskill, *Crime and mentalities*, pp. 68, 94.

in the *Historical essay* mirrored what Hutchinson hoped to do in real life: the clergyman in the book reminded the advocate what the safe principles were and what the consequences would be if he did not abide by them. The clergyman and the advocate were then expected to work together to persuade the jurymen, their educational and social inferiors, that the suspected witch should be acquitted.

It will be argued below that since, in 1718, Hutchinson felt obliged to publicly demonstrate that the *Historical essay* was backed by influential men, this illustrates his belief that it would prove controversial upon publication. However, the fact that he went out of his way to gain permission to dedicate his book to eminent lawmen (the Lord Chief Justice of England, Sir Thomas Parker, the Lord Chief Baron of Exchequer, Sir Peter King, and the Lord Chief Justice of the Common Pleas, Sir Thomas Bury) in 1718, just as he had in 1712 with Judge Powell, further shows that Hutchinson held a desire to influence the legal profession: if leading Whig lawmen approved of his book, then it would carry more weight among those lower down the judicial ladder.[126] Hutchinson was probably able to secure these men's approbation for the *Historical essay* because he was in a better position socially in 1718 to ask such a thing of men of such high social standing than he had been in 1712. Then he was a self-confessed 'obscure country parson', unable to approach Powell himself,[127] whereas in 1718 he was a royal chaplain and 'courtier'.[128] Although the court, during the reigns of George I and II, lost ground as a political institution, it retained political significance as a place of political brokerage and theatre, where political negotiation between low-ranking officials and ministers was conducted and where patronage was sought from the king, members of the royal family and household, and the leading lights of Church and state.[129]

Parker's approbation for the *Historical essay* was probably the easiest to procure, since in 1712 he had declared himself publicly to be, as Hutchinson himself noted in the *Historical essay*, no friend to witchcraft accusers, in particular those who 'tested' suspects using the dangerous 'swimming' or 'water' test:

> And as great numbers of poor creatures have been destroy'd, and the justice of the nation reproach'd for this custom of swimming, and yet

---

[126] Hutchinson, *Historical essay*, sig. A3ʳ; for Parker's patronage of Hutchinson, see pp. 132–3 below.
[127] Hutchinson to Sloane, 3 Apr. 1712 (B.L., Sloane MS 4043, fo. 38).
[128] Hutchinson to Charlett, 17 July 1718 (Bodleian, Oxford, Ballard MS 38, fo. 27).
[129] Hannah Smith, 'The court in England, 1714–1760: a declining political institution?' in *History*, xc, no. 297 (2005), 23–41.

out countrey-people are still fond of it, as they are of bear baiting or bull: I will take leave to publish in as solemn a manner as I can, that at the summer assizes held at Brentwood in Essex, in the year 1712, our excellent Lord Chief Justice of England, the right honourable the Lord Parker, by a just and righteous piece of judgement, hath given all men warning, that if any dare for the future to make use of that experiment, and the party lose her life by it, all they that are the cause of it are guilty of wilfull murder.[130]

Swimming the witch (also known as the 'water ordeal' or 'trial by water') was used throughout the seventeenth century, but was never formally recognised legally as a proof of witchcraft. Nevertheless, juries and judges often accepted it as such, and figures of authority in local communities, such as constables, clergymen and magistrates, often organised and sanctioned the ordeal itself, or at least they did so up until the end of the seventeenth century. Elite opinion, however, may have begun to turn against swimming as early as 1645, when Parliament condemned it outright in reaction to the excesses of witch-finders Hopkins and Stearne during the East Anglian witch-hunts. Furthermore, almost as soon as it began to be used in the early seventeenth century, learned demonologists, such as William Perkins, and sceptics, like John Cotta, poured their scorn upon it.[131]

Hutchinson claimed that the recent low numbers of witchcraft prosecutions were a direct result of the legal establishment's sticking to safe common-law principles when weighing up the evidence presented before them.[132] Hutchinson believed that if these safe principles were followed, and similarly if pernicious principles were avoided, then it would be almost impossible to convict a suspect witch. In order to continue the low rate of prosecution that had marked recent years, Hutchinson codified two sets of principles to ensure magistrates, grand juries and judges had a clear guide to follow.

The first set were 'sober principles of those times and places that have been troubled with few witches' and they can be summarised thus: 1. Do not intrude into things you have not seen; 2. Evidence reliant upon the testimony of spirits, whether they were good or bad spirits,

---

[130] Hutchinson, *Historical essay*, pp. 139–40.
[131] Davies, *Witchcraft, magic and culture*, pp. 88–90; idem, 'Witchcraft: the spell that didn't break' in *History Today* (August, 1999), 10. When swum in a local river or pond, suspects had their waists tied with two ropes and their thumbs bound to their toes. Their innocence was proved if they sank, but if they floated it was taken that God had forsaken them on account of their guilt. The victim was often subjected to physical and mental abuse, both before and after the test.
[132] Hutchinson, *Historical essay*, pp. 48, 50.

is inadmissible in court; 3. It is imprudent to blame a neighbour for one's misfortune when the devil is ever ready to work evil without the agency of the witch; 4. The old proofs of witchcraft – swimming, scratching or touching – are insufficient; 5. Confessions are not to be believed if they do not tally with prevailing notions pertaining to what is probable and improbable; 6. When something anomalous appears, and it cannot be fitted into a normal system of belief, it is to be disregarded until it can be accounted for; 7. When there are no prevailing principles to judge something by, then it is better to delay judgment; 8. It is better to err on the side of caution in cases of witchcraft, because in doing so one is showing faith in God's providence.[133]

Bostridge asserts that numbers 1, 6, and 7 of the first set of positive principles mirror those which Newton put forward in Book Three of his *Principia Mathematica*. He argues that Hutchinson's first principle simply reiterates Newton's declaration that we should not 'relinquish the evidence of experiments for the sake of dreams and strange fictions of our own devising'.[134] A re-examination of what Hutchinson wrote – '1. Do not intrude into things you have not seen, Col. 2:18' – reveals that he was actually quoting from the Bible, from St Paul's Epistle to the Colossians, and not alluding to the *Principia Mathematica*.[135] He even used the same quotation four years later in a Church of Ireland catechism:

> Col. 2:18 let no man begile you of your reward in a voluntary humility, and worshipping of angels, intruding into those things which he hath not seen, vainly puffed up by his fleshy minds.[136]

It is more than possible that Hutchinson's sixth and seventh principles were a tribute to Newton's famous phrase that one should frame no hypothesis,[137] but the rest of his principles can be traced back to the

---

[133] Ibid., pp. 55–63.
[134] Bostridge, *Witchcraft and its transformations*, p. 146.
[135] Hutchinson, *Historical essay*, p. 54.
[136] Hutchinson, *The church catechism in Irish, with the English placed over and against it in the same karakter. Together with prayers for sick persons, and some texts of Scripture, and a vocabulary explaining the Irish words that are used in them* (Belfast, 1722), pp. x–xi. The preface of this text is printed with boxes for the page numbers but, owing to a contemporary printing error, no page numbers appear. I have added my own, from the first page of the preface to the 14th page.
[137] Translated from the Latin, Newton's phrase read: 'But hitherto I have not been able to discover the cause of those properties of gravity from phenomena, and I frame no hypothesis; for whatever is not deduced from phenomena ought to be called a hypothesis, and hypotheses of this kind, whether metaphysical or physical, whether of occult qualities or mechanical, have no place in experimental philosophy', quoted in Pravas Jivan Chaudhury, 'Newton and hypothesis' in *Philosophy and Phenomenological Research*, xxii, no. 3 (1963), 344–5.

works of other sceptical witchcraft theorists, being precisely those 'proofs' of the crime of witchcraft they found unsatisfactory.[138]

The second set of principles Hutchinson described as 'a catalogue of the principles of those times and men that have been troubled with and have hang'd great numbers'. It is necessary to list these principles in full before we examine their origin: 1. The belief that a person labouring under fits or illness induced by 'devillery' always witnesses an apparition of the witch responsible; 2. The belief that this type of 'spectral' evidence is a sufficient proof of witchcraft; 3. The belief that if a bewitched person reacts to the touch of a witch, then this is sufficient proof of witchcraft; 4. The belief that the inability to speak the Lord's Prayer is yet another proof of witchcraft; 5. The belief that the swimming of a witch was a prudent and reliable way to test for suspected witches; 6. The belief that a lack of tears is a sufficient proof of witchcraft; 7. The belief that if a person accused of witchcraft possesses areas in his or her body which are insensible to pain then this is a sure sign that he or she is a witch; 8. The belief that the devil's mark might take the shape of something indistinguishable from a natural mark or blemish on the skin, such as a flea-bite or a mole; 9. The belief that Satan was more powerful when he used the agency of human beings; 10. The belief that any persons, no matter their character or background, should be treated as reliable witnesses; 11. The belief that torture is a legitimate way to extort confessions from people suspected of witchcraft; 12. The belief that it is acceptable for interrogators to use ill-disguised forms of torture, such as sleep deprivation or starvation, in order to extract confessions from suspects; 13. The belief that suspected witches should be watched until an imp or familiar appears, and that this creature could take any shape; 14. The belief that evidence relating to other matters, including those long past, constitutes acceptable evidence in court; 15. The belief that the ill-fame of close relatives or ancestors is also sufficient proof of witchcraft; 16. The belief that familiars were detectable by their odour and that any odour present in the suspect's home is sufficient proof of ownership of such a creature; 17. The belief that rules and proofs used in court procedure are to be revered without first deciding whether

---

[138] John Wagstaffe, *The question of witchcraft debated, or a discourse against their opinion that affirm witches, considered and enlarged* . . . (2nd edn, London, 1671), pp. 14–15, 114–15; Sir Robert Filmer, *An advertisement to the jury-men of England, touching witches. Together with a difference between an English and Hebrew witch* (London, 1653), pp. 18, 11, 10; Reginald Scot, *Scot's discovery of witchcraft: proving the common opinions of witches contracting with divels, spirits, or familiars* . . . (1584, repr. London, 1651), pp. 15, 52–3; Hitchcock, 'George Gifford', p. 93.

or not they are reasonable; 18. The idea that any one of the above 'proofs' is sufficient to convict someone of the crime of witchcraft.[139]

These principles were designed to persuade the reader that suspects should not be criminally convicted of witchcraft on the strength of these sorts of proofs and legal procedures. Once again, these principles were those that sceptical writers had long disapproved of, doubted or dismissed.[140] This second list, however, does contain principles that are directly derived from the 'sceptical' canon. Principle 9 further highlights Hutchinson's belief in a temporally active Satan, while Principles 17 and 18 are indictments of the English legal system, in particular the type of faulty court procedure he believed worked to convict innocents of witchcraft.

V

Bostridge suggests that the combined facts that Hutchinson was able to publish the *Historical essay* only in 1718 when he knew his book would slip quietly without controversy into the educated mainstream, and that a discursive silence on the subject of witchcraft ensued after its publication, proves his contention that witchcraft, by the second half of the 1710s, had become a marginal concern for educated culture.[141] As has been indicated, it is clear that Hutchinson decided to publish the *Historical essay* in 1718 in direct response to the publication of Boulton's *Compleat history of . . . witchcraft* (1715–16). Furthermore, there is much to suggest that witchcraft was still a controversial matter in 1718 and that Hutchinson was well aware of this.

Firstly, the *Historical essay* received a mixed response from the general public and the clerical profession alike. In early 1720, Hutchinson boasted to the Archbishop of Canterbury, William Wake, that his 'book of witchcraft hath had a second impression' and that he had received 'thanks' for his book from individuals of 'both high and low' social standing.

---

[139] Hutchinson, *Historical essay*, pp. 55–8.
[140] Wagstaffe, *The question of witchcraft debated*, pp. 14–15; John Cotta, *The triall of witch-craft, shewing the true and right methode of the discovery: with a confutation of erroneous wayes* . . . (London, 1624), pp. 144, 127–37; Scot, *Scot's discovery of witchcraft*, p. 19; John Webster, *The displaying of supposed witchcraft, wherein is affirmed that there are many sorts of deceivers and impostors, and divers persons under a passive delusion of melancholy and fancy* . . . (London, 1677), p. 83; Ady, *Candle in the dark*, pp. 127–9; Hitchcock, 'George Gifford', p. 95; Filmer, *An advertisement to the jury-men of England*, pp. 9–10, 12, 10, 12–13, 9; John Gaule, *Select cases of conscience touching witches and witchcrafts* . . . (London, 1646), pp. 78, 77–8, 80, 78–9.
[141] Bostridge, *Witchcraft and its transformations*, pp. 141–54.

However, he also admitted that by writing the book he had been 'forced to provoke many ingenious men still living'.[142] Secondly, Hutchinson still felt the need to demonstrate that his views on witchcraft had the backing of leading members of the judiciary, Parker, King and Bury. He was also more than grateful to gain the support of Arthur Charlett, master of University College, Oxford and, until 1717, a fellow royal chaplain.[143] Immediately after the publication of the *Historical essay*, Hutchinson wrote to Charlett (in July 1718) to say that 'having ventur'd to write upon so dark and unpopular a subject . . . it was great satisfaction to hear so good a judge approving what I had done'.[144] It follows that if Hutchinson knew his book was going to enter the educated mainstream without any fuss he would not have felt the need to gain the support of such men in exactly the same manner as he had with Powell in 1712. Thirdly, in spite of the support he gained from these men, Hutchinson was still ready, in mid-1718, to distance himself from the opinions contained in the book if the criticism against it proved too difficult to bear:

> But I think that the principles that I had lay down . . . are . . . very right as well as safe and prudential, I am apt to think that time will confirm them, if ever experience doth shew the contrary, I have no interest to tempt me to shut my eyes against it, I hope in such a case I should have virtue enough to make me . . . change notions . . . but at present I am of the same mind with my book.[145]

The initial levels of criticism that the *Historical essay* aroused, however, did not reach an unbearable level of intensity, as Hutchinson felt no need to distance himself from the book. In fact two years later, in 1720, high sales warranted a second edition.

The changes he made to this second edition in no way affected or altered the overall meaning or arguments of the first edition, and represented nothing more than the addition of further evidence to back up assertions already made. For example, to the chronological table of witchcraft presented in the first edition, Hutchinson added the example of an impostor, Martha Brossier (a 'victim', who, in France in 1599, had mimicked the sins of demonic possession), along with the tale of an execution in Rome in 1633 of a man who had tried to 'kill Pope Urban

---

[142] Francis Hutchinson to William Wake, 14 April 1720 (C.C., Wake Letters, vol. 21, no. 215).
[143] R. H. Darwall-Smith, 'Charlett, Arthur (1655–1722)' in *OxDNB*.
[144] Hutchinson to Charlett, 17 July 1718 (Bodleian, Oxford, Ballard MS 38, fo. 27).
[145] Ibid.

the 8th by a waxen image struck with pins and needles'.[146] Hutchinson collected this new evidence from friends and acquaintances. His patron, Sir Thomas Parker, for example, informed him of a case in Rouen, France, where a number of people accused of witchcraft were later acquitted.[147] Furthermore, in July 1718, Hutchinson not only thanked Charlett for his approval of the first edition of the *Historical essay*, but he asked him to proofread it and inform of 'any later executions either in England or foreign parts' which 'would be proper to have ... added' to the second edition.[148] This second edition was not the end of the publication story, as extracts from the *Historical essay* were published in German in 1727.[149]

Bostridge's argument that the *Historical essay* marked an end to educated debate on witchcraft is problematic. In *Witchcraft and its transformations*, Bostridge's chosen methodology, which in turn relies upon a precise epistemology, is that, within a particular culture, the vitality of a belief system (such as witchcraft) can be gauged by how much it appears as a matter of discussion in public discourse. In this way discursive silence is seen to equal non-belief. Bostridge's concept of what actually constitutes both discursive silence and vitality is both protean and, at times, arbitrary. For example, he argues that the *Historical essay* met with discursive silence, whereas Boulton's 1715–16 book, *A compleat history ... of witchcraft*, provoked a discursive controversy. However, each book gained one literary response. The *Historical essay* provoked Boulton's 1722 book, *The possibility or reality of magick, sorcery and witchcraft, demonology or a vindication of a compleat history of magick sorcery and witchcraft. In Answer to Dr Hutchinson's Historical essay*; and, as has already been discussed, Hutchinson claimed that he had written the *Historical essay* as a reply to Boulton's first book *A compleat history of magick, sorcery and witchcraft*.[150]

Bostridge is able to take this seemingly contradictory stance because he argues that the *Vindication*, unlike the *Historical essay*, 'was ignored

---

[146] Francis Hutchinson, *An historical essay concerning witchcraft with observations upon matters of fact; tending to clear the texts of the sacred Scriptures, and confute the vulgar errors about that point. And also two sermons: one in proof of the Christian religion; the other concerning good and evil Angels. The second edition, with considerable alterations* (2nd edn, London, 1720), pp. 45, 49.
[147] Hutchinson to Charlett, 17 July 1718 (Bodleian, Oxford, Ballard MS 38, fo. 27).
[148] Ibid.
[149] Francois de Saint Andre, *Mr. de St André ... lesenwürdige briefe an einige seiner freunde uber die materie von der Saubery ... gedruckt zu Paris 1725 ... statt eines suplements zum Hutchinson aus dem Frantzosischen ins Teutsche übersetzt ... von Theodoro Arnold* (Leipzig, 1727).
[150] Bostridge, *Witchcraft and its transformations*, pp. 141–2, 202.

by its target and dismissed by contemporaries'. He bases this latter inference on the fact that 'Jacques Daillon, in his *Daimonologia* of 1723, viewed Boulton's efforts as beneath contempt'.[151] Hutchinson may have been the target of Boulton's *Vindication* but, far from ignoring it, he actually wrote a reply to it. In a commonplace book dating from the 1730s, Hutchinson noted that in his library lay 'Mr Boulton's answer to my *Historical essay* and my reply to that with a sermon concerning the right use of Scriptures in readiness but not yet printed'.[152] Hutchinson probably penned this reply, which is no longer extant, immediately after the *Vindication* appeared. It remains unclear why he never published it. The fact that Boulton died two years after the publication of the *Vindication* must have lessened the necessity in Hutchinson's mind to publish a written response to Boulton's animadversions on his *Historical essay*.[153] Furthermore, the social threat posed by witchcraft trials, which spurred him to condemn witchcraft in the first place, must have seemed negligible in Ireland. Although there was legal provision for the prosecution of witches, and belief in witchcraft extended across denominational boundaries, from Catholic to Protestant, witchcraft trials in seventeenth- and eighteenth-century Ireland were extremely rare.[154] This not to say Hutchinson was unaware of Irish credulity. In a commonplace book he kept during the 1720s, he carefully noted reported instances of fairies and witchcraft, such as the case of a Mr Smith and a Mr Higgison who claimed to have, respectively, vomited straw and pins.[155] He was so convinced that witchcraft in Ireland was a socially and politically innocuous belief system that by 1723 he was using it as an improvement metaphor: 'trade is witchcraft and works wonders'.[156]

Hutchinson's *Historical essay* received as much of a mixed response from the Protestant elite in Ireland as it had in England, angering some and amusing others. Just after Hutchinson had been nominated to the bishopric of Down and Connor in December 1720, the then Church of Ireland Bishop of Kilmore and future Archbishop of Cashel, Timothy Godwin, informed the Archbishop of Canterbury, William Wake:

[151] Ibid., p. 142.
[152] Hutchinson's commonplace book, 1731–9 (D.R., p. 536); see also, ibid., p. 534.
[153] Harold J. Cook, 'Boulton, Richard (*bap.* 1674, *d. c.*1724)', *OxDNB*.
[154] Sean J. Connolly, *Religion, law, and power: the making of Protestant Ireland, 1660–1760* (Oxford, 1992), pp. 196–7; Raymond Gillespie, 'Women and crime in seventeenth century Ireland' in Margaret MacCurtain and Mary O'Dowd (eds), *Women in early modern Ireland* (Edinburgh, 1991), pp. 45–7; E. C. Lapoint, 'Irish immunity to witch-hunting, 1534–1711' in *Eire–Ireland*, xxvii (1992), 76–92.
[155] Hutchinson's commonplace book, 1721–30 (P.R.O.N.I., MS DIO/1/22/1 (unpaginated).
[156] Francis Hutchinson, *A letter to a member of Parliament, concerning the imploying and providing for the poor* (Dublin, 1723), p. 16.

I know Dr Hutchinson a little, and I think he has always maintained a good character, but he must expect to be attacked by his Grace of St Sepultures [the Archbishop of Dublin William King, 1650–1729] for his book about witchcraft, but I suppose he will keep as much he can out of his way.[157]

Furthermore, an anonymous ballad published in Dublin in 1726 with the strict intention of ridiculing Hutchinson's various schemes and publications satirised the *Historical essay* thus:

Least witches and spirits our children should fright,
He on that occasion did learnedly write,
And at tea told her Grace t'was no breach of the law,
Tho' men should spew pins and old women spit straws.[158]

This stanza also hints that Hutchinson lacked grace in social situations, a part of his public persona examined in the next chapter.

VI

It has been the contention of this chapter that Hutchinson attacked traditional witchcraft belief because he believed it to be a virulent form of religious enthusiasm and, as such, inimical to his vision of an improved polite, ordered, civil society. This was a social ideology that fitted perfectly with his Low-Church, Latitudinarian-Whig politics. The experience of attending witchcraft trials, as well as living in a county that had witnessed some of the previous century's most intense spells of witch-hunting, deepened this scepticism. Hutchinson's path to witchcraft scepticism thus bears out Elmer's, and to a lesser extent Sharpe's, contention that elite belief in witchcraft and the witchcraft trials in early modern England were distinct phenomena, but they were not largely unconnected.

Although the methodology employed by Hutchinson in the *Historical essay* to attack traditional witchcraft beliefs was similar to that used by other English sceptics, and to a lesser degree that of authors of anti-enthusiastic literature, the structure of the book was also shaped by his attempt to influence two sectors of English society, the literate lower orders and the judiciary. Hutchinson argued that the prosecution rate for witchcraft would remain low if the judiciary continued to regard

---

[157] Timothy Godwin to William Wake, 28 December 1720 (C.C., Wake Letters, vol. 13, no. 216). Archbishop King's credulity about witchcraft has been noted elsewhere, in relation to his concern in the early 1690s over the Salem witchcraft trials; see Connolly, *Religion, law, and power*, p. 196.

[158] Anon., *An excellent new ballad* (Dublin, 1726).

the accusations and evidence of witchcraft brought before them with caution and scepticism. He was also convinced that the power to prevent witchcraft trials occurring in the first place lay with the lower orders, for it was they who made the bulk of witchcraft accusations. He consequently designed the *Historical essay* so as to appeal to this target audience and convince them of the erroneous nature of traditional witchcraft beliefs. Furthermore, not only did the publication of the *Historical essay* in 1718 create controversy, but it cannot be seen to have marked the beginning of a discursive silence on the subject of witchcraft. This in its turn backs up Davies' contention that witchcraft belief still held some attraction for the educated of Britain and Ireland and not just those of the radical fringe.

Part II
Ireland

6

The Bishop of Down and Connor and the established Church and state in Ireland, 1721–39

Despite a recent flurry of interest in the Church of Ireland clergy,[1] as T. C. Barnard has pointed out, 'the characteristics and functions of this profession can only be guessed until the origins, education, careers and wealth of its members have been clarified through prosopographical studies of particular cohorts of graduates and ordinands, and of individual dioceses'.[2] The latter study would be particularly welcome in the case of the diocese of Down and Connor, upon which little academic

---

[1] For overviews of the functions and background of the eighteenth-century episcopate, see Jeremiah Falvey, 'The Church of Ireland episcopate in the eighteenth century: an overview' in *Eighteenth-Century Ireland*, viii (1993), 103–14; Francis James, *Lords of the ascendancy: the Irish house of Lords and its members, 1600–1800* (Dublin, 1995), pp. 131–49, and Irvin Ehrenpreis, *Swift: the man, his works, and the age* (3 vols, London, 1962, 1967, 1983), iii, 166–86. For a general overview of the incomes and backgrounds of the clergy as a whole, see Toby Barnard, *A new anatomy of Ireland: the Irish Protestants, 1649–1770* (London, 2003), chapter 4; and J. L. McCracken, 'The ecclesiastical structure, 1714–60' in T. W. Moody and W. E. Vaughan (eds), *A new history of Ireland: eighteenth-century Ireland, 1691–1800* (Oxford, 1985), iv, 84–5. For a discussion of the attitudes and outlooks of the High-Church majority in particular, see David Hayton, 'High-Churchmen in the Irish Convocation' in idem (ed.), *Ruling Ireland, 1685–1742: politics, parties, politicians* (Suffolk, 2004), pp. 131–58 and Sean J. Connolly, 'Reformers and high-flyers: the post-Revolution Church' in A. Ford, J. McGuire and K. Milne (eds), *As by law established: the Church of Ireland since the Reformation* (Dublin, 1995), pp. 152–65. Much work has also been done on the activities of the small group of reforming clergymen who filled the upper ranks of the Church of Ireland in the early eighteenth century: see T. C. Barnard, 'Improving clergymen', pp. 136–51; F. G. James, *North country bishop: a biography of William Nicolson* (New Haven CT, 1956); Philip O'Regan, *Archbishop William King of Dublin, 1650–1729, and the constitution in Church and state* (Dublin, 2000); and A. R. Winnet, *Peter Browne: provost, bishop, metaphysician* (London, 1974). The various attempts by Irish clergy to convert the majority, Catholic population to Protestantism using the Irish tongue and through elementary education are dealt with in detail in Chapter 7.

[2] Barnard, 'Improving clergymen' in Ford, McGuire and Milne (eds), *As by law established*, p. 137.

research has been done.³ The logical place to start a new study of Down and Connor would be to examine the careers of its bishops. Francis Hutchinson is particularly fitted for such a study because, despite the loss of most of the established Church records in the Four Courts Fire of 1922, there is enough extant primary source material to enable a detailed picture to be built up of his time as bishop between 1721 and 1739. Consequently, it is possible to detail the events surrounding his rise to the episcopacy, the reaction in Ireland to his appointment, and his relationship with his clergy and fellow bishops. His performance of the spiritual and temporal duties of his new office will also be assessed.

I

In George I's reign, the main consideration that the Whig ministry in Westminster had in mind when choosing bishops was their potential for political reliability. In the Irish House of Lords, the Irish episcopate exercised a disproportionate amount of political power in relation to their numbers because they comprised the majority of its active membership. The active members not only attended Parliament on a regular basis, but they became involved in the various committees set up during the course of a session and introduced or presented Heads of Bills or bills to the house. A loyal episcopate was therefore essential to the building of a tractable Irish Parliament. On the death of Queen Anne the majority of bishops in the Irish House of Lords were Tories. Soon afterwards, the aspiring Whig hegemony began its bid to break this dominance. As bishops could not in normal circumstances be removed once appointed, it became the policy of successive ministries between 1714 and 1724 to fill the Irish bishoprics with men who were particularly favourable to the Whig administration and the House of Hanover. Of the 32 appointments made in the years 1714 to 1727, 62 per cent were given to Englishmen. Most of these appointments were made as translations of tried and tested men into the more sought-after dioceses, such as Derry and Raphoe; the rest were given to ordinary clerics who happened to have powerful patrons. English-born bishops were favoured because they were more likely to be loyal to the Whig administration at Westminster than Irish clerics who might be inclined to serve the Irish interest.⁴

---

³ Some notable exceptions are: J. B. Leslie, *Clergy of Connor: from patrician times to the present day* (Belfast, 1993); [Ulster Historical Foundation], *Clergy of Down and Dromore*; James O'Laverty, *An historical account of the Diocese of Down and Connor: ancient and modern* (5 vols, Dublin, 1878–95).

⁴ Patrick McNally, 'Irish and English interests: national conflict within the Church of Ireland episcopate in reign of George I' in *Irish Historical Studies*, xxxix (1995), 296; Falvey, 'Church of Ireland episcopate', pp. 107–12; James, *Lords of the ascendancy*, pp. 131–3, 140–2, 148.

The Irish interest was led by the philosopher, writer and Whig statesman, Robert, Viscount Molesworth and two leading churchmen, the Archbishop of Tuam, Edward Synge, and the Archbishop of Dublin, William King. It resulted primarily from the anti-English tension created by the appointment of apparently unqualified political puppets imported from England as prelates in the Church of Ireland. The extent of this practice was frequently exaggerated by the Irish interest. This tension between English and Irish bishops took on a political character between 1717 and 1721 because of the constitutional implications of the Sherlock-Annesley case and the Declaratory Act. The Irish 'patriot' interest in the Irish House of Lords in the 1719 session of Parliament used a legal wrangle over property between an English and an Irish landlord (the Sherlock *versus* Annesley case) to question the right of the English House of Lords to act as the final court of appeal in Irish court cases. The Whig government in Westminster reacted to this perceived attempt by the Irish Parliament to increase its legal powers by passing the Declaratory Act (6 George I, chap. 5). This Act stated that the Dublin Parliament was subordinate to, and dependent on, its counterpart at Westminster, specifically denying the Irish Parliament any right to independent judicial and legislative powers. The Sherlock-Annesley affair, along with the controversy created by William Wood's doomed attempt in the mid-1720s to issue copper farthings and halfpence in Ireland, formed the central part of an intermittent political struggle by an Irish patriot Protestant interest, intent on controlling its own political and economic destiny in the face of what it perceived to be unwarranted and detrimental British interference. Religious tension added fuel to this political conflict. The Irish interest saw Ulster Presbyterians as posing a threat to Anglican ascendancy equal to that posed by Catholics, or even greater. They were thus opposed to any civil or religious relief being given to Protestant Dissenters and were content to leave the Penal Laws that affected Catholics as they were. English Whig bishops were, on the whole, more sympathetic to Protestant Dissenters and were convinced that further penal legislation should be enacted to deal with the threat to political security posed by the Catholic majority.[5]

Hutchinson, like all English-born bishops imported into Ireland after the Hanoverian succession by the Whigs at Westminster, was a man of exemplary Whig credentials. Furthermore, in common with many

---

[5] P. McNally, *Parties, patriots and undertakers: parliamentary politics in early Hanoverian Ireland* (Dublin, 1997), pp. 52–4, 148–73; idem, 'Wood's half-pence, Carteret, and the government in Ireland, 1723–6' in *Irish Historical Studies*, xxx (1997), 354–76; Barnard, *New anatomy*, pp. 98–9; Isolde Victory, 'The making of the Declaratory Act of 1720' in Gerald O'Brien (ed.), *Parliament, politics and people: essays in eighteenth-century Irish history* (Dublin, 1989), pp. 8–24.

ordinary clerics promoted to the Irish episcopacy, Hutchinson was a former chaplain to one of the ruling elite and so had powerful Whig patrons. Hutchinson's rise to the Irish episcopate began on 24 March 1715, when he was appointed chaplain-in-ordinary to George I.[6] Possession of an influential patron and unquestioned loyalty to the Hanoverian dynasty and the Court Whig administration were the defining characteristics of those clergymen asked to join the Chapel Royal as one of the king's 48 royal chaplains.[7] By 1715, Hutchinson's patron was the Whig grandee and fellow Bury St Edmunds resident, John Hervey, first Earl of Bristol. After several unsuccessful attempts in Queen Anne's reign (from 1708 onwards) to reach the king's ear, via various officers of the royal household, Hervey informed Hutchinson on 15 March 1715 that Francis, second Earl of Godolphin, the cofferer (one of the three main treasurers of the royal household) to George I, had succeeded in persuading the king to bestow his favour on him.[8] It is not entirely clear why Hervey sought to promote Hutchinson's interest for such a long period at such a high level. What is certain is that, like other local Whigs, Hervey admired Hutchinson's intellectual powers and renowned merit as a pulpit champion of the Whig cause.[9]

Royal chaplains prepared to toe the Court line were usually guaranteed high preferment.[10] In practice, those clergy who had accompanied George I to Hanover, and thereby gained his further favour, were advanced first.[11] Hutchinson was never afforded this privilege and thus, in common with any other preferment-hungry chaplain, he began the search for a powerful patron to recommend him to the leading Whig statesmen (in Hutchinson's case, the Secretary of the Treasury, Charles Stanhope, and the Northern Secretary, Charles Spencer, 3rd Earl of Sunderland) who, for all intents and purposes, controlled the patronage attached to many of the higher offices in the Anglican church, including the episcopacy. By early 1720 Hutchinson had gained the patronage of the Lord Chief Justice of England, Sir Thomas Parker.[12] This patronage

---

[6] Lord Chamberlain's appointment books, series II, 1660–1851 (T.N.A., Records of the Lord Chamberlain and other officers of the Royal household, LC 3/63), p. 86.
[7] Mischler, 'Political sermons', p. 36.
[8] John Hervey to Francis Hutchinson, 24 July 1708, *Letter books of John Hervey, first earl of Bristol* (3 vols., Wells, 1894), i, 237–8; John Hervey to Francis Hutchinson, 15 March 1714/15, *Letter books of John Hervey*, i, 396; G. C. Boase, 'Godolphin, Francis, second earl of Godolphin (1678–1766)', rev. Philip Carter in *OxDNB*.
[9] John Hervey to Francis Hutchinson, 24 July 1708, and John Hervey to Francis Hutchinson, 15 March 1715 in *Letter books of John Hervey*.
[10] W. A. Speck, Stability and strife in England, 1714–1760 (London, 1977), p. 98.
[11] Sykes, *Church and state*, pp. 151–61.
[12] Hutchinson to Wake, 14 Apr. 1720 (C.C., Wake Letters, vol. 21, no. 215).

may have grown out of the contact Hutchinson had had with Parker two years earlier, when he persuaded him to become one of the three dedicatees of the *Historical essay*.[13] Parker's ecclesiastical recommendations were taken seriously by the Whig elite, and by Sunderland in particular.[14] He also controlled the disposal of a considerable proportion of the Crown's smaller livings.[15]

The patronage of a leading lay Whig was, however, sometimes not enough to secure high preferment quickly because Sunderland and Stanhope relied upon the advice of an ecclesiastical adviser, the Archbishop of Canterbury, William Wake.[16] Hutchinson realised, after his name had been unsuccessfully put forward to Stanhope and Sunderland by Parker on numerous occasions, that to gain advancement he would also have to win the favour of Wake.[17] He used the last resort of a benefice-hungry clergyman, self-recommendation.[18] In a letter to Wake dated 14 April 1720, he informed Archbishop Wake that he was the most 'senior of all the chaplains who never had any mark of the kings favour'.[19] He also claimed that he was a Whig born and bred, before listing all the books and pamphlets he had written in support of the Whig cause during the rage of party.[20] Hutchinson's letter of self-recommendation had the desired effect, for only eight months later he was made Bishop of Down and Connor.[21] Shortly after his appointment he wrote from Ireland, thanking Archbishop Wake for his help:

> tho' the inclosed be not a present worthy too cross the water, yet being so small that it will come in a letter I gladly lay hold of the opportunity of acknowledging the obligations I have received from your Grace.[22]

II

The Irish interest had hoped that an Irishman would replace the High-Church Tory, Edward Smythe, as Bishop of Down and Connor when

---

[13] See p. 117 above.
[14] Lord Sunderland to Thomas Parker, 14 May 1715 (B.L., Add. MS 61452, fos. 285–6).
[15] List of ecclesiastical benefices disposed of by Thomas Parker 1718–24 (B.L., Stowe MS 119, fos. 119–35).
[16] Norman Sykes, *William Wake, Archbishop of Canterbury, 1657–1737* (2 vols, Cambridge, 1957), ii, 111–12, 119, 129–31, 133, 144–9.
[17] Hutchinson to Wake, 14 April 1720 (C.C., Wake Letters, vol. 21, no. 215).
[18] William T. Gibson, ' "Unreasonable, and unbecoming": self-recommendation and place-seeking in the Church of England, 1700–1900' in *Albion*, xxvii (1995), 43–65.
[19] Hutchinson to Wake, 14 Apr. 1720 (C.C., Wake Letters, vol. 21, no. 215).
[20] Ibid.
[21] [Ulster Historical Foundation], *Clergy of Down and Dromore*, part 2, p. 22.
[22] Francis Hutchinson to William Wake, June 1721 (C.C., Wake Letters, vol. 13, no. 251).

he died on 15 October 1720. Two weeks after Smythe's death, William King wrote to the head of the Irish executive, the Lord Lieutenant, Charles Fitzroy, Duke of Grafton, to ask him to present the vacant bishopric to the Irish Dean of Clogher and chaplain to the House of Commons, William Gore. Gore was brother to the Chancellor of the Irish Exchequer, Ralph Gore, and both men were prominent members of the Irish interest.[23] King was particularly eager that an Irishman should fill the diocese of Down and Connor because he believed that the 'patronage' attached to it was 'very considerable'.[24] If appointed, Gore would thus be in a perfect position to ensure that worthy Irishmen were promoted to livings in the diocese. Down and Connor was a relatively desirable prelacy for other reasons. First and foremost, it generated – so the Bishop of Meath, John Evans, reckoned in December 1720 – a yearly revenue of about £1,100.[25] Furthermore, although it lacked an episcopal palace, it was relatively close to Dublin, the largest and most developed city in Ireland, and possessed fewer Catholics than Protestants.[26]

A week after King's letter to Grafton, in November 1720, John Stearne, a supporter of the Irish interest and Gore's diocesan, broke the news to King that his recommendation to Grafton had been ignored.[27] King wrote soon afterwards to Stearne to inform him that it was now inevitable that the bishopric would be given to 'some chaplain' that had 'never served cure' and who would think it 'ungenteel to trouble his head' with the spiritual duties of his office.[28] Thus when, in early December 1720, the news that Francis Hutchinson, a Whig royal chaplain, had been appointed to Down spread to Ireland, Archbishop William King was reported to have given 'Dr Hutchinson . . . his fair share of censure, and reflexion'.[29] The fact that Hutchinson was sceptical in matters of witchcraft, when King was not, could have served only to have increased King's dislike of him.[30]

Harsh words were soon complemented with harsh deeds. When the time came in January 1721 for Hutchinson to be consecrated bishop, it transpired that the Primate of All Ireland and Archbishop of Armagh,

---

[23] William King to Charles Fitztroy, 29 Oct. 1720 (Trinity College Dublin [hereafter T.C.D.], William King coll., MS 750/6, pp. 98–9).
[24] William King to John Stearne, 20 Nov. 1720 (T.C.D., Wm King coll., MS 1995–2008/1964); for a list of Hutchinson's collations to livings under his control, see Hutchinson's commonplace book, 1721–30 (P.R.O.N.I., MS DIO/1/22/1), pp. 142–70 [2nd pagination].
[25] John Evans to William Wake, 9 Dec. 1720 (C.C., Wake Letters, vol. 13, no. 211).
[26] McCracken, 'Ecclesiastical structure', pp. 84–5; Falvey, 'Church of Ireland', p. 110; Phil Kilroy, *Protestant Dissent and controversy in Ireland* (Cork, 1994), pp. 25–7.
[27] John Stearne to William King, 4 Nov. 1720 (T.C.D., MS 1995–2008/1962).
[28] William King to John Stearne, 12 Nov. 1720 (T.C.D., Wm King coll., MS 750/6, p. 155).
[29] John Evans, to William Wake, 9 Dec. 1720 (C.C., Wake Letters, vol. 13, no. 211).
[30] See pp. 124–5 above.

Thomas Lindsay, was unable to consecrate him, owing to a recent stroke. Since the aged and increasingly infirm Archbishop of Cashel, William Palliser, was also unable to perform the ceremony, the task passed to the two remaining archbishops, King and Synge. Synge asked to be excused from performing the ceremony on account of the fact that he was too ill to travel, whilst King simply refused to do so. A commission of bishops was finally formed to perform the consecration in St Peter's Drogheda on 22 January 1721, comprising the Irish-born Bishop of Raphoe, Nicholas Forster, and two English-born bishops, Welbore Ellis of Kildare and Henry Downes of Elphin.[31] This charade was repeated a year later when Gore was again denied a bishopric by another English chaplain Josiah Hort: King refused to consecrate Hort and once again a commission of mostly English bishops was formed to perform the ceremony.[32]

During the early 1720s, English bishops in Ireland constantly complained of being abused by their Irish counterparts.[33] Whereas the Bishop of Derry, William Nicolson, found this victimisation almost unbearable,[34] Hutchinson bore it with ease: 'my younger brother Down is sometimes made sensible of the inconveniences of his having been born in England. But he bears pretty sturdily against all the jests and peevish remarks that the native wits pass upon him'.[35] Evans, Downes and Nicolson took solace from these attacks in their friendship with one another. Hutchinson, however, made no attempt to join their clique. Evans remarked in 1723 that, though Hutchinson was both 'honest and good', he was 'often indifferent in common behaviour', something which Evans regarded as 'by no means truly episcopall'.[36] He went on to say that although Hutchinson 'was fond of asking advice' he generally stuck to his own company.[37] Given Hutchinson's deep attachment to notions of politeness and sociability, Evans's comments take on a somewhat ironic hue.[38]

---

[31] William Nicolson to William Wake, 24 Jan. 1721 (B.L., Add. MS 6116, fo. 133); [Ulster Historical Foundation], *Clergy of Down and Dromore*, part 2, p. 22.

[32] William King to William Wake, 20 Jan. 1722 (B.L., Add. MS 6117, fo. 105); William Nicolson to Wake, 4 Mar. 1722 (B.L., Add. MS 6116, fos. 120–1); Edward Synge to William Wake, 26 Mar. 1722 (B.L., Add. MS 6117, fos. 162–3); McNally, *Parties, patriots, undertakers*, pp. 166–7.

[33] See William Nicolson to William Wake, 21 Aug. 1724 (B.L., Add. MS 6116, fos. 130–1); John Wilkins to William Nicolson, 17 Nov. 1719, and Henry Downes to William Nicolson, 20 Feb. 1719–20 in John Nichols (ed.), *Letters on various subjects literary, political, and ecclesiastical, to and from William Nicolson D.D.* (London, 1809), pp. 493, 509–10; McNally, *Parties, patriots, undertakers*, pp. 158–9.

[34] William Nicolson to William Wake, 2 Oct. 1719 (C.C., Wake Letters, vol. 13, no. 113).

[35] Ibid., 19 Mar. 1721 (B.L., Add. MS 6116, fo. 134).

[36] Evans to Wake, 20 Apr. 1723 (C.C., Wake Letters, vol. 14, no. 72).

[37] Ibid.

[38] See chapters 4 and 5.

III

In common with the Irish interest in the House of Lords, the High-Church Irish parish clergy took the growth of Presbyterianism in Ulster more seriously than they did the Catholic threat. This does not imply that the Irish clergy (whose numbers by the early eighteenth century stood somewhere between 800 and 1200, of whom 90 per cent were of Irish birth and education) were unconcerned with Catholic Dissent or with bringing the Reformation to Ireland. It nonetheless fed their opposition to the Whig party, upon whose perceived ambivalent attitude to the growth of Dissent and irreligion they poured derision. In common with members of the Irish interest, many of Ireland's curates, vicars and rectors resented the fact that a high proportion of the best livings were given to Englishmen – a trend, it was often noted, not reciprocated in England for those of Irish birth and education.[39] It was for these reasons that the Down and Connor clergy came to despise their new spiritual leader, Francis Hutchinson, during his first years in the diocese. Unlike his predecessor, Hutchinson aligned himself with the English interest and was an outspoken Latitudinarian-Whig. The fact that during his first decade in Ireland he showed more concern with the temporal duties of his new office (attending the House of Lords as a peer of the realm) than with the spiritual concerns of his diocese served only to increase this antipathy.

Despite the contrary opinion of contemporaries, Westminster's appointment policy did not lead to the Irish bench of bishops becoming crowded with politically loyal incompetents. Bishops were usually required to have doctorates, and political appointees were not necessarily negligent or corrupt. In the Church of Ireland, as in the Church of England, the day-to-day running of the Church was handled by the lower clergy, which left bishops with three main duties: to perform regular visitations of their diocese, to ensure the Church had a ready supply of ordinands and to confirm the laity. Most Irish bishops met the standard set by canon law and custom relating to these, because the labour involved was light in comparison to that of much larger and more populous English dioceses.[40] The dictates concerning ordination were laid down in the ecclesiastical canons of 1604 and in royal letters and injunctions. Candidates had to prove their religious, intellectual and moral qualifications by producing letters of testimonial. They then took an examination designed by their bishop to test their scriptural knowledge and grasp

---

[39] Hayton, 'High-Churchmen', pp. 154–8; Barnard, *New anatomy*, pp. 82, 88, 98–9.
[40] Connolly, *Religion, law and power*, pp. 179–84; Falvey, 'Church of Ireland episcopate', pp. 106, 113; Sykes, *Church and state*, pp. 98–145.

of classical languages. The ordination practices of bishops varied enormously in Ireland as they did in England: some followed the canons to the letter; others were lax or inconsistent. All bishops, however, were guilty to some degree or other of nepotism.[41]

The clerical profession in Ireland did not really suffer as a result of this inconsistent recruiting policy because, on the whole, candidates were usually well qualified and not just well connected.[42] Since the 1980s, historians of the early eighteenth-century Irish Church have revised the hitherto accepted picture of the Church of Ireland as an institution both materially poor and beset by problems of nepotism, non-residence, absenteeism, pluralism, clerical negligence and ignorance. The Church of Ireland is now seen as a relatively well-run institution, in the sense of its ability to execute its pastoral duties, possessing more than enough resources to serve the small numbers of Irish Anglicans if not the population as a whole. It also possessed a core of bishops and influential reforming clergymen committed to raising clerical standards in the parishes. This programme was to be facilitated by institutional improvement of the finances and buildings of individual churches. Nicolson, King and the Archbishop of Armagh, Hugh Boulter, were notable examples of this type of reforming churchman.[43]

Hutchinson failed adequately to fulfil the three main spiritual duties of his new office.[44] Custom and canon law held that the confirmation of laymen was to be carried out every three years, but Hutchinson made just one confirmation tour between 1721 and 1728.[45] Bishops were also expected to carry out annual visitations, which formed the mark of diligence by which bishops were judged.[46] Hutchinson managed to conduct

---

[41] Pruett, *Parish clergy*, pp. 48–53; James, *North country bishop*, pp. 137–42, 257–61; Sykes, *Church and state*, pp. 98–115; Thomas Newcome, *The life of John Sharp, D.D., Lord Archbishop of York* (2 vols, London, 1825), i, 116–17, 137–142; O'Regan, *William King*, p. 128; Sykes, *William Wake*, i, 213–18, 243–6; Barnard, *New anatomy*, p. 97.

[42] McCracken, 'The ecclesiastical structure, 1714–60', p. 85; William Gibson, 'Unreasonable and unbecoming', pp. 45–59.

[43] Connolly, *Religion, law, power*, pp. 177–85, 187–90; Barnard, 'Improving clergymen', pp. 137–48; David Hayton, 'Did Protestantism fail in early eighteenth century Ireland? Charity schools and the enterprise of religious and social reformation, c.1690–1730' in *As by law established*, p. 167; James, *North country bishop*, pp. 259–62; O'Regan, *William King*, pp. 125–30, 144–51.

[44] No visitation records exist for the diocese of Down and Connor. Hutchinson's performance of his episcopal duties has been examined through his commonplace book for the years 1721 to 1730.

[45] Hutchinson's commonplace book, 1721–30 (P.R.O.N.I., MS DIO/1/22/1 [unpaged section]).

[46] O'Regan, *William King*, pp. 128–30; Falvey, 'Church of Ireland episcopate', p. 105; Sykes, *Church and state*, pp. 115–17.

only two visitations between 1721 and 1728, including his compulsory primary visitation.[47] Hutchinson may have maintained a healthy flow of ordinands,[48] but it is impossible to tell with certainty how well he followed canon law when judging the suitability of potential candidates. We do, however, have a detailed description of one of Hutchinson's ordinations, that of James Hely in 1726. Although Hutchinson's whole ordination policy should not be judged on the strength of this one case, it nonetheless demonstrates that, in the 1720s at least, he was willing to throw away the rule book even when his fellow prelates Bishop Ellis and Archbishop King were set against it, if and when he had a mind to ordain a particular individual. James Hely was the son of Sir John Hely, successively Chief Baron of the Irish Exchequer and Chief Justice of the Common Pleas. A former soldier who had never attended university, he decided to join the clergy only when Henry Moore, 4th Earl of Drogheda, promised him title to a living in the archdiocese of Dublin.[49] It was, by the eighteenth century, customary for bishops to insist that prospective ordinands were university-educated.[50]

In his primary visitation sermon, delivered at Lisburn, County Antrim, on 3 May 1721, Hutchinson exhorted his clergy to 'live up to the holy character that we have upon us, and be diligent in the right discharge of that sacred, important, and difficult work to which we are called'.[51] In practice, however, he took no steps to raise the standards of worship in his diocese: he made no attempt to cut down on pluralism or absenteeism, or to raise educational standards among his clergy, and the only church that he built in his diocese before 1729 was one designed to facilitate his conversion programme on Rathlin Island. He did at least, as was expected of early eighteenth-century bishops, reside in his

---

[47] Hutchinson, *Sermon preached... 3 May 1721*; Hutchinson's commonplace book, 1721–30 (P.R.O.N.I., MS DIO/1/22/1 [unpaged section]).

[48] Hutchinson's commonplace book, 1721–30 (P.R.O.N.I., MS DIO/1/22/1 [unpaged section]).

[49] William King to James Hely, 16 Aug. 1725 (T.C.D., Wm King coll., MS 1995–2008/2131); James Hely to William King, 29 June 1726 (T.C.D., Wm King coll., MS 1995–2008/2168); William King to Thomas Trotter, 4 July 1726 (T.C.D., Wm King coll., MS 750/8, pp. 118–19; William King to James Hely, 12 July 1726 (T.C.D., Wm King coll., MS 750/8, p. 130); William King to Welbore Ellis, 13 July 1726 (T.C.D., Wm King coll., MS 750/8, pp. 124–6); Thomas Trotter to William King, 20 July 1726 (T.C.D., Wm King coll., MS 1995–2008/2156); William King to Welbore Ellis, 29 July 1726 (T.C.D., Wm King coll., MS 750/8, pp. 135–6); William King to Thomas Trotter, 13 July 1726 (T.C.D., Wm King coll., MS 750/8, pp. 126–7); Thomas Trotter to William King, 30 June 1726 (T.C.D., Wm King coll., MS 1995–2008/2151); William King to Francis Hutchinson, 22 Oct. 1726 (T.C.D., Wm King coll., MS 750/8, p. 952).

[50] Barnard, *New anatomy*, p. 107.

[51] Hutchinson, *Sermon preached... 3 May 1721*, p. 11.

diocese. Since there was no episcopal palace in his diocese, Hutchinson and his family lived from 1721 to 1729 in a town house in Lisburn, County Antrim, which cost him £330.[52] With a population of about 4,000, Lisburn was the eighth largest town in Ireland. In common with most provincial towns in this period, it was regarded as a bastion of English and Protestant values. It also provided access to a richer and more varied social life, and a wider range of consumer goods.[53] Hutchinson left Lisburn in January 1730. His new estate and manor house (O'Neill's Castle) lay on the banks of Lough Neagh, near the hamlet of Portglenone in rural County Antrim, in an immediate demesne of 139 acres. His country pile cost him the princely sum of £8,200.[54]

In Post-Convocation Ireland,[55] attempts to promote the welfare of the Church were left to bishops in Parliament, an example of which was the attempt in the 1730s to increase clerical tithe yields.[56] Hutchinson himself played no role in this type of parliamentary action. In fact, although an unusually regular attender of the Irish House of Lords between 1721 and 1739, he played little part in the house's legislative production process: he was never called on to introduce or present a bill or heads of a bill and only ever reported from (in March 1736), or formed part of, one committee.[57] Furthermore, this select committee was charged with examining an 'improvement' heads of a bill rather than a clerical welfare bill, namely an 'Act for repairing the road from Maryborough, through Mountrath, Castletown, Borris in Ossory, and Roscrea, to Tomivaragh' (9 George II c. 22).[58]

The hypocritical disparity between Hutchinson's own clerical performance and his public exhortations on the need to raise clerical standards

---

[52] Hutchinson's commonplace book, 1721–30 (P.R.O.N.I., MS DIO/1/22/1, p. 57 [2nd pagination]).

[53] Connolly, *Religion, law, power*, pp. 45, 146; Toby Barnard, 'The cultures of eighteenth-century Irish towns' in Peter Borsay and Lindsay Proudfoot (eds), *Provincial towns in early modern England and Ireland: change, convergence and divergence* (Oxford, 2002), p. 222.

[54] Hutchinson's commonplace book, 1721–30 (P.R.O.N.I., MS DIO/1/22/1, p. 15 [1st pagination]).

[55] Convocation or the National Synod of the Church of Ireland was suspended in 1713 owing to an unparalleled level of party conflict between the High- and Low-Church factions.

[56] Barnard, *New anatomy*, p. 99; David Hayton, 'The development and limitations of Protestant ascendancy: the Church of Ireland laity in public life, c.1660–1740' in R. Gillespie and W. G. Neely (eds), *The laity and the Church of Ireland, 1000–2000: all sorts and conditions* (Dublin, 2002), p. 128.

[57] *Journals of the Irish House of Lords* [hereafter *LJ*] (8 vols, Dublin, 1779–1800), ii, 684–856; ibid., iii, 1–435.

[58] *LJ*, iii, 258; for details of turnpike roads in Ireland, see David Broderick, *The first toll roads: Ireland's turnpike roads, 1729–1858* (Cork, 2002).

not only fulfilled Archbishop King's prophecy but no doubt increased the antipathy his High-Church Tory clergy already felt towards him on account of his politico-religious stance.[59] The disaffection of the Protestant clergy and gentry of Down and Connor to the Hanoverian Whig regime in Ireland was of particular concern to those English bishops, such as John Evans, appointed to Ulster sees after 1714.[60] Hutchinson did little to dissipate this tension, not attempting to disguise his Latitudinarian-Whig views on Protestant Dissent. In fact, he was so forthright in downplaying the importance of the theological differences between Anglican and Presbyterian as to shock even the forward-thinking, Presbyterian moral philosopher, Francis Hutcheson.[61] Evans informed Archbishop Wake in January 1722 that Hutchinson was 'in much contempt among' clergy and gentry alike. Evans was concerned that only a truly well affected dean could help Hutchinson mend relations with his clergy. Evans felt that if Charles Brandon Fairfax, English-born and educated at Westminster School and Oxford University, were to be appointed to the then-vacant deanery of Down, which he feared would be the case, the situation in the diocese would only worsen.[62] In Evans's opinion there 'never came a greater Tory out of the Westminster school than Fairfax', a man who conversed 'with none but those reported to be disaffected'.[63] Unfortunately for Hutchinson, Fairfax was appointed in February 1722 and Evans's fears were realised.[64] In April 1723, Evans informed Archbishop Wake that the Bishop of 'Down and Connor advises us there is a combination hatcht among his clergy against him headed by his dean now their side'.[65] This 'combination' took the form of a protracted campaign to use ecclesiastical courts to prosecute for fornication those Presbyterians who had been married by their own minister rather than an Anglican divine. In doing so they revived an old controversy, last aired in the 1690s. The episode was ended by Fairfax's death in July 1723. Fairfax's actions had the further effect of persuading

---

[59] It must be pointed out, however, that some early eighteenth-century parish clergy actually resented the work of reforming bishops, regarding their increasing demands on their time and finances as unreasonable. See Hayton, 'High-Churchmen', p. 151.
[60] John Evans to William Wake, 28 Oct. 1720 (C.C., Wake Letters, vol. 13, no. 201); John Evans to William Wake, 15 Nov. 1720 (C.C., Wake Letters, vol. 13, no. 205).
[61] Francis Hutcheson to his father, 4 Aug. 1726 in *Christian Moderator*, ii (May 1827–April 1828), 353.
[62] John Evans to William Wake, 12 Jan. 1722 (C.C., Wake Letters, vol. 13, no. 224); Toby Barnard, 'Fairfax, Charles Brandon (1684–1723)', *OxDNB*.
[63] Evans to Wake, 12 Jan. 1722 (C.C., Wake Letters, vol. 13, no. 224).
[64] [Ulster Historical Foundation], *Clergy of Down and Dromore*, part 2, p. 21.
[65] John Evans to William Wake, 20 Apr. 1723 (C.C., Wake Letters, vol. 14, no. 72).

the Presbyterian synod of Ulster to try, unsuccessfully, to pressure Irish MPs in the 1723 session of Parliament to pass a relief act relating to Presbyterian marriage.[66]

Unfortunately for his parishioners and clergy, Hutchinson failed to become more involved in pastoral reform in the 1730s, or indeed with clerical agitation in the Lords on behalf of the established Church. He did, however, become more concerned with the material condition of his diocese. In 1735, and mainly at his own expense, he built a chapel of ease in Portglenone, County Antrim. Although served by curates, chapels of ease were not parish churches in their own right but adjuncts to nearby vicarages or rectories. The Portglenone chapel of ease formed part of the nearby rectory of Ahoghill, where Peter Leslie was incumbent. Church of Ireland bishops were allowed to build one or two chapels of ease anywhere in their dioceses where a number of Protestants lived five measured miles from the nearest parish church. The prelate did not need the patron's or the incumbent's consent to begin building work, but they did have to get the consent of local Protestants. The diocesan, however, retained the power to set the curate's stipend.[67]

Hutchinson also exhorted the clergy and laity of his diocese to build their own chapels. In late 1729 he stated that if any minister in his diocese employed a curate 'in a place where a chapelry is wanted' then 'my own purse shall never be shut upon such an occasion'.[68] He called on large and small landowners to donate houses and glebe lands, and encourage their tenants to build their own chapels.[69] In order to make this sort of endeavour more attractive to would-be philanthropists, he went on to state that he would 'always accept' their 'nomination of a regular conforming curate' and would do anything else in his power 'towards making the place a parish, and the benefactor the patron of it'.[70]

Hutchinson's interest in church building was not only proactive but reactive. During a visitation of May 1733, he noted:

[66] Henry Downes to William Wake, 4 Feb. 1724 (C.C., Wake Letters, vol. 14, no. 158); J. C. Beckett, *Protestant Dissent in Ireland, 1687–1780* (London, 1958), pp. 121–2; Toby Barnard, 'Fairfax, Charles Brandon (1684–1723)', OxDNB.

[67] Hutchinson's commonplace book, 1731–9 (D.R., p. 492); Purvis, *Introduction to ecclesiastical records*, pp. 18–19; Richard Mant, *History of the Church of Ireland: from the Revolution to the Union of the churches of England and Ireland* (London, 1840), pp. 476–7; Sibbet, *The shining Bann: records of an Ulster manor, for all touring in Northern Ireland*, pp. 171–4.

[68] Francis Hutchinson, *Advices concerning the manner of receiving popish converts...* (Dublin, 1729), p. 14.

[69] Ibid., p. 15.

[70] Ibid.

at the complaint of the minister and churchwarden that the church of Belfast was not safe for them to meet in I made a rule that the parish should provide a safe place for the worship of God and if they built a new church I promised 20 guinneas.[71]

In August 1732 he informed Edward Southwell, whose family at that time owned the town of Downpatrick, that when building work for a new church got under way there, he would contribute a small sum towards the project.[72] In 1733, Hutchinson backed Lady Anne Midelton's project to build a church in the parish of Breda at her own expense. The project however was opposed by Lady Ikkerin of Castle Hill, who complained to the Primate and Archbishop of Armagh, Hugh Boultor, that parishioners of her own parish church in Knock would flock west to attend the new church in Breda. Boulter took the part of both Hutchinson and Midelton, and the new church at Breda was finally completed in 1737.[73]

The records that we need to determine how well Hutchinson performed the spiritual duties of his new office are even more sparse for the 1730s than they are for the 1720s. Source material relating to his conduct of visitations and ordinations stops suddenly in 1733 and there are no records of confirmation. On the basis of this, albeit incomplete, evidence it may still be argued that in the 1730s Hutchinson was more diligent in the conduct of his episcopal duties than he had been in the 1720s. Between 1729 and 1733, he performed a visitation every two years (in May 1730 and then again in May 1733) compared to the period 1721–8 when he conducted one every three and a half years.[74] Hutchinson's ordination policy also seemed to become stricter after 1728: on two separate occasions he refused to ordain prospective candidates until they provided proof that they possessed titles to livings.[75]

If Hutchinson was lax in the performance of the spiritual part of his episcopal duties in the 1720s, he seemed more devoted to the temporal duties of his prelacy, maintaining, as we have seen, regular attendance

---

[71] Hutchinson's commonplace book, 1731–9 (D.R., p. 121); for a discussion of the dilapidated condition of this church in the mid-eighteenth century, see Raymond Gillespie, *Early Belfast: the origins and growth of an Ulster town to 1750* (Belfast, 2007), p. 132.

[72] Francis Hutchinson to Edward Southwell, 6 Aug. 6 1732 (B.L., Add. MS 21131, fo. 93); John Stevenston, *Two centuries of life in Down, 1600–1800* (Belfast, 1990), p. 218.

[73] Hutchinson's commonplace book, 1731–9 (D.R., pp. 121, 123); Peter Carr, *The most unpretending of places: a history of Dundonald, County Down* (Belfast, 1988), p. 84.

[74] Hutchinson's commonplace book, 1731–9 (D.R., pp. 121–2).

[75] Hutchinson's commonplace book, 1721–30 (P.R.O.N.I., MS DIO/1/22/1, pp. 3, 38 [1st pagination]).

in the House of Lords throughout the 1720s and 1730s.[76] A high attendance rate was expected of Whig political appointees. The fact that throughout this period he also used his various invitations to preach state sermons to cast George I and his Whig ministry in the role of saviours of Protestant rule and religion in Ireland must have also pleased the Whig hierarchy in England.[77] However, it was not until the 1730s that Hutchinson became willing to engage head-on with the Whig administration's political opposition, the 'patriot' interest in the Irish Commons and Lords, as he had done in England.

Before examining how Hutchinson dealt with patriot opposition in the mid-1730s, it is first necessary to look at the pattern of high politics in that period. In the late 1720s and 1730s, parliamentary politics in Ireland were relatively calm, despite periodic eruptions of the type of 'patriotic' opposition that had proved so troublesome for the English interest in the late 1710s and early 1720s. The economic issues over which they fought had changed little in the intervening period. For example, in 1729 England was accused of draining the country of wealth through the unfavourable balance of trade, and absentee landlords were lambasted for spending the profits they made in Ireland in other countries, especially in England. In 1737, a low-key repeat performance of the Wood's halfpence affair was played out in Parliament.[78]

Given the political situation in Ireland at that time, it was not unreasonable for Hutchinson to believe that a full-scale revival of 'patriotic' opposition of the kind that plagued Irish politics in the late 1710s and early 1720s was not only probable but likely. He was convinced that the Irish 'patriotic' interest would stray beyond merely challenging Westminster on economic matters to re-opening the constitutional wounds that the Declaratory Act had aimed to stitch shut. He consequently defended the constitutional implications of the Declaratory Act (1720)[79] and Poynings' Law (1494–5) in print for the first time.[80] Poynings' Law restricted the legislative powers of the Irish Parliament by subordinating it to the Irish and British privy councils. In so doing, as Sean Connolly points out, it was the 'most important mechanism by

---

[76] See p. 139 above.

[77] Hutchinson, *Sermon preached . . . 1 Aug. 1721*, pp. 3–5; idem, *Sermon preached . . . 5 November 1731*, pp. 24, 26.

[78] R. E. Burns, *Irish parliamentary politics in the eighteenth century, 1714–30* (2 vols, Washington DC, 1990), i, 236–63; idem, *Irish parliamentary politics in the eighteenth century, 1730–60*, ii, 1–38; McNally, *Parties, patriots and undertakers*, p. 56; Moody and Vaughan, *A new history of Ireland*, iv, 106–8.

[79] Hutchinson, *Sermon preached . . . 5 Nov. 1731*, p. 30.

[80] Hutchinson, *Defence of the antient historians*, p. 128.

which the proceedings of the Irish Parliament were controlled from London'.[81]

Hutchinson also became increasingly enamoured of the idea of a closer union between Ireland and England. In the 1720s and 1730s, historical and antiquarian writing in Ireland began to show new enthusiasm for pre-Norman Ireland, along with a willingness to portray its culture in a flattering light. This enthusiasm crossed the religious and cultural divide and was evident in historical works written by English Whig, Irish, and native Irish Catholic authors alike.[82] The attraction of this new view of ancient Irish culture to English Whig Churchmen such as William Nicolson, in his *Irish historical library* (1724), and Francis Hutchinson, in his *Defence of the antient historians* (1734), stemmed from two main causes. It emphasised the independence of Ireland from Rome in early Christian times and, more importantly for Hutchinson, justified a closer union between Ireland and England.[83] 'Because Gaelic culture', Jacqueline Hill argues, was 'to be found in Ireland, Scotland and Wales', it possessed 'the capacity to serve as an integrating factor for the different "British dominions"'.[84]

'Ireland is an antient nation',[85] Hutchinson argued in *Defence of the antient historians*, and was, 'as most of the northern nations', of the 'Gothic breed'.[86] He took the great age of the Irish language to be one of the sure signs of this antiquity and even reckoned it to be one of the 'mother tongues'.[87] He also noted its similarity to the 'the Samaritan character, in which the Jewish traditions, and even the ten commandments and the five books of Moses were written'.[88] He argued that Irish and ancient Hebrew not only possessed an eighteen-letter alphabet but also shared an extremely similar orthography.[89] Irish, in contrast to Hebrew however, had remained in an 'imperfect' condition right up to the modern day.[90] As early as 1721 Hutchinson was expressing the view that the Irish language was 'backward', but at this early stage did not

---

[81] Connolly, *Religion, law, power*, p. 34.
[82] Ann De Valera, 'Antiquarian and historical investigations in Ireland in the eighteenth century' (Master's thesis, University College Dublin, 1978), pp. 17–51.
[83] Jacqueline Hill, 'Popery and Protestantism, civil and religious liberty: the disputed lessons of Irish History, 1690–1812' in *Past and Present*, cxiii (1988), 102–4.
[84] Hill, 'Popery and Protestantism', 104.
[85] Hutchinson, *Defence of the antient historians*, p. 39.
[86] Ibid., p. 58.
[87] Ibid., p. 39.
[88] Ibid., p. 45.
[89] Ibid., pp. 44–6.
[90] Ibid., p. 45.

venture any explanations of why this might be the case.[91] He chose to do so in 1734 because, by then, his interest in Irish was sparked more by antiquarian zeal and less by its use as a converting tool.

Having, he hoped, convinced the reader of the antiquity of the Irish nation, Hutchinson went on to praise the ancient Irish for their cultural achievements. First of all he attacked Sir William Temple (historian, influential diplomat and Jonathan Swift's employer and mentor) for condemning the ancient inhabitants of Ireland on account of 'the bold and fierce part of their character'.[92] Hutchinson maintained that, though it might have been true that the Irish were an aggressive and warlike people in pagan times, they became more civilised under the influence of early Christianity, their culture in this era being marked by piety, learning, temperance and generosity.[93] Furthermore, he argued that by 'the time of the Saxons' Ireland had begun to enjoy the leadership of 'very good kings',[94] as well as the benefits of 'some kind of Justice' system.[95]

Hutchinson unsurprisingly showed support for other authors who propounded the same view of ancient Irish civilisation as his own. He owned William Nicolson's *Irish historical library* and expressed considerable admiration for it.[96] Furthermore, like Nicolson, he was a subscriber to Henry Rowland's *Mona antiqua restaurata: an archaeological discourse on the antiquities, natural and historical, of the Isle of Anglesey, the ancient seat of the British Druids* (1723). In the decades after its publication, Rowland's book became popular among writers on Celtic religion and druids.[97] In Ireland then, publication by subscription was usually the only way that an author who lacked wealth, reputation or patronage could get his work published.[98]

Hutchinson not only defended the English interest in print, but was also quick to take the side of the English government when the Irish Parliament tried to increase its legislative power. In September 1733, the English ministry ordered the Lord Lieutenant, Lionel Cranfield Sackville, 1st Duke of Dorset, to try to repeal the Test Clause that formed part of the 1704 'act to prevent the further growth of popery' (2 Anne, c. 6).

---

[91] See p. 160 below.
[92] Hutchinson, *Defence of the antient historians*, pp. 64–5.
[93] Ibid., pp. 62–4.
[94] Ibid., p. 63.
[95] Ibid., p. 64.
[96] Ibid., p. vii; Hutchinson's commonplace book, 1731–9 (D.R., p. 527).
[97] De Valera, 'Antiquarian and historical investigations', pp. 32–5.
[98] Mary Pollard, *Dublin's trade in books 1550–1800* (Oxford, 1989), p. 196.

This clause prevented Irish Protestant Dissenters from enjoying the same civil and legal rights as communicants of the Church of England. By early December it was apparent that there was little chance that a repeal bill would ever make it through the Irish House of Lords. Westminster consequently dropped the matter. However, a group of lay peers in the Irish Lords remained convinced that the bishops there would bow to government pressure and force the bill through Parliament. To prevent this situation arising, a resolution was passed on 5 December 1733 stating that all bills were to be communicated between both houses of Parliament before being presented to the Lord Lieutenant. The English ministry took this resolution to be a direct attempt by the Irish Parliament to increase its initiative powers. Westminster's fears were soon dispelled when a dispute over a tithe limitation bill persuaded the Lords to pass a resolution putting an end to this practice.[99] Hutchinson, along with some other bishops and lay peers, lodged a written objection to the 5 December resolution on two separate occasions during the session.[100]

Although resident in his diocese, during his first decade in Ireland, Hutchinson seemed to fulfil the prophecies of the leading members of the Irish interest, who regarded the English-born bishops, imported into Ireland after 1714 as part of the English administration ploy to build a controllable Irish House of Lords, as mere political puppets, more concerned with the revenue of their see than its spiritual needs. During the 1720s, Hutchinson displayed little interest in pastoral improvement or indeed with dispatching the relatively light spiritual duties attached to his new office and rather more on attending the House of Lords. This apparent indifference to his spiritual duties, combined with the fact that he was an English-born, Latitundinarian-Whig, blind to the perceived Presbyterian threat to the established Church, caused a major rift between Hutchinson and his Irish-born, High-Church, Tory clergy during the first few years of his prelacy.

In reality, Hutchinson was as concerned with maintaining the welfare of the Church of Ireland and serving the Whig and Hanoverian regime as he had been in England. As will be argued in the next chapter, Hutchinson in the 1720s was merely convinced that the Church and state in Ireland would be better served by devising and implementing conversion schemes designed to remove the political threat posed by the mass of the population's adherence and political deference to Roman Catholicism and the pope. Once this sense of Catholic threat retreated

---

[99] Burns, *Irish Parliamentary politics*, ii, pp. 17–22; Edith Mary Johnston, *Ireland in the eighteenth century* (Dublin, 1974), p. 29.
[100] *LJ*, iii, 245–6.

in Hutchinson's mind during the early 1730s, he became less concerned with conversion and set about defending the Whig/Hanoverian regime and the established Church in much the same way as he had done in England a decade earlier: through increased effort in the dispatch of his clerical duties and by defending the Whig and Hanoverian regime against parliamentary opposition, both with his pen and in person in the Irish House of Lords.

7

'Darkness must be expell'd by bringing in the light': the conversion of Irish Catholics, c.1721–34

In the early to mid-eighteenth century the majority of Irish Protestants would have given lip service to the benefits of converting the native Irish Catholic population to the Protestant religion. These benefits were perceived to be three-fold. Conversion was seen as a way to increase the political security of the Irish Ascendancy, as it was an ingrained part of Irish Protestant culture to view Irish Catholics as a potential security threat because of their temporal and spiritual allegiance to the pope, the arch-enemy of all Protestant countries. This threat would only be removed when Ireland was made Protestant. Many Irish Protestants regarded it as part of their religious duty to save the souls of a Catholic population who would otherwise be damned as a result of their adherence to a 'superstitious' and 'idolatrous' faith. Catholicism was also seen to be inimical to economic development owing to its discouragement of individual responsibility, an overabundance of holy days and the possession of a clergy that posed a financial burden on their congregations. Therefore, until made Protestant, Ireland would remain economically backward and underdeveloped.[1]

Early modern Irish Protestants took one of two approaches to the problem of conversion. The first mooted that Catholics would convert in large numbers if their religion was suppressed by penal legislation.[2] By the time Hutchinson reached Ireland in January 1721, Catholics were able to practise their religion, primarily because those Penal Laws (passed piecemeal by the Irish Parliament between 1695 and 1750) that related specifically to religious worship were by now enforced only at

---

[1] Connolly, *Religion, law, and power: the making of Protestant Ireland, 1660–1760* (Oxford, 1992), pp. 294–5; Michael Brown, Charles Ivar McGrath and Thomas P. Power, 'Introduction: converts and conversion in Ireland, 1650–1850' in idem (eds), *Converts and conversion in Ireland, 1650–1850* (Dublin, 2005), p. 17.

[2] Connolly, *Religion, law, and power*, pp. 295–9.

times of acute political crisis, in particular during Jacobite invasion or rebellion scares. It was at these times that Irish Protestants' sense of the Catholic threat became almost hysterical in intensity.[3] By contrast, the Penal Laws relating to the ownership of land and political activity were consistently and rigorously enforced.[4] It was thus those Catholics who owned land or had pretensions to political power, or both, that stood to gain most by conversion, namely those near or at the top of the Catholic social ladder. And many members of the leading Catholic families, such as the Butlers, Dillons and Nugents, did convert.[5] The English-born Whig bishops, imported into Ireland after 1714 were, for the most part, convinced that the Catholic population was on the brink of internal rebellion. They were consequently among the most vehement advocates of toughening the Penal Laws.[6] The Whig administration in London at that time had a 'let sleeping dogs lie' attitude to the Catholic situation and was, as far as possible, keen to prevent the Irish Parliament adding to the existing body of penal legislation.[7]

By the late 1720s, the fact that the Penal Laws had failed to disable the Catholic Church and bring about mass conversion was becoming widely acknowledged by the majority of Irish Protestants. This was confirmed by a report of the House of Lords' committee 'on the state of popery' delivered on 8 March 1732. The report concluded that the Catholic Church in Ireland possessed a high level of ecclesiastical organisation. The numbers of secular priests had all but outstripped demand, the numbers of the regular clergy were steadily increasing and most dioceses possessed a bishop. Ireland was also well-stocked with friaries, convents, mass-houses and Catholic schools. In most locales, the Catholic Church was not only tolerated but the persecution of priests had all but ceased. The Catholic population was growing steadily, and in Dublin an Irish literary, devotional and intellectual scene flourished. It is therefore unsurprising that by the early 1730s most Anglicans had all but lost their faith in the Penal Laws and become resigned to the fact that Ireland would remain a Catholic country. Even the Irish Parliament, where the calls for more penal legislation had traditionally been the loudest, began

---

[3] Maureen Wall, 'The Penal Laws, 1691–1760' in Gerald O'Brien and Tom Dunne (eds), *Catholic Ireland in the eighteenth century: collected essays of Maureen Wall* (Dublin, 1989), pp. 17–30; for a list of the Penal Laws, see Charles Ivar McGrath, 'The provision for conversion in the Penal Laws, 1695–1750' in Brown, McGrath and Power, *Converts and conversion*, pp. 57–8.

[4] McNally, *Parties, patriots and undertakers*, p. 26.

[5] Thomas Bartlett, *The fall and rise of the Irish nation: the Catholic question, 1690–1830* (Dublin, 1992), p. 23.

[6] McNally, 'Irish and English interests', pp. 302–4.

[7] Connolly, *Religion, law, and power*, pp. 272–4, 287.

to drift towards the same conclusion. This acceptance of the Catholic religion had much to do with the fact that the Protestant fear of Catholics in the 1730s had dropped to an almost negligible level. This should not obscure the fact that most Irish Protestants still viewed Catholics as a potential threat and that there were still some in the Irish House of Commons committed to ecclesiastical prohibition of Catholicism.[8]

The second approach to conversion adopted by Irish Protestants was the use of the Irish language to evangelise the native population. The underlying assumption of this method was that the main barrier to conversion was the fact that most Catholics were monoglot, speaking only Irish. In the sixteenth and seventeenth centuries, there had been various attempts to convert in this manner but all had been conspicuously unsuccessful. In 1571 the Archbishop of Canterbury, Matthew Parker, published a catechism, a selection of prayers and the twelve articles of religion in Irish. In the 1680s, the Irish-born natural philosopher, Robert Boyle (who had learned Irish as a boy), published a catechism and the old and new testaments in Irish, assisted by the Irish-speaking Archbishop of Dublin, Narcissus Marsh. The results were deemed disappointing and many of the bibles and catechisms went unsold and unread. Boyle and Marsh also encouraged several ministers to preach in Irish. In the early years of the eighteenth century, the lower house of the Irish Convocation stated its support for preaching in Irish and the publication of basic religious texts, but it was not until 1711 that a full-scale conversion programme was set in motion by John Richardson, rector of Belturbet in County Cavan. In *A proposal for the conversion of the popish natives of Ireland to the established religion* (Dublin, 1711), Richardson called for Irish-language bibles to be provided for Irish-speaking Anglican clergy who were to instruct monoglot Irish adult Catholics in Irish using custom-made Gaelic catechisms and simple religious manuals. Catholic children, on the other hand, were to be taught the principles of Protestantism in English in free schools. Although Richardson's scheme received tacit approval from the lower house of the Irish Convocation, the Tory bishops in the upper house ensured that he received no further support.

Richardson later received money from the government and generous donations from reformers based in England, via the agency of the S.P.C.K. in London. This enabled him to print in 1711 and 1712 a new Irish-language version of the *Book of common prayer*, a catechism and

---

[8] Bartlett, *Fall and rise*, pp. 24–9; Connolly, *Religion, law, and power*, pp. 287–90; Patrick J. Corish, *The Irish Catholic experience: a historical survey* (Dublin, 1985), pp. 123–6; Patrick Fagan, *Divided loyalties: the question of the oath for Irish Catholics in the eighteenth century* (Dublin, 1997), pp. 72, 74; Michael A. Mullet, *Catholics in Britain and Ireland, 1558–1829* (London, 1998), pp. 135–7.

a selection of five sermons. Richardson was able to sell only a fraction of these texts and made little headway to providing the established Church with Irish-speaking ministers. Around this time, the S.P.C.K. in London backed away from Gaelic conversion schemes and as a consequence the grassroots support for it among English reformers began to wane. After 1714, the Irish and English governments received few requests to pursue a sustained programme of proselytising in Irish. The majority of clerical strategists were now, albeit erroneously, convinced that literate monoglot Irish speakers were few and the native Irish were increasingly becoming English speakers. Furthermore, those individuals worried about the state of Protestantism in Ireland had concluded that their money would be better spent on supporting charity schools.[9]

Charity schools were established in Ireland in increasing numbers in the early eighteenth century, first through private and parish initiatives and then under the auspices of a national society in Dublin, set up in 1717 and modelled on the S.P.C.K in England. In charity schools, Catholic children were to be made Protestant through a slow process of linguistic and cultural assimilation. This educational process was also meant to make pupils more industrious, pious, well mannered and deferential to their social superiors. In practice, these schools were more concerned with the educational needs of poor Protestant children than those of Catholic children.[10] As David Hayton points out 'in 1733 the charity schools were reborn with a different set of priorities: proselytization first; moral reformation, social discipline and economic reconstruction all given a subsidiary role'.[11] The Irish charter school system, whose official title was the *Incorporated Society for promoting English Protestant working schools in Ireland* was a national organisation which attracted widespread support from the lower and higher clergy alike, as well as the Protestant laity. It was set up primarily through the efforts of the vehemently anti-Catholic, English-born, Whig Archbishop of Armagh, Hugh Boulter.[12]

[9] Connolly, *Religion, law, and power*, pp. 299–303; Toby Barnard, 'Protestants and the Irish language, c.1675–1725' in *Journal of Ecclesiastical History*, xliv (1993), 247–65; Michael MacCraith, 'The Gaelic reaction to the Reformation' in Steven Ellis and Sarah Barber (eds), *Conquest and union: fashioning a British state, 1485–1725* (London, 1995), pp. 140, 144; Betsey Taylor Fitzsimon, 'Conversion, the Bible, and the Irish language: the correspondence of Lady Ranelagh and Bishop Dopping' in Brown, McGrath and Power, *Converts and conversion*, pp. 157–82.

[10] David Hayton, 'Did Protestantism fail in early eighteenth-century Ireland? Charity schools and the enterprise of religious and social reformation, c.1690–1730' in Ford, McGuire and Milne, *As by law established*, pp. 166–86.

[11] Hayton, 'Did Protestantism fail', p. 181.

[12] Kenneth Milne, *The Irish charter schools, 1730–1830* (Dublin, 1997), pp. 12, 22–5; idem, 'Irish charter schools' in *Irish Journal of Education*, viii (1974), 5–6; Barnard, *New anatomy*, p. 97.

Despite the priority given to proselytisation in the charter school system, it nonetheless represented simply a face-saving exercise by the Anglican ascendancy in the face of the knowledge that Ireland would remain Catholic.[13]

Although it is certain that by the 1720s the cultural stock of Gaelic conversion schemes was at a low ebb among the Irish Protestant elite, it would be unwise to suggest it had become a concern only of English-born antiquaries such as Hutchinson and the Bishop of Derry, William Nicolson.[14] Just as a minority continued to believe in the effectiveness of the Penal Laws and charter schools in obtaining large-scale conversion, after the majority of their countrymen had lost faith in them, so a minority continued to support Gaelic conversion after Richardson's scheme failed. William King remained committed to preaching and printing in Irish far into the 1720s, as did the Archdeacon of Raphoe, Andrew Hamilton, and the Bishop of Raphoe and later Archbishop of Tuam, Edward Synge. At the same time the Bishop of Cloyne, George Berkeley, in his *Querist*, published in Dublin from 1735 to 1737, suggested that Irish Catholic adults should be converted using Irish-speaking ministers and minors through a Protestant education conducted in English.[15] Bishop Francis Hutchinson was yet another clergyman who championed Gaelic. The author of two Gaelic conversion schemes, he continued to believe in the worth of Irish as a conversion tool right up until the early 1730s, when his sense of Catholic danger began to wane.

I

Hutchinson supported conversion in Ireland for the same reasons as he had in England. Roman Catholics quite simply posed an unacceptable threat to the Whig and Hanoverian regime and the established Church. To him, this threat was much greater in Ireland than in England, primarily because most of the population were Catholic.[16] He was convinced that a bloody rebellion by the Catholic majority was imminent:

> eleven parliaments are not enough to settle us, tho' upon the next Protestant legal blood, that we have to rest on. God's Providence overturning all

---

[13] Bartlett, *Fall and rise*, p. 26.
[14] See Barnard, 'Irish language', p. 265.
[15] Charles Simeon King (ed.), *A great Archbishop of Dublin: William King, 1650–1729: his autobiography, family and a selection from his correspondence* (London, 1906), pp. 234, 292; Barnard, 'Irish language', pp. 258, 260; idem, *New anatomy*, pp. 93–4; Connolly, *Religion, law, and power*, p. 303.
[16] Francis Hutchinson, *A letter to the gentlemen of the landed interest in Ireland, relating to a bank* (Dublin, 1721), p. 26.

opposition is of no weight with them; nor are their own most solemn and repeated oaths and abjurations, and receiving protection of any moment upon their consciences. Our Protestant and just Prince must be murdered, a massacre must be made, and a popish Pretender be brought from Rome.[17]

The best way to remove this threat and render Catholics loyal to their Protestant monarch was to convert them to the Church of Ireland:

> It wou'd make them better subjects to a Protestant Prince, when they shall be of the same religion with him ... That unnaturall and unfortunate fondness, that they have towards popish nations, and the pope himself, will be taken away; and if at any time those foreign nations invade us, instead of opening their arms to receive them, they will joyn with us, in defending our holy religion and liberty against them.[18]

The political pacification of the native population may have been foremost in his mind when advocating conversion, but he also noted its economic benefits. A leading exponent of improvement, Hutchinson believed that, though the Irish and Ireland could be improved by the Protestant minority while the island remained Catholic, the process would be swifter and easier if the country were Protestant.[19] The 'Protestant religion', he maintained, was 'much better suited to a trading nation than the popish', as popery had 'too many holy-days, and monks and nuns, and expensive vanities and idle errands to take them off from their business'.[20] Surprisingly, Hutchinson never couched his support of conversion in religious terms though, as will be argued below, he never tired in Ireland as in England of commenting on what he and other Protestants deemed the theological and doctrinal shortcomings of Catholicism.

The 'superior judgement that their education gives them', Hutchinson argued, along with the penalties that penal legislation imposed on their property ownership and religious observance, had persuaded the Catholic nobility and gentry to 'come off from the gross errors of popery'.[21] However, unlike the majority of Protestants, he was convinced, by the early 1720s, that the Penal Laws had done all they could to convert both

---

[17] Hutchinson, *Sermon preached ... 30 Jan. 1723*, p. 9.

[18] Francis Hutchinson, *The church catechism in Irish, with the English placed over against it in the same karakter. Together with prayers for sick persons, and some texts of scripture, and a vocabulary explaining the Irish words that are used in them* (Belfast, 1722), p. 25.

[19] See p. 181 below.

[20] Francis Hutchinson, *A letter to a Member of Parliament, concerning the imploying and providing for the poor* (Dublin, 1723), p. 10.

[21] Francis Hutchinson, *An Irish-English almanack for the year, 1724. Being bissextile, or leap-year. And from the creation of the world, about 5686 ...* (2nd edn, Dublin, 1724), p. iv. The 2nd edition of this pamphlet lacks proper pagination. The pagination used here allots pp. ii–vi to the preface and pp. 9–30 for the main text.

the Catholic clergy and the mass of the Catholic population: 'the number of the popish Priests is greater than it hath been formerly ... a sign that the people are not fewer'.[22] In 1721 he calculated that 'Ireland hath three or four, perhaps five papists to one Protestant, and therefore, if the name was to follow number, must be called a popish, rather than a Protestant nation'.[23] Throughout the 1720s, Hutchinson kept a careful note of this perceived growth of the Catholic threat by listing in his commonplace book the names, and sometimes the whereabouts, of Catholic priests, laymen and unregistered mass houses.[24]

Hutchinson concluded that if coercive means had failed to change the religious make-up of Ireland, then persuasive means, and persuasive means alone, had to be used to convert the 'common people'.[25] Not only was this section of society 'ignorant and bigoted',[26] but it spoke only Irish. The 'greatest obstruction' to conversion, he stated in 1721, lay 'in the difficulty of applying the means of religion and learning to them in English because Irish is at present their mother tongue'.[27] His assessment was more accurate than those of some of his contemporaries. It has been calculated that, as late as 1731, two-thirds of the population may have used Irish as their everyday language, particularly poorer Catholics living outside Plantation Ulster.[28] Hutchinson argued that Irish Catholics thus only had to be informed in their native tongue of the ways in which the Catholic religion had corrupted the true word of God.[29] This was, he said, 'the method that was taken in England, at the time of the Reformation', when the first 'reformers translated the bible into English, set up the Holy Scriptures upon the very walls of the churches', 'read them in the known tongue' and published 'the common-prayer in the langwage that every body understood'.[30] It was common for Gaelic enthusiasts such as Hutchinson to defend

---

[22] Hutchinson, *Almanack* (2nd edn), p. iv.
[23] Hutchinson, *A letter ... relating to a bank*, p. 26.
[24] Hutchinson's commonplace book, 1721–30 (P.R.O.N.I., MS DIO/1/22/1, pp. 174–5 [2nd pagination]); idem, p. 22 [1st pagination]).
[25] Hutchinson, *Almanack* (2nd edn), p. iv.
[26] Ibid., p. iv.
[27] Francis Hutchinson, *The state of the case of Raghlin* (Dublin, 1721), p. 1.
[28] Connolly, *Religion, law, and power*, p. 147; Ciaran Devine, 'The Irish language in County Down' in Lindsay Proudfoot (ed.), *Down history and society: interdisciplinary essays on the history of County Down* (Dublin, 1997), p. 431; Reg Hindley, *The death of the Irish language: a qualified obituary* (London, 1990), pp. 7–8; Brian O Cuiv, 'Irish language and literature, 1691–1845' in T. W. Moody (ed.), *A new history of Ireland: eighteenth-century Ireland, 1691–1800* (8 vols, Oxford, 1992), iv, 383.
[29] Hutchinson, *Almanack* (2nd edn), p. iv; idem, *Church catechism in Irish*, p. v.
[30] Hutchinson, *Church catechism in Irish*, p. v.

proselytising in Irish by reference to the Protestant religious imperative of evangelising the populace in the vernacular.[31]

In common with those first Protestant reformers, and indeed previous Irish lobbyists, Hutchinson maintained that an essential part of any Gaelic conversion programme was to ensure that public worship was conducted in the vernacular by Irish-speaking clergy.[32] In practice, however, Hutchinson took no practical steps to encourage this, being of the belief that those converted by the printed word were likely to be more committed to their new religion than those converted by a Protestant preacher, since the former had been converted by 'conviction like reasonable creatures'.[33] Hutchinson had been an exponent of clerical reform in England and as such had laid stress on the value of the written word when endeavouring to impose right religion on the laity. Religious commitment, as has already been suggested, was often associated by English reformers with understanding, which in its turn was thought to be best achieved by individuals reading about Christianity for themselves.

Hutchinson claimed to have discovered the reason why the schemes of the 'pious and learned Mr Boyle, Mr Richardson, and other good men' to proselytise Irish Catholics using the printed word had had 'no good effect'.[34] It was because 'not one in twenty thousand' could 'write nor print, nor read' their own language.[35] The negative effect that high illiteracy rates could have on clerical reform had been made clear to Hutchinson early in his career. He ceased distributing catechisms among the poor of Bury St Edmunds when he realised they could not read them.[36] It thus became Hutchinson's self-appointed mission to enable a large proportion of the Irish Catholic majority to read the Protestant message for themselves in their native tongue. To make this goal more achievable, he proposed to concentrate on Irish charity school children.[37] Hutchinson's experience of founding and running charity schools in Suffolk not only made this demographic familiar to him, but the charity school system was a national organisation spread throughout Ireland.[38]

In order to make it easier for monoglot Catholic children to learn to read Irish, Hutchinson devised a new method of presenting their

[31] Barnard, 'Irish language', p. 244.
[32] Hutchinson, *Almanack* (2nd edn), p. iii; Francis Hutchinson to Sir Hans Sloane, 12 Oct. 1723 (B.L., Sloane MS 4047, fos. 67–8).
[33] Hutchinson, *Almanack* (2nd edn), p. v.
[34] Ibid., p. v.
[35] Hutchinson, *Church catechism in Irish*, p. viii.
[36] See p. 32 above.
[37] Hutchinson, *Church catechism in Irish*, pp. vii, x.
[38] For Hutchinson's involvement with charity schools in Bury St Edmunds, see pp. 34–6 above.

tongue.[39] He employed this new form of Irish for the first time in his 1722 work, the *Church catechism in Irish*. The *Catechism* was to be the first of a series of Protestant texts written in phonetic Irish, to include 'primmers ... psalters, common-prayer books' and the New Testament.[40] Aware of the cultural proscription among the Protestant elite of proselytising in Irish, especially among those connected with charity schools, Hutchinson knew he would have to demonstrate the effectiveness of his new phonetic Irish in a working school if it was to have any chance of being adopted elsewhere.[41]

He chose Rathlin Island, off the coast of north Antrim in Ulster, for the site of this pilot scheme and for very particular reasons. Rathlin not only lacked a resident Catholic priest to upset his plans for the island,[42] but it was one of the few places in his diocese where a large concentration of monoglot, Irish Catholics lived: 'as my diocese lies amongst these Scotch Presbyterians and not amongst the natives I have less opportunity of pushing it [Gaelic conversion] forward'.[43] In the early eighteenth century, the counties of Antrim and Down possessed the smallest proportions of Catholics of all the counties in Ireland.[44] Rathlin, however, as Hutchinson reckoned in 1721, contained some 'four hundred and ninety souls', the vast majority of whom were Catholic monoglots.[45]

A major flaw in Hutchinson's plan was that Rathlin did not own a charity school or a parish church of its own, as it formed part of the parish of Ballintoy on the mainland. In order to pay for the printing of the *Catechism*, and to furnish the island with a school and church, Hutchinson began to raise subscriptions from the great and good of Protestant Ulster in early 1721. Their names, 13 in all, including that of Archbishop of Dublin, William King, were published in *The state of the case of Raghlin*. This was a two-sided advertisement published in 1721 to attract further funding for the Rathlin project. *The state of the case of Raghlin* fulfilled Hutchinson's expectations, attracting 33 more subscribers, whose names were printed at the back of the *Catechism* in 1722.[46]

---

[39] See pp. 158–9 below.

[40] Hutchinson, *State of the case of Raghlin*, p. 1.

[41] Hutchinson, *Church catechism in Irish*, p. x; idem, *State of the case of Raghlin*, p. 2; Francis Hutchinson to John Richardson, 22 Apr. 1721(P.R.O.N.I., Rathlin Island Catechism, MS D3577/3A).

[42] Hutchinson, *State of the case of Raghlin*, p. 1.

[43] Hutchinson to Sloane, 12 Oct. 1723 (B.L., Sloane MS 4047, fos. 67–8).

[44] Connolly, *Religion, law, and power*, p. 146.

[45] Hutchinson, *State of the case of Raghlin*, p. 1.

[46] See Andrew Sneddon, 'The production, impact and reception of *The Church catechism in Irish*' (1722), forthcoming in *Oxford history of the Irish book, vol. ii: the Irish book in Irish*.

In the same year, in a bid to secure more funding from subscribers in England, Hutchinson sent a copy of the *State of the case of Raghlin* to the S.P.C.K. in London. He received no financial support from the S.P.C.K., but they did offer to supply him with excess copies of Richardson's catechisms and common prayer books, which at that time lay rotting in the society's store somewhere in Ireland.[47] Unfortunately we do not know whether Hutchinson took up this offer.

In early 1722, with donations to his scheme coming in steadily, Hutchinson gave the order for building work to begin on Rathlin. He also sent to the island Daniel McNeil, a schoolmaster who could speak Irish and came on the recommendation of William King.[48] On 20 April 1722, Hutchinson secured an Act of the Irish Privy Council to sever Rathlin from Ballintoy, a rectory served by the vehement Tory, Archibald Stewart, to create the new rectory of Rathlin. Given Hutchinson's problems with troublesome Tory clergy at the time, it must have pleased him immensely to see Rathlin prised from the control of a man of Stewart's political stamp. He persuaded Stewart to surrender the small tithes attached to Rathlin and bought, using money donated by Queen Anne's bounty, the great tithes from the Earl of Antrim, Randall Macdonnell. These tithes were to provide a future incumbent with a suitable stipend.[49]

In November 1722 Hutchinson consecrated the Rathlin parish church and confirmed 30 or 40 local children, despite the fact that construction work on the church, school, parsonage and library had recently ground to a halt owing to a lack of funds, and even though a Catholic priest, Father Dominick O'Brallaghan, had recently arrived on the island with the precise intention of preventing the ceremony from going ahead.[50] Convinced that enough money had been raised to cover the cost of all the building work, Archbishop William King, a subscriber and manager of the project, advised Hutchinson, for his reputation's sake, to immediately raise a loan to finish what he had begun.[51] King was unaware that Hutchinson had just lent the project £200 of his money, albeit at

---

[47] Minute books, 29 May 1722 (C.U.L., S.P.C.K. records, MS A1/10 (1722–24), p. 48); Minute books, 31 July 1722 (C.U.L., S.P.C.K. records, MS A1/10 (1722–24), p. 65).

[48] Archibald Stewart to William King, 21 Jan. 1722 (T.C.D., Wm King coll., MS 1995–2008/2025); Hutchinson's commonplace book, 1731–9 (D.R., p. 119).

[49] Catherine Gage, *A history of the island of Rathlin* (1851, repr. Coleraine, 1995), pp. 64–5; G. Hill, 'The Stewarts of Ballintoy' in *Ulster Journal of Archaeology*, old series, vi (1900), 107.

[50] Francis Hutchinson to Cox Macro, 12 Nov. 1722 (B.L., Add. MS 32556, fo. 151); William King to Francis Hutchinson, 22 Dec. 1722 (T.C.D., Wm King coll., MS 750/7, pp. 260–2).

[51] William King to Francis Hutchinson, 22 Dec. 1722 (T.C.D., Wm King coll., MS 750/7, pp. 260–2).

a punitive interest rate of 30 per cent, secured against future Rathlin tithes.⁵² St Thomas's Church on Rathlin was completed on 28 October 1723 and the rest of the buildings in November 1724.⁵³

While managing the institutional side of the Rathlin project, Hutchinson simultaneously oversaw the publication of the *Catechism*. This was, in common with many Anglican catechisms of the period, based on that contained in the English *Book of common prayer*, written in 1549 and revised in 1604. The *Catechism* differed from earlier Irish-language catechisms in three main ways.⁵⁴ Firstly it employed a new form of Irish that deviated from the orthographic conventions of traditional, literary Irish. This type of Irish is exemplified by Richardson's Irish catechism and *Book of common prayer* of 1712.⁵⁵ As Cathair O' Dochartaigh points out, this form of written Irish was 'more representative in its graphemic-phonemic correspondences of the spoken language of the twelfth century than of that of the eighteenth'.⁵⁶

Hutchinson modified the orthography of this Irish to make it more phonetic and thus bear a closer resemblance to English. He was of the opinion that many of the letters in written Irish words were 'quiescents', in that they were not pronounced when spoken: 'the word in the title of the Church-Catechism, as it stands in the common character; the word is, ionfnoghlomtha to be learned, which is spoken only inoloma; fourteen letters, and seven of them quiescents'.⁵⁷ In Hutchinson's view these quiescents were to be 'cast out' of Irish words.⁵⁸ In practice, O' Dochartaigh argues, this occasioned 'the removal or modification of graphemes representing historic fricative consonants which have been lost or vocalised, with or without concomitant effects on the surrounding vowels' and the deletion, albeit inconsistently, of 'graphemes used ... to indicate the quality of consonants ... following the rule of *caol le caol agus leathan le leathan*'.⁵⁹ Furthermore, with respect to capitalisation

---

⁵² Hutchinson's commonplace book, 1721–30 (P.R.O.N.I., MS DIO/1/22/1, pp. 56, 67 [2nd pagination]); ibid., c.1731–9 (D.R., p. 118).

⁵³ Hutchinson's commonplace book, 1731–9 (D.R., p. 118); ibid., 1721–30 (P.R.O.N.I., MS DIO/1/22/1, p. 67 [2nd pagination]).

⁵⁴ For an exposition of the linguistic significance of this *Catechism*, see Cathair O' Dochartaigh, 'The Rathlin catechism' in *Zeitschrift fur Celtische Philologie*, xxxv (1976), 175–233.

⁵⁵ John Lewis and John Richardson, *The Church catechism explain'd by way of question and answer; and confirm'd by scripture proofs* (London, 1712); *The book of common prayer, and administration of the sacraments* (Dublin, 1712).

⁵⁶ O' Dochartaigh, 'Rathlin catechism', pp. 178, 204.

⁵⁷ Hutchinson, *Church catechism in Irish*, p. ii.

⁵⁸ Ibid., p. ix.

⁵⁹ O' Dochartaigh, 'Rathlin catechism', p. 183.

(Hutchinson capitalised most nouns and verbal nouns) and punctuation, the Irish text in the *Catechism* followed, for the most part, eighteenth-century printing conventions. Hutchinson did however use hyphens and apostrophes to make certain words more phonetic: the word 'guidhim', for example, is written as 'gui-ham'.[60]

Hutchinson also argued that the traditional Irish alphabet proved difficult for learners to grasp because it had 'neither h in its proper sound, nor k, nor i consonant, nor v, nor w, nor x, y, z, and yet they had the sounds of them all'.[61] He consequently increased the number of the letters in the Irish alphabet from 18 to 26, making it identical to English.[62] He believed Irish was a survival language, redolent of English, 'about 11 hundred years . . . before time and printing had given it a smoother and better turn'.[63] Therefore, his 'introduction of a new character' was 'not a wanton needless changing of a thing well setl'd, but only improving a very bad one'.[64] Consequently, although his phonetic Irish was conceived as a conversion tool, it fitted perfectly with his other main concern of the period, improvement.

Secondly, the *Catechism* was translated into the dialect of the area where it was to be used, County Antrim,[65] and it included a short grammatical introduction, some useful conversational phrases and a vocabulary. The grammatical introduction outlined some dimensions of morphology, such as auxiliary verbs, noun declensions, pronouns and word formation. The vocabulary mainly consisted of words that were used in the *Catechism* itself,[66] with samples of conversation, which he envisaged Irish monoglots using in conversation with English speakers, presented at the end. These took the form of a series of questions and answers, such as 'K[est]. In lavirin tu Bearl?' (Question. Can you speak English?) and 'Fre[gra]. Lavirim nee lavirim, lavirim began' (Answer. Yes – no – a little).[67] Unsurprisingly, John Richardson's 1712 catechism contained none of these features.[68]

Hutchinson designed his *Catechism* to enable children to learn to read Irish quickly, but also to read English 'by the common method of teaching French', placing the Irish version and its English translation

---

[60] Ibid., pp. 184–6.
[61] Hutchinson, *Church catechism in Irish*, p. ii.
[62] Ibid., pp. ii–iii, xii, 36–50.
[63] Ibid., p. ix.
[64] Ibid., p. i.
[65] O' Dochartaigh, 'Rathlin catechism', pp. 180, 204–16.
[66] Hutchinson, *Church catechism in Irish*, pp. 30–5, 36–50, 3–16.
[67] Ibid., p. 55.
[68] See Lewis and Richardson, *Church catechism explain'd*.

on opposite pages since 'the easiest way of learning a new language, is by having the known tongue and the tongue to be taught in two columns placed over against one another'.[69] He also employed a Roman rather than a Gaelic typeface. The Roman typeface was not only far cheaper to produce but, he conjectured, those who learned to read Irish in it would become familiar with written English.[70] He included a phonetic alphabet – in which, for example, 'b' was written as 'bee' and 'h' as 'atch'[71] – and altered some words in the English translation to make them slightly more phonetic and thus easier to read: so 'Christian' and 'commandments' appear as 'Kristian' and 'kommandments'.[72] To appreciate the novelty of the English spellings in the *Catechism*, one has only to compare it to the *Book of common prayer*, printed in English in Dublin in 1721 for the charity-school market.[73] Furthermore, even if Richardson expressed a desire to make Irish Catholics speak English, unlike Hutchinson he did not design his catechism accordingly.[74]

By the inclusion of these aids to learning English, Hutchinson sidestepped the accusation that had been aimed at previous Gaelic converters: that promoting Irish perpetuated linguistic differences and prevented the assimilation of the native Irish Catholics into Irish Protestant culture.[75] This should not be taken to mean that Hutchinson was insincere in his commitment to making Ireland an English-speaking country. It 'would be a great happiness and wonderful improvement to the kingdom of Ireland', he stated in 1724, that 'if without knowing any distinction of English, Scotch or Irish all its inhabitants were united in one language and way of living'.[76]

By turning the native Irish into English speakers, Hutchinson also believed he was 'improving' them. English was in his view 'the noblest and more perfect and most used language' whereas Irish, even in its improved, phonetic form, was a 'less honourable' and 'imperfect' form of communication.[77] He nonetheless believed that even English could be improved[78]

---

[69] Hutchinson, *State of the case of Raghlin*, p. 1.
[70] Hutchinson, *Church catechism in Irish*, pp. xii, 2, 4, 6, 8, 10.
[71] Ibid., p. xii.
[72] Ibid., p. 3.
[73] *Book of common prayer*; Scott Mandelbrote, 'John Baskett, the Dublin book-sellers, and the printing of the Bible, 1710–1724' in Arnold Hunt, Giles Mandelbrote and Alison Shell (eds), *The book trade and its customers: historical essays for Robin Myers* (Winchester, 1997), pp. 117, 121.
[74] Lewis and Richardson, *Church catechism explain'd*, p. 261.
[75] Barnard, 'Irish language', p. 255.
[76] Hutchinson, *Almanack* (2nd edn), p. ii.
[77] Ibid., p. vi.
[78] Hutchinson to William Wake, 14 Apr. 1720 (C.C., Wake Letters, vol. 21, no. 215).

because it contained numerous grammatical 'ambiguities and faults'.[79] In a bid to cleanse his mother tongue of these frailties he claimed, in the 1730s, to have written and published a book entitled 'an English grammar' while living in Bury St Edmunds.[80] It has proved impossible to track down this work, most probably because Hutchinson had from the outset intended to print it 'either without a name, or under the name of a neglected author'.[81]

It would appear from this discussion of the linguistic novelty of the *Catechism* that Hutchinson was both an ingenious and innovative Gaelic scholar. In reality, he could neither read nor write Irish, a fact commented upon in a ballad of 1726:

And cause we can't read, nor yet understand,
The language that's spoken in old England?
First taught a catichize wrote in his own;
In an easy new method, before never known . . .

. . . But what's more surprising to you I'll relate,
To shew his fine genius, and knowledge so great,
And indeed it is strange, yet some folks so say,
He can't read a word on't himself to this day.[82]

Hutchinson consequently relied upon the translating skills of John Richardson and Archibald McCollum.[83] McCollum was an Irish-speaking curate, resident in the parish of Ramoan, County Antrim, a supporter of proselytising in Irish and a cohort of Richardson.[84] Sometime in early 1721, Hutchinson received from Richardson an 'account of the steps by which the common prayer-book and the sermons are got into the Irish tong'.[85] A few months later Hutchinson asked Richardson to translate part of the *Catechism* for him.[86] The extant manuscript of the *Catechism*, however, is in McCollum's handwriting. This manuscript version is far less phonetic than its printed counterpart, suggesting it is the only survivor of multiple drafts made by McCollum while preparing the *Catechism*.[87]

---

[79] Hutchinson to Richardson, 22 Apr. 1721 (P.R.O.N.I., MS D3577/3A).
[80] Hutchinson's commonplace book, 1731–9 (D.R., p. 495).
[81] Hutchinson to Wake, 14 Apr. 1720 (C.C., Wake Letters, vol. 21, no. 215).
[82] Anon., *An excellent new ballad*.
[83] Hutchinson, *Church catechism in Irish*, pp. iii, xiii.
[84] Ibid., pp. iii, xiii; John Richardson, *A short history of the attempts to convert the popish natives of Ireland, to the estabish'd religion: with a proposal for their conversion* (London, 1712), pp. 29–30, 50.
[85] Hutchinson to Richardson, 22 April 1721 (P.R.O.N.I., MS D3577/3A).
[86] Ibid.
[87] The Rathlin catechism, 1721 (P.R.O.N.I., Diocesan records, MS D3577/1A, pp. 22–77).

Hutchinson rewarded McCollum's linguistic talents by presenting him at the end of 1721 to a living that lay in his diocese: the vicarage of Loughguille, County Antrim, worth a respectable £60 a year.[88]

N. J. A. Williams argues that Hutchinson borrowed the idea for phonetic Irish from Thomas Wilson, Bishop of Sodor and Man, who had devised and used a phonetic form of Manx in a catechism published in 1707.[89] In the same style as Hutchinson's *Catechism* published ten or so years later, Wilson's catechism was printed in English and phonetic Manx, in two columns opposite each other on the same page.[90] Nevertheless, it is apparent that Hutchinson's *Catechism* was also heavily indebted to J. Daubichon's *A French grammar: or, a new and easy method for to learn to speak French in a short time*, printed in Dublin in 1721. Daubichon's book supplies the reader with a phonetic alphabet, a vocabulary, some familiar phrases and a list of grammatical principles. This way of presenting French was Daubichon's own invention, devised to enable readers to learn French quickly and easily.[91] Hutchinson owned many French grammars and dictionaries, of whose contents he had more than a passing knowledge.[92]

But it was the linguistic innovation of the *Catechism* that ultimately plunged the Rathlin project into controversy: school, church and conversion were things no clergyman could publicly deny were worthwhile, whereas altering the conventions of a written language smacked of heterodoxy. On 7 July 1722, Hutchinson wrote to Archbishop King to request that he arrange a meeting of those bishops still in Dublin after their attendance at the recent session of Parliament. Hutchinson was convinced that if he secured the approval of the Irish episcopate for the *Catechism* this would ensure the success of his project. On 22 August 1722, King wrote back to Hutchinson to inform him that he had been unable to arrange such a meeting as most of the bishops who had been in Dublin had already returned to their dioceses.[93] Hutchinson consequently sacrificed official approval in order to see the *Catechism* in print:

---

[88] Hutchinson's commonplace book, 1721–30 (P.R.O.N.I., MS DIO/1/22/1, p. 144 [2nd pagination]).

[89] N. J. A. Williams, 'Thomas Wilson, Francis Hutchinson agus Litirui na Gaeilge' in *Eighteenth-Century Ireland*, i (1986), 204–7.

[90] Thomas Wilson, *The principles and duties of Christianity, being a further instruction for such as have learned the Church catechism; for the use of the diocese of Man. In English and Manks* (London, 1707), pp. 1–136.

[91] J. Daubichon, *A French grammar or a new and easy method for to learn to speak French in a short time* (Dublin, 1721), pp. 55–6, 172–85, 9, 62–171, unpaginated introduction.

[92] Hutchinson's commonplace book, 1731–9 (D.R., pp. 498–500, 506, 508, 513, 524–5); idem, *Almanack* (2nd edn), p. vi; idem, *Church catechism in Irish*, p. vii.

[93] William King to Francis Hutchinson, 22 Aug. 1722 (T.C.D., King MS, MS 750/7), p. 185.

on 24 August 1722, he paid James Blow £15 to publish an unknown number of copies of it.[94] What we do know is that the majority of the print-run was sent to Rathlin island. Subscribers to the project were given a single copy each, while multiple copies were sent to those Down and Connor clergy who had supported the project, to sell to interested parties. McCollum, for example, received six copies, while the treasurer of Down Cathedral, Charles Ward, was given twenty-four.[95]

Unaware that the *Catechism* was already in print, King wrote to Hutchinson on 6 November 1722 to inform him that an unnamed committee of Irish bishops had approved of his proposal to publish a catechism in Irish, but had unanimously condemned his phonetic Irish and English.[96] In another letter a month later, King pleaded with him to take some 'sounde advice' and forgo its publication.[97] Arguing that Hutchinson would realise how foolish it was to alter the spelling of English or Irish if he took the time to read some 'books which have bin written on . . . [the] subject', King enclosed a 'pamphlet of about 150 pages', which he believed to have been written in England sometime after the Restoration.[98]

Other subscribers to the project were also critical of Hutchinson's linguistic enterprises. James Smythe, prebendary of Cairncastle, informed his father, the Bishop of Raphoe, William Smythe, that Hutchinson's Irish pamphlets were 'generally turned to their proper use almost as soon as printed, for he always favours me with waste paper'.[99] Hutchinson was well aware of the controversy surrounding the *Catechism*. In November 1722, he informed his friend and Suffolk clergyman, Dr Cox Macro, that his 'Irish pamphlet' had put him 'at a disfavour . . . in the country'.[100] The arrival of a new year did nothing to improve his standing in Ireland. In a letter addressed to Archbishop Wake and dated 12 January 1723, the English-born Bishop of Meath, John Evans, summed up Hutchinson thus:

> He is honest and well affected, but very-narrow-souled, imprudent and almost incapable of brotherly advice . . . In short (my Lord) he shames us

---

[94] Hutchinson's commonplace book, 1721–30 (P.R.O.N.I., MS DIO/1/22/1, p. 52 [2nd pagination]).
[95] The Rathlin catechism, 1721 (P.R.O.N.I., MS D3577/1A, p. 5); Hutchinson's commonplace book, 1731–9 (D.R., p. 118).
[96] William King to Francis Hutchinson, 6 Nov. 1722 (T.C.D., MS 750/7, pp. 236–7).
[97] William King to Francis Hutchinson, 22 Dec. 1722 (T.C.D. MS 750/7, pp. 260–2).
[98] Ibid., pp. 260–2.
[99] James Smythe to William Smythe, 5 Dec. 1729 (National Library of Ireland, Smythe of Barbarvilla Papers, PC 449). I would like to thank Dr Toby Barnard for providing this quotation.
[100] Hutchinson to Cox Macro, 12 Nov. 1722 (B.L., Add. MS 32556, fo. 151).

all. The Lord Lieutenant[101] disowns him ... 'Bishop, what!' says Dublin[102] to the Lord Chief Justice [Sir Richard] Levinge, 'Have you sent us the flower of Derby to be an ornament to Ireland?'[103]

II

Hutchinson's crusade to convert Ireland had its basis in his political-anti-Catholicism. His belief that the Penal Laws had done all they could for the Catholic problem, and that the best way to reform an Irish-speaking country was to evangelise the populace in print in the vernacular, persuaded him to try to convert the Catholic charity-school children of Rathlin to Protestantism using a catechism written in an easy-to-read, phonetic form of Irish. He hoped the success of the Rathlin project would inspire charity schools throughout Ireland to use proselytising material written in his phonetic Irish, thereby setting the seeds for mass conversion of the Catholic population. Institutionally, the scheme can be regarded as a success because a charity school, a church and a parsonage were built on Rathlin. However, he failed to reach his main objective, as no charity school in Ireland ever used his phonetic Irish for proselytising purposes, apart presumably from the one on Rathlin. Given the general level of hostility among the Protestant elite to Hutchinson's phonetic Irish, the failure of the Rathlin project was fairly predictable. It is thus no surprise to find that Hutchinson was unable to find subscribers to fund the publication of a planned set of phonetic common prayers and bibles, as well as the Psalms that McCullom had already translated.[104] Due to a lack of Church records, it is impossible to really know whether the scheme even altered the religious make-up of Rathlin, far less the whole of Ireland. It is interesting to note that the convert rolls for Ireland in the eighteenth century suggest no conversions were made on Rathlin.[105]

Despite the failure of the Rathlin project, Hutchinson remained convinced of the converting power of his new form of presenting the Irish language. The project nonetheless showed him that there was little point in trying to persuade the proprietors of charity schools to proselytise using his new Irish. The publication in 1724 of *An Irish–English Almanack* represented Hutchinson's next attempt at conversion. His new target

---

[101] Charles Fitzroy, 2nd Duke of Grafton.
[102] William King, Archbishop of Dublin.
[103] Quoted in Irvin Ehrenpreis, *Jonathan Swift: the man, his works, and his age* (3 vols., London, 1983), iii, 29.
[104] Hutchinson to Richardson, 22 Apr. 1721 (P.R.O.N.I., MS D3577/3A).
[105] Eileen O'Byrne (ed.), *The convert rolls* (Dublin, 1981).

audience was Catholic adults, whom he aimed to bombard with 'bibles and common prayers, and the offices of religion in their own tongue'.[106] Hutchinson hoped that his *Almanack* would succeed where the Rathlin project had failed and convince Irish lay Protestants of the effectiveness of his new form of Irish, which in its turn would persuade them to use their own money to carry his scheme forward.

In late 1723, Hutchinson told Sir Hans Sloane, his erstwhile philosophical adviser, that he hoped the Irish and English almanac he was preparing would not only 'draw some eyes towards'[107] his phonetic Irish, but would also demonstrate 'how easy it may be learnt'.[108] In turn, he hoped this would help to bring it 'into use by degrees'[109] because, he noted, 'I cannot boast that it finds much encouragement as yet'.[110] The *Almanack* was eventually published in 1724, replete with phonetically spelt Irish, Roman typography and an English translation, printed on the page opposite the Irish text.[111] In the *Almanack*, Hutchinson lost no time in pleading for 'some charitable hand or other' to 'procure more, and other ways of instruction' in his new Irish.[112] He went on to declare, somewhat hyperbolically: 'The ice is broken. The press is open. Every printer in Ireland or Europe may print Irish as well as English. They may write in it letters as all other nations in Europe write theirs'.[113]

To ensure that the *Almanack* did indeed demonstrate the effectiveness of his new method in enabling Irish speakers to read texts written in their mother tongue for the first time, Hutchinson decided to try to tilt the odds in his favour. He did this by designing his almanac to appeal primarily to those 'native Irish, who have had such education that they can read and write English'.[114] As has already been suggested, Hutchinson was convinced that it was easier for a person to learn to read texts written in a foreign language if they were provided with translations. By this rationale, he believed that those Irish speakers who could already read English (but not Irish) would find it easier to learn to read his new phonetic Irish (which of course always came supplied with English translations) than those Irish speakers who could read neither English nor Irish.

---

[106] Hutchinson, *Almanack* (2nd edn), p. v.
[107] Francis Hutchinson to Sir Hans Sloane, 11 Dec. 1723 (B.L., Sloane MS 4047, fo. 110).
[108] Francis Hutchinson to Sir Hans Sloane, 12 Oct. 1723 (B.L., Sloane MS 4047, fos. 67–8).
[109] Francis Hutchinson to Sir Hans Sloane, 11 Dec. 1723 (B.L., Sloane MS 4047, fo. 110).
[110] Francis Hutchinson to Sir Hans Sloane, 12 Oct. 1723 (B.L., Sloane MS 4047, fos. 67–8).
[111] Hutchinson, *Almanack* (2nd edn), pp. 9–30.
[112] Ibid., p. vi.
[113] Ibid.
[114] Ibid., p. iii.

The fact that Hutchinson targeted the *Almanack* at literate Catholics is also reflected in its content. The English translations of Irish text in the *Almanack* are not spelt phonetically, as they had been in the *Catechism*, because the intended reader of the *Almanack*, unlike that of the *Catechism*, did not need to be taught English. The removal of the phonetic English may also have been a deliberate attempt to make the *Almanack* less controversial than its predecessor. Hutchinson chose the format of the almanac because he believed this was the type of publication that literate, rather than learned, Catholics would read. He also expunged from the *Almanack* the kind of vitriolic anti-Catholic rhetoric so willingly espoused in many of his other books and pamphlets. This omission is all the more conspicuous given the fact that almanacs in the Georgian period were often used as platforms for religious and political polemic, especially anti-Catholicism and anti-Jacobitism.[115]

Hutchinson copied the astronomical data given in his *Almanack* from other almanacs. His 'table of the eclipses of the sun and moon for 17 years next ending, from this present year, 1724, till the year 1740' was based 'on the calculations of Mr. Charles Leadbetter, published, 1715'.[116] This was almost certainly Charles Leadbetter, editor of the extremely popular *Partridge's Almanac*. Hutchinson informed the reader that the 'holy-days and state-days of both churches, the beginning and ending of the terms, the rising and setting of the sun, the changes of the moon are in this as in others [almanacs]'.[117] The inclusion of the holy days of the Catholic Church was a further concession he made to attract a Catholic readership.

The toning down of the astrological content was in this period common to both Irish and English almanacs, which tended to place a higher value on amusement and instruction. This was largely due to the fact that astrology by the beginning of the eighteenth century, had all but lost its credibility among all sectors of genteel or polite society in England and Ireland, from the nobility and gentry down to the nascent middling orders, because it was now solidly identified with lower class enthusiasm.[118] Given his view of religious enthusiasm in general, Hutchinson unsurprisingly

---

[115] J. R. R. Adams, *The printed word and the common man, 1700–1900* (Belfast, 1987), pp. 2–74; Bernard Capp, *Astrology and the popular press: English almanacs 1500–1800* (London, 1979), pp. 250–1.

[116] Hutchinson, *Almanack* (2nd edn), un-paginated fold-out table resting between pages 22 and 23.

[117] Ibid., p. iii.

[118] Patrick Curry, *Prophecy and power: astrology in early modern England* (Cambridge, 1989), pp. 7, 11–12, 19–57, 105–12, 155–7; Bridgit A. Fitzpatrick, 'The development of the Irish almanac, 1612–1724' (Master's Thesis, T.C.D., 1990), pp. 46–7.

contended that the judicial astrology in traditional almanacs not only 'ridiculed' the common people but perpetuated their ignorance by filling their heads 'with stories of what the sun, moon and stars say about the quarrels, weddings, and deaths of princes'.[119] He also attacked natural astrology and its 'idle predictions about the weather, and that senseless column in every month, of the sign's being in the head, back or breech'.[120]

Consequently, Hutchinson replaced astrological predictions in his *Almanack* with snippets of useful knowledge, which he believed would help in his quest to effect the 'improvement of common life' of the native Irish.[121] He noted that as well as keeping the native Irish in the manacles of Catholicism, their illiteracy also kept them in a backward condition culturally and educationally because it distanced them from the 'useful learning and other knowledg which other nations have and they only have hithertoo neglected'.[122] They were, in his view, as ignorant of 'knowledge of times past, and arts and sciences' as they were of 'written contrakts, akkounts, bills bonds, wills and all the written affairs of life'.[123] He was thus convinced that if Protestants could 'put a little sense, and intelligence and knowledge of things into their minds' it would 'make them more capable of other improvement and service of their country'.[124] He subsequently included, in the last seven pages of the *Almanack*, 'examples of receipts, and other helps in business',[125] such as 'acquittances, general discharges, promissory notes, last wills and bonds'.[126]

In conjunction with these templates, Hutchinson provided 'such observations about the work or weather of the seasons, as time and wise men have contracted into proverbial speech and rhimes'.[127] Some of these proverbs informed the reader of the right time to perform a particular agricultural task for optimum efficiency: 'make hay while the sun shines'; 'sow wheat in a mud, and it will come up like a wood'; 'while the grass grows, the seed starves'.[128] Others constituted general observations about the movement of the seasons: 'a swarm of bees in July is not worth a butterfly' and 'one swallow makes no summer'.[129]

---

[119] Hutchinson, *Almanack* (2nd edn), p. ii.
[120] Ibid., p. iii.
[121] Ibid., p. v.
[122] Hutchinson, *Church catechism in Irish*, p. 35.
[123] Ibid.
[124] Hutchinson, *Almanack* (2nd edn), p. v.
[125] Ibid., p. ii.
[126] Ibid., sig. A1^V [title page].
[127] Ibid., p. iii.
[128] Ibid., pp. 16, 18, 13.
[129] Ibid., pp. 16, 14.

Although it ran to two editions identical in content,[130] the *Almanack* failed to persuade other authors to publish texts that used phonetic Irish. In fact no other Protestant work was published in Irish in Ireland for the next 66 years.[131] Furthermore, the only time it was mentioned after publication was in a satirical context:

> And since he has spoke, to his praise be it told,
> An *ALMANACK*, since that will never grow old?
> For whilst we doe practice his *PROVERB* so wise,
> His works never fail, and his name never dies . . .
>
> . . . O! Whaley,[132] thy loss we now shou'd lament.
> Hadn't providence this good *ASTROLOGER* sent;
> To converse in the clouds, with the stars sun and moon,
> And to find out their haunts at night morn and noon.[133]

III

What demonstrates a great deal about Hutchinson's character was that after the *Almanack* failed to achieve its objective he remained convinced of the worth of his phonetic Irish.[134] However, its failure did convince him of the need to pursue conversion in another, more localised, less ambitious and less controversial manner. This was to be done by furnishing the ministers of his diocese with a set of guidelines to make 'the entrance into our churches' easier for would-be clerical and lay converts.[135] These guidelines comprised two parts, one for lay converts and one for their clerical counterparts, and were published in Dublin in 1729 as *Advices concerning the manner of receiving popish converts*. Once more, political anti-Catholicism fuelled this conversion scheme. 'Our modern papists', he wrote in 1729, 'tho' they receive protection from their Princes', 'like ill subjects, foresake their side, imbroil their affairs, and always help not only the Pope, but forren Princes'.[136] Even the loyal

---

[130] Francis Hutchinson, *An Irish–English almanack for the year, 1724, being bissextile, or leap-year . . .* (1st edn, Dublin, 1724); see n. 21 above for details of the 2nd edition.
[131] L. M. Cullen, 'Patrons, teachers, and literacy in Irish 1700–1850' in Mary Daly and David Dickson (eds), *The origins of popular literacy in Ireland: language change and educational development 1700–1920* (Dublin, 1990), p. 47.
[132] John Whalley, Dublin astrologer and almanac maker, who died in April 1724.
[133] Anon., *An excellent new ballad*.
[134] In a single sheet at the end of *Advices . . . receiving popish converts*, Hutchinson placed the Apostle's Creed, printed in standard English and phonetic Irish. He did this again five years later in his *Defence of the antient historians . . .* (1734), p. 174.
[135] Hutchinson, *Advices . . . receiving popish converts*, p. 1.
[136] Ibid., p. 6.

address, presented in 1727 to George II by Lord Devlin and leading Catholic aristocrats, in which they declared that the Roman Catholic population of Ireland not only recognised the Hanoverian monarch as their rightful ruler but pledged their full allegiance to him, did little to alter Hutchinson's sense of Catholic threat.[137]

It was common practice in early eighteenth-century Ireland to compel converts to declare the errors of Rome publicly in front of their new clergymen and congregation.[138] Hutchinson felt it necessary to provide his clergy with a new declaration to be made by a convert on the day they joined their new congregation because, he contended, the one currently used 'put harder terms upon converts than are necessary'. Consequently, many would-be Anglican converts turned 'to the Dissenters' because they required 'no such declarations'.[139] In Hutchinson's schema, only clergymen were expected to make any public denouncement of Catholic liturgy or doctrine.[140] Lay converts needed only to declare that they intended to become a sincere and committed part of their new congregation and would do all that they could for the 'welfare and good' of the established Church.[141]

Hutchinson not only believed that it was important to make the conversion ceremony itself more palatable, but that it was also crucial to make the actual daily experience of worshipping in an Anglican Church as un-intimidating for the new convert as possible. This, he maintained, would encourage converts to be more devoted to their new religion and keep them from backsliding into Catholicism. According to Hutchinson, ministers could make converts feel more at home by making slight alterations to the form of public worship they provided in their churches. Betraying his moderate, Latitudinarian bent, Hutchinson argued that this was a discretionary power open to all Anglican ministers and would not place those who exercised it outwith the realms of liturgical or doctrinal orthodoxy.[142]

For example, he argued that although ministers were not to encourage the saying of masses for the dead (which, he alleged, served only to encourage the unscriptural and idolatrous practice of praying souls out of Purgatory), they could comfort the sick or dying (or a relative thereof) with a slightly altered version of collects already provided for in the Anglican liturgy, such as that used for the office of the burial of

---

[137] Fagan, *Divided loyalties*, pp. 62–71.
[138] Marianne Elliott, *The Catholics of Ulster: a history* (London, 2000), p. 171.
[139] Hutchinson, *Advices . . . receiving popish converts*, p. 1.
[140] Ibid., pp. 8–12.
[141] Ibid., pp. 8–9.
[142] Ibid., pp. 17, 20.

the dead.[143] Finally, if converts felt the need to confess, ministers could give them absolution by the laying-on of hands and by uttering a few solemn words similar to those formerly used by their Catholic priests.[144] This practice, he proposed, was 'part of the ministry of reconciliation committed to us by Christ' and had only become objectionable to Protestants when Catholic priests had made it 'necessary to confess all faults' and had convinced their parishioners 'that the forgotten and unconfess'd sins would be unpardoned'.[145]

Hutchinson also wanted to encourage Catholic priests to convert. He believed that many would-be clerical converts were discouraged from joining the established Church because little financial provision was made for them by the Protestant communities where they lived. He thus advised his rectors and vicars to employ clerical converts as curates whenever possible.[146] He himself promised to 'turn every stone to find a reasonable subsistence for such a converted priest' in his own diocese.[147] Financial support was to be coupled with the provision of friendly advice and theological guidance because, he mooted, newly converted priests were 'wonderfully at a loss for officiating and preaching the Gospel in our way'.[148]

Hutchinson may have wanted to make the conversion process easier, but he was careful to note that, if converts wanted to gain 'legal advantage' over the penal legislation by their conversion, they would still have to 'do what the law requires at [the court of] quarter-sessions'.[149] In short, he was reassuring the reader that his new guidelines would not make it easier for insincere converts to escape the rigour of the Penal Laws. In the late 1720s, along with the realisation of Protestants that the Penal Laws had failed to rid the country of Catholicism, came the insight that many converts were in fact occasional conformists who used their new-found positions of power to help further the Catholic cause. This was thought to be especially true of convert lawyers.[150] To ensure this type of clerical convert did not infiltrate the ranks of the established clergy, Hutchinson drew up some guidelines that Anglican ministers could follow to ascertain a priestly convert's sincerity. First of all he advised

---

[143] Ibid., pp. 18–20.
[144] Ibid., p. 21.
[145] Ibid.
[146] Ibid., pp. 13–14.
[147] Ibid., p. 14.
[148] Ibid., pp. 14–15.
[149] Ibid., p. 2.
[150] T. P. Power, 'Converts' in T. P. Power and Kevin Whelan (eds), *Endurance and emergence: Catholics in Ireland in the eighteenth-century* (Dublin, 1990), p. 111.

them to discover the precise reasons why the priest had decided to convert. They were also to inform themselves of what the convert intended to preach in their new living before they were allowed to do so. This was to prevent them from sowing the seed of subversion in their new parishes. Finally, they were to constantly remind the convert of the manifold errors and corruptions of the Catholic faith, such as belief in, and support of, fraudulent and feigned miracles, the withholding of the Scriptures from the people and the active discouragement of free knowledge in natural philosophy. Converted priests, Hutchinson further stated, must also not be allowed to come alone into the Anglican Church, but were to bring some of their old congregation with them.[151]

In England, as in Ireland, Hutchinson saw conversion as a way to politically pacify Catholics. His approach to the practical problem of securing these conversions, however, differed dramatically in the two countries. He maintained that English Catholics, in contrast to their Irish counterparts, could be made to convert by both coercive and persuasive means: by implementing penal legislation and by convincing his target audience of educated Catholic gentry, using theologically complex tracts written in English, that they could convert to the established Church without compromising their existing religious beliefs.[152]

IV

Shortly after the publication of the *Advices . . . receiving popish converts*, Hutchinson's view of the Catholic problem in Ireland began to change. His sense of Catholic threat had dropped considerably and thus, more than ever before, his view of it resembled that of his fellow countrymen. The experience of living in his newly purchased castle and estate in Portglenone in County Antrim during a period of famine and general economic distress had convinced him that only a minority of Irish Catholics were intent on, or capable of, overthrowing Protestant religion and rule in Ireland and that the poverty-stricken majority were to be more pitied than feared. With the main motivation for conversion gone, Hutchinson no longer felt the need to devise and implement conversion schemes and became willing to accept the idea that Ireland would in all probability remain a Catholic country.

Two years after the publication of the *Advices . . . receiving popish converts*, Hutchinson was asked to preach a gunpowder sermon in Christ Church Cathedral in Dublin before an audience of members of the Irish

[151] Hutchinson, *Advices . . . receiving popish converts*, pp. 2–3, 13.
[152] See pp. 75–6 above.

House of Lords.[153] In the late seventeenth and eighteenth centuries, these sermons were preached before both houses of the Irish Parliament on 5 November to commemorate both England's escape from the Gunpowder plot and William III's landing at Torbay in Devon. The well connected preachers of these sermons usually used them to espouse anti-Jacobite and anti-Catholic rhetoric.[154] However, by the 1730s even the deliverers of these sermons had begun to display a more benevolent attitude to the Catholic population. In 1731, Henry Jenney, chaplain to the Irish House of Commons, delivered such a sermon to the Commons at their place of worship in St Andrew's Church, Dublin. In his sermon he called for Christian charity to be extended towards the Catholic poor and a continued blind eye to be turned toward the enforcement of the Penal Laws as long as the Catholic population remained politically docile.[155]

Complementing Jenney's sermon to the Commons, Hutchinson preached to the Lords a thematically similar sermon, in which he claimed to be optimistic that 'the quiet and respite that we have had of late' would continue.[156] This optimism stemmed from his new-found belief that most Catholics were moderate 'papists', ever 'ready to defend the Prince that protects them'.[157] Irish Protestants had rewarded this deferential disposition, he went on, by allowing Catholics to worship according to their own fashion, a situation he suggested might be given legislative legitimacy in the future in repayment for good behaviour.[158] Contrariwise, he mooted that it was now only a minority of bigoted Catholics, who had been 'brought up in the Pope's colleges' and were 'sworn to his obedience',[159] who wanted to repeat 'the inhuman butchery that they made in 1641'.[160] The 1641 uprising and the alleged massacre of Protestants that followed were viewed by eighteenth-century Irish Protestants as a co-ordinated and systematic attempt at Protestant genocide. Sir John Temple's *The Irish rebellion* (1646) played a central role in shaping this perception.[161] Hutchinson not only owned a copy of

[153] *LJ*, iii, 158.
[154] Toby Barnard, 'The uses of 23 October 1641 and Irish Protestant celebration' in *English Historical Review*, cvi (1991), 895–901.
[155] Desmond Bowen, *History and the shaping of Irish Protestantism* (New York, 1995), p. 135.
[156] Hutchinson, *Sermon preached . . . 5 Nov. 1731*, p. 25.
[157] Ibid., p. 27.
[158] Ibid., pp. 27, 25.
[159] Ibid., p. 27.
[160] Ibid., p. 29.
[161] Bartlett, *Fall and rise*, pp. 6–7.

Temple's book, but made extensive notes from it in the early 1720s.[162] Consequently, in Hutchinson's opinion, any modern 'bigoted papists' who were similar in character to those of 1641, were to be shown little mercy: 'they ought to know, that altho' it is against our principles to burn hereticks, it is not against our conscience to hang traitors'.[163]

By 1734, Hutchinson's willingness to attest to the loyalty of the majority of the Catholic population had grown rather than diminished. In the *Defence of the antient historians* (1734), Hutchinson praised Ireland's 'present happy state of peace'[164] and stated that although Irish Catholics were 'froward to one another . . . they are in perfect obedience to their priests and landlords, and will disturb no government'.[165] He even congratulated them on their lack of avarice and greed, being in his view people who had 'the least use and enjoyment of riches . . . of any under the sun, and yet are the best contented without them'.[166] So tolerant was the attitude displayed by the *Defence of the antient historians* that the Bishop of Killala and Achonry, Robert Clayton, took the trouble in 1733 to publish a preface vindicating it.[167] Clayton embraced the Enlightenment values of the Molesworth Circle, of which religious toleration – even of Catholics – featured as one of the most prominent. The Molesworth Circle met regularly in Dublin in the 1720s and comprised such philosophical luminaries as Robert Molesworth, Francis Hutcheson and John Toland. It played a central role in shaping Irish philosophy during the early eighteenth century.[168]

Unsurprisingly, Hutchinson's interest in conversion schemes declined proportionately with his sense of Catholic threat: for him, the underlying rationale for conversion schemes was that they provided a perfect antidote to the Catholic threat. Becoming convinced that this threat was slight, he saw little point in expending time and energy on conversion schemes. It was for this reason that Hutchinson showed little interest

---

[162] Hutchinson's commonplace book, 1731–9 (D.R., p. 524); Various notes in the hand of Bishop Francis Hutchinson, c.1726 (Royal Irish Academy [hereafter R.I.A.], Irish Manuscript Collection, Antrim Box XIV, Lisburn, pp. 108–15).
[163] Hutchinson, *Sermon preached . . . 5 Nov. 1731*, p. 28.
[164] Hutchinson, *Defence of the antient historians*, p. 130.
[165] Ibid., p. 68.
[166] Ibid.
[167] See Robert Clayton, *A letter to the Right Reverend the Lord Bishop of *****, concerning his defence of the antient historians, &c. Which may serve as a postscript to his Lordship's preface* (Dublin, 1733).
[168] David Berman, 'Enlightenment and counter-Enlightenment in philosophy' in *Archiv fur Geschichte der Philosophie*, liv (1982), 150; idem, 'The culmination and causation of Irish philosophy' in ibid., pp. 257–61, 278–9; A. R. Winnet, 'An Irish heretic bishop: Robert Clayton of Clogher' in *Studies in Church History*, ix (1972), 311, 314, 316–18.

in the proselytising efforts of the charter schools system. He did subscribe £40 to the charter schools between 6 February 1733 and 16 July 1734,[169] but once he had made this token gesture of support of to what after all was a church-backed venture, he let his subscription lapse and cut all ties with the charter schools.

So why did Hutchinson's attitude towards Catholics change so radically between 1729 and 1731? Unfortunately, Hutchinson left no indication why he had this change of heart and we are left to draw conclusions about it from what we know of his life and experiences in that period. It is clear that he became acquainted with the devastation wrought to the lives of the people of Ulster, especially the Catholic poor, by the famine of the winter of 1728/9 and the economic distress that followed.[170] The human cost, however, must only have been hammered home to him in 1730 when he left polite, Protestant, civilised town life in Lisburn to live near Portglenone in the Ulster countryside, where living conditions for the poor were harsh: 'many of their houses now, tho' above ground, yet have neither chimneys, windows or doors: their beds, diet, and furniture are as mean as their houses'.[171] The fact that his, probably limited, dealings with such down-trodden people were likely to have been cordial may have helped to increase his benevolent attitude towards them. Early eighteenth-century Ulster Catholics, after all, rarely disturbed the public order and for the most part enjoyed harmonious relationships with their Protestant neighbours and landlords. This helped to make Ulster society relatively stable in the first half of the eighteenth century.[172] In short, at Portglenone, Hutchinson was confronted with a picture of Irish Catholics that conflicted with that painted by the popular and political anti-Catholicism that had so influenced him until that point. However, though he no longer believed that the Catholic population were a political threat, he continued throughout the 1730s to voice the standard Protestant denunciations of certain Catholic religious beliefs and practices; such as the doctrines of purgatory and transubstantiation, the worship of saints and images and not using the vernacular in public worship.[173]

---

[169] Incorporated Society cash book no. 1, 1733–78 (T.C.D., Charter School records, MS 5419).
[170] See pp. 181–3, 189–90 below.
[171] Hutchinson, *Defence of the antient historians*, p. 68.
[172] Elliott, *Catholics of Ulster*, pp. 177–9; W. H. Crawford, 'The influence of the landlord in eighteenth-century Ulster' in L. M. Cullen and T. C. Smout (eds), *Comparative aspects of Scottish and Irish economic history, 1600–1900* (Edinburgh, 1979), pp. 197–8.
[173] Hutchinson, *Sermon preached ... 5 Nov. 1731*, pp. 7–19; idem, *Certainty of Protestants*, p. 9; idem, *Defence of the antient historians*, pp. 110, 129.

V

Hutchinson's first few years in Ireland were a baptism of fire, snubbed by his fellow English and Irish-born bishops, as well as his own clergy, for a lack of sociability, his English blood, a lack of commitment to his spiritual duties and a deep attachment to the religious politics of a Low-Church Whig.[174] Unfortunately for him his first foray into conversion only served to increase this antagonism.

Convinced that conversion would immediately remove the perceived political threat posed by an inherently hostile and disloyal Catholic majority, Hutchinson launched his first scheme to effect this almost immediately after landing on Irish shores. He contended that since the Penal Laws had failed to achieve this end, the only way forward was to use more persuasive methods and proselytise them in Irish. His faith in the converting power of Irish stemmed from his belief that, despite contemporary opinion to the contrary, most Irish Catholics spoke only Irish, so his use of the vernacular emulated the first Protestant reforms as well as fulfilling one of the key tenets of Protestantism; he also believed he had found a solution to the reason why previous conversion schemes had failed: monoglot Irish Catholics were illiterate and thus unable to read the key tenets of the Anglican faith even if written in their own language. Hutchinson reasoned that, if he could enable Irish-speaking Catholic charity-school children to read such material in Irish, he could convert them in large numbers. This, he maintained, could be achieved quickly and easily by a new method of presenting the Irish language which centred around a newly created phonetic form of Irish, first showcased in his *Catechism* of 1722. This conversion scheme fed into his other main concern of the period, improvement. First of all he maintained that phonetic Irish was an improvement on traditional literary Irish. He also designed his *Catechism* to enable its readers to learn to read and speak English, a more linguistically perfect language. Finally, he believed that the conversion of the Catholic population would remove the final barrier to improvement schemes, as Catholicism was inimical to economic development.

Acutely aware that there was little regard, within the country at large but especially among charity school enthusiasts, for proselytising in Irish, he believed that if he could demonstrate the effectiveness of his new Irish in his own charity school other schools would soon start to use it. Hutchinson chose Rathlin Island as the site for a pilot scheme, but unfortunately his phonetic Irish quickly plunged the project into

---

[174] See Chapter 6 above.

controversy. Consequently, his *Catechism* (1722) was the only one of many planned phonetic devotional aids to be published. Even then, Rathlin was the only place where the *Catechism* was ever used.

Undeterred, he began, a year or so later, to advertise his new form of Irish by printing a bilingual almanac. Hutchinson hoped the *Almanack* would persuade Irish Protestants to invest their money in schemes to produce proselytising material, such as bibles and prayer-books, written in his new form of Irish. He then intended to distribute this material among Irish-speaking adults and thereby effect their conversion. The *Almanack*, however, met with almost universal indifference and confirmed him as a figure of ridicule among Dublin wits. Nonetheless, he continued his conversion campaign unabated. In 1729 he published the *Advices . . . receiving popish converts*, the main purpose of which was to furnish his own clergy with a set of guidelines on how lay and clerical converts should be treated by their new Protestant congregation in order to make the conversion process easier and thus a more attractive proposition for Catholics.

By the early 1730s, Hutchinson's sense of a Catholic threat had lowered dramatically and he now believed that political anti-Catholic ideology was applicable only to a small proportion of the Irish Catholic population. The experience of living among Catholics in his estate at Portglenone in County Antrim, between 1729 and 1731, had convinced him of this fact. This new, lower sense of political threat had the effect of draining his conversion schemes of their ideological rationale, and from that time he showed little or no interest in supporting them, far less developing or implementing them. As a result of this change of outlook Hutchinson's view of the Catholic problem had become similar to that held by the majority of his fellow Irish Protestants.

8

'Improve everything that is improveable': the social, economic and cultural improvement of Ireland and the Irish, 1721–39

The various attempts, between the late sixteenth and mid-eighteenth centuries, to convert the largely Irish-speaking, Catholic native population to Protestantism, through charity and charter schools, the employment of Irish-speaking clergy and the publication of key religious texts in Irish have been discussed in the last chapter. Irish Protestants wanted not only to convert Ireland but also to civilise it and its inhabitants. In the seventeenth century, various attempts were made by the Irish Protestant elite to civilise and improve Ireland by bringing its governmental and legal infrastructures into line with those of England and by encouraging the spread of English dress, language, industries and agriculture.[1]

While the Irish Protestant landowning elite, in the late seventeenth and early eighteenth centuries especially, fostered agricultural improvement (by experimenting with agricultural techniques and crops, either on their own demesne farms or by rewarding improving tenants with longer leases), developed the linen industry, especially in Ulster, facilitated urban modernisation (by playing pivotal roles in the planning, establishment and operation of provincial towns), and constructed conspicuous country houses and demesne parks according to the polite

---

[1] T. C. Barnard, 'The Hartlib Circle and the cult and culture of improvement in Ireland' in Mark Greengrass, Michael Leslie and Timothy Raylor (eds), *Samuel Hartlib and universal reformation, studies in intellectual communication* (Cambridge, 1994), pp. 281–97; idem, 'Gardening, diet and "improvement" in later seventeenth-century Ireland' in *Journal of Garden History*, x (1990), 71–85; Patricia Coughlan, 'Natural history and historical nature: the project for a natural history of Ireland' in *Samuel Hartlib*, pp. 298–317.

fashions of the day.² The Church of Ireland clergy distinguished themselves from lay improvers in two main ways: by initiating moral programmes to reform manners and suppress vice, and by disseminating the cult and culture of improvement. This was achieved by contrasting activity with idleness, and civility (in manners, dress, language and housing) with 'barbarism', in their sermons and in making their clerical households models of civility, hospitality and charity.³ Although much work remains to be done on the role of the Dublin Parliament in fostering improvement in the long eighteenth century, public money was channelled into local committees and subsidiary panels, such as the privately financed turnpike trusts set up in various parts of Ireland in the middle decades of the eighteenth century.⁴ Irish Protestants set up and ran improving societies, such as the Dublin Philosophical Society (1683), the Irish Linen Board (1711), the Dublin Society for the Improvement of Husbandry and Other Useful Arts (1731) and the Physico-Historical Society (1744).⁵

The question remains: why did Irish Protestants find the cause of improvement so alluring? Wealth and opportunity are necessary, but not sufficient, as explanatory mechanisms because many of the elite possessed

---

² Lindsay Proudfoot, 'Land ownership and improvement ca. 1700 to 1845' in Lindsay Proudfoot and William Nolan (eds), *Down history and society: interdisciplinary essays on the history of an Irish county* (Dublin, 1997), pp. 212–19, 221–2, 226; Peter Borsay and Lindsay Proudfoot, 'The English and Irish urban experience, 1500–1800: change, convergence, and divergence' in idem (eds), *Provincial towns in early modern England and Ireland: change, convergence, and divergence* (Oxford, 2002), pp. 2, 24; W. H. Crawford, 'The creation and evolution of small towns in Ulster in the seventeenth and eighteenth centuries' in *Provincial towns*, pp. 102–3; idem, 'Economy and society in eighteenth-century Ulster' (PhD thesis, Queen's University, Belfast, 1983), p. 19; idem, 'The influence of the landlord in eighteenth-century Ulster' in L. M. Cullen and T. C. Smout (eds), *Comparative aspects of Scottish and Irish economic history, 1600–1900* (Edinburgh, 1979), pp. 199–200; T. C. Barnard, *The Kingdom of Ireland, 1641–1760* (Basingstoke, 2004), pp. 80–9; idem, 'The cultures of eighteenth-century Irish towns' in *Provincial towns*, pp. 195–6.

³ T. C. Barnard, 'Reforming Irish manners: the religious societies in Dublin during the 1690s' in *Historical Journal*, xxxv, no. 4 (1992), 805–38; idem, 'Improving clergymen', pp. 137, 146.

⁴ Eoin Magennis, 'Coal, corn and canals: Parliament and the dispersal of public moneys, 1695–1772' in D. W. Hayton (ed.), *The Irish Parliament in the eighteenth century: the long apprenticeship* (Edinburgh, 2001) pp. 71–86; Broderick, *The first toll-roads*, pp. 27–83.

⁵ K. T. Hoppen, *The common scientist in the seventeenth century: a study of the Dublin Philosophical Society, 1683–1708* (London, 1970); H. D. Gribbon, 'The Irish Linen Board, 1711–1828' in *Comparative aspects of Scottish and Irish economic and social history*, pp. 77–87; James Livesey, 'The Dublin Society in eighteenth-century Irish political thought' in *Historical Journal*, xlvii, no. 3 (2004), 615–40; Eoin Magennis, 'A land of milk and honey: the Physico-Historical Society and the surveys of mid-eighteenth-century Ireland' in *Proceedings of the Royal Irish Academy*, no. 102c, (2002), 199–217.

both but were largely unconcerned with improvement.[6] The influence of humanist and Christian charitable impulses, a non-political sense of patriotism or the need to see themselves as leaders of taste and style in Ireland can be regarded as central motivators for improvers.[7]

Despite our increased knowledge of Irish improvement and improvers, the historiography of the subject still lacks a solid body of case studies of the activities of individuals. Such studies are essential lest too much homogeneity is afforded to the ways in which, and the reasons why, Protestants tried to reshape Ireland and the Irish in the eighteenth century. Most current studies are dedicated to national figures such as the Archbishop of Dublin, William King, and the economic pamphleteer and future governor of North Carolina, Arthur Dobbs.[8] This chapter seeks to help address this imbalance by presenting a case study of a relatively unknown improver, Francis Hutchinson. The scope and depth of Hutchinson's commitment to improvement is not only exceptional but is illustrative of the fact that enlightened, Latitudinarian-Whig ideology could motivate Irish improvers. He is also one of the few Ulster improvers and the only one where the closely connected goals of conversion and improvement come together in the activities of a particular individual.

I

In a sermon preached in early 1723, Hutchinson exhorted the Protestant elite gathered before him in Christ Church Cathedral, Dublin, to improve the country they governed:

> Let us with as much diligence apply our minds to the more pleasing arts of improving all things improvable in our island. There is learning, language, useful arts, and knowledge; imploying and providing for the poor;

---

[6] Lindsay Proudfoot, *Property ownership and urban village improvement in provincial Ireland* (Edinburgh, 1997), p. 212.
[7] McNally, *Parties, patriots and undertakers*, p. 75; Barnard, *Kingdom of Ireland*, pp. 78–80; idem, *New anatomy*, p. 96; Hayton, 'Limitations of Protestant Ascendancy', pp. 129–31.
[8] Susan Reilly, 'William King and the idea of improvement' in Christopher J. Fauske (ed.), *Archbishop William King and the Anglican Irish context, 1688–1729* (Dublin, 2003), pp. 148–59; Desmond Clarke, *Arthur Dobbs, esquire, 1689–1765: Surveyor-General of Ireland, prospector and governor of North Carolina* (London, 1958); idem, *Thomas Prior, 1681–1751: founder of the Royal Dublin Society* (Dublin, 1951); C. G. Caffentzis, 'Why did Berkeley's bank fail? Money and libertinism in eighteenth-century Ireland' in *Eighteenth-Century Ireland*, xii (1997), 100–15; James Kelly, 'Jonathan Swift and the Irish economy in the 1720s' in *Eighteenth-Century Ireland*, vi (1991), 7–36; Robert Mahoney, 'Protestant dependence and consumption in Swift's Irish writings' in S. J. Connolly (ed.), *Political ideas in eighteenth-century Ireland* (Dublin, 2000), pp. 84–104.

educating youth; carrying on publick works; and in short, mending the state of every thing that can be made better amongst us.⁹

Hutchinson practised what he preached. During the 1720s he published a number of economic tracts that suggested ways in which Ireland could escape its economic backwardness by developing its indigenous resources. The creation of the Dublin Society for improving husbandry, manufactures and other useful arts in June 1731, combined with his purchase of an estate and manor house near Portglenone in County Antrim in October 1729, allowed him to widen his improving repertoire. He became an active member of the Dublin Society and used his newly purchased Ulster estate to disseminate the culture of improvement. He even helped to get a road improvement bill through Parliament.¹⁰

The source of Hutchinson's dedication to the cause of improvement is not to be found in patriotism, nor did it stem from a belief that it was a form of practical piety and as such part of his Christian duty. There is also no evidence to suggest that it was a result of the influence of other Ulster-based projectors, such as Arthur Dobbs.¹¹ Dobbs wrote *An essay on the trade and improvement of Ireland* (published in two volumes in Dublin in 1728 and 1730), built the Newry Canal and was a founding and active member of the Dublin Society. Thomas Coote, of Cootehill in County Cavan, and Samuel Waring of County Down were both avid private promoters of the linen industry and members of the Linen Board created in 1711 to encourage it. In the 1730s at Ballycastle, County Antrim, Hugh Boyd built up a colliery, a salt-works, a tannery, an ironworks, a brewery, a bleach green and a glassworks.¹² Improvement, as an ideology, fitted perfectly with Hutchinson's Latitudinarian-Whig views, which envisaged a stable, commercial, ordered society, guided by a sociable and reasonable national religion.¹³ Hutchinson had supported improvement in England, but as he admitted himself, his own contribution to this programme had been more rhetorical than tangible, stating in the early 1720s that his 'maggotty projecting brain'¹⁴ had been put 'to little purpose' there.¹⁵ Only in Ireland did he receive the spur to action.

He was moved to act by the experience of living in a country almost always in the grip of economic crisis and by his gaining the resources

---

⁹ Hutchinson, *Sermon preached . . . 30 January 1723* (Dublin, 1723), p. 7.
¹⁰ For details of this bill, see p. 139 above.
¹¹ Robert M. Calhoon, 'Dobbs, Arthur (1689–1765)' in *OxDNB*.
¹² Connolly, *Religion, law and power*, p. 57; Barnard, *Kingdom of Ireland*, pp. 85–7.
¹³ See Chapter 4.
¹⁴ Francis Hutchinson to Cox Macro, 12 Nov. 1722 (B.L., Add. MS 32556, fo. 151).
¹⁵ Francis Hutchinson to Sir Hans Sloane, 12 Oct. 1723 (B.L., Sloane MS 4047, fos. 67–8).

and opportunities needed to actualise his projecting potential. The money and time came from his relatively large episcopal income and his light burden of episcopal duties.[16] After all, publishing pamphlets, joining improving societies, and purchasing and beautifying estates all cost considerable amounts of time and money. Implicit in Hutchinson's support of improvement was his acquiescence to the increasingly widespread Protestant belief that, although the native Irish were backward, barbaric and ignorant, they were nonetheless improvable, their backward state being environmentally and historically conditioned rather than the by-product of racial inferiority.[17]

II

James Kelly has argued that the economic pamphlets published during the 1720s helped to broaden 'the focus of Irish economic thinking, hitherto obsessed with the restrictive impact of British mercantilist regulations and stimulated interest in and enthusiasm for schemes that encouraged indigenous development'.[18] Hutchinson's contributions to this larger economic debate formed part of smaller, more specific debates: the debate in 1720–1 over a proposal to furnish Ireland with a national bank and a paper credit; the debate in 1723–4 on how best to deal with Ireland's increasing numbers of poor; and a debate over the depressed state of the Irish economy that arose in the aftermath of the subsistence crisis of 1728–9.

It is impossible to understand the economic debates of the 1720s without first examining the economic backdrop. Sean Connolly suggests that, in the first half of the eighteenth century, 'the dominant characteristics of the Irish economy remained those of underdevelopment: a pattern of trade in which imports of manufactured goods were paid for by the export of a narrow range of basic products, a sparse population, recurrent subsistence crises, and widespread poverty'.[19] This was the general picture but, for most of the population, conditions in the 1720s were far worse. The early eighteenth century was the most famine-prone era in Irish history.

The harvest failures of 1720–1, coupled with rising bread prices, caused the death rate to double. The years 1722, 1723 and 1724 produced better harvests, but tenants struggled to make up for the losses incurred

---

[16] See Chapter 6 above.
[17] D. W. Hayton, 'From barbarian to burlesque: English images of the Irish, c.1660–1750' in *Irish Economic and Social History*, xv (1988), 8–9.
[18] Kelly, 'Swift', p. 7.
[19] Connolly, *Religion, law and power*, p. 41.

during the bad years. Rents were not lowered to aid recovery because many landlords had themselves fallen on hard times, largely as a result of the collapse of the joint-stock enterprise, the South Sea Company, in which they had invested heavily. The good harvests also failed to aid a general economic recovery because the woollen and provisions markets were still depressed. Ireland was also plagued by a shortage of low-denomination coins created by the recent outflow from Ireland of large amounts of silver coin. Population growth, in conjunction with economic stagnation, meant that beggary and vagrancy increased dramatically during the early 1720s. The situation reached its nadir in 1725, when the national debt increased three-fold and the summer proved to be the wettest in living memory. Grain and flax harvests and low demand for beef, butter, tallow and hides made a firm dent in the finances of tenant farmers; bread prices rose once more and by winter, as weather conditions worsened, the situation had become critical.[20]

Another poor harvest in 1726, combined with insufficient imports, caused the prices of oatmeal and wheat to rise to record levels, carrying with them the rate of exchange. In the summer of 1727, Ireland witnessed a further subsistence crisis and this time widespread starvation and the emigration of Ulster Presbyterians were the two primary results. The situation had worsened by the summer of 1728, as a bad harvest, along with a scarcity of low-denomination coin, pushed up wheat, barley and oatmeal prices. To make matters worse, work was also in short supply. By December 1728, the already high bread prices reached record levels and by that time the country had already been in the grip of famine for nearly six months. In December 1728 in response to the situation, the English-born, staunchly Whig Archbishop of Armagh, Hugh Boulter, set up a famine relief fund in the form of a subscription list. In early eighteenth-century Ireland, subscription lists played a major role in poor relief. Boulter himself subscribed £500, whilst other notables gave varying sums of money, including Hutchinson, who donated £100.[21]

Although the fund managed to save some from immediate want (especially in Ulster, one of hardest-hit areas), it did not stop large numbers from dying of starvation. Others emigrated to the American colonies or rioted. Poor relief, along with food transfers from Munster to areas of chronic need like Dublin and Ulster, ensured that Ireland did not

---

[20] James Kelly, 'Harvests and hardship: famine and scarcity in Ireland in the late 1720s' in *Studia Hibernica*, xxvi (1991–2), 65; L. M. Cullen, *An economic history of Ireland since 1660* (2nd edn, London, 1972), pp. 43–9.

[21] Cullen, *Economic history*, p. 49; Kelly, 'Harvests and hardship', pp. 78–9, 82, 86–7, 90; Kelly, 'Swift', p. 28; Printed transcript of a subscription list drawn up by the Archbishop of Armagh, Hugh Boulter, to relieve the poor of Ireland, c.1729 (P.R.O.N.I, T/656/1, p. 187).

suffer a famine in the spring and summer of 1729, and the autumn brought with it a bumper harvest. Nonetheless, the country was still in the grip of economic crisis: trade was almost at a standstill, tenant farmers were still heavily burdened with debts and tithes, landlords still experienced difficulty collecting their rents and the ranks of the poor were still swollen. In Ulster, emigration continued apace.[22]

III

Hutchinson's first involvement with the vagaries of the Irish economy came shortly after he took his seat on the bench of bishops in the Irish House of Lords on 12 September 1721.[23] Just over a month later, on 14 October, the heads of a bill 'for establishing a bank in Ireland', which would have a paper credit, private shareholders and a structure closely modelled on the Bank of England, founded over twenty years earlier, was thrown out of the Irish House of Commons without any attempt to discuss its content.[24] Objections were summarily raised by the bank's supporters and it was resolved that a committee of the whole house would reconvene after two months. Shortly afterwards, on 7 November, the Irish House of Lords passed a resolution stating that a national bank would prove detrimental to Ireland's economic fortunes. Lords Limerick, Ferrard, Strabane and Boyne, along with Ralph Lambert, Bishop of Dromore, and Hutchinson, entered a protest against this resolution on the grounds that the committee of the whole house charged with examining the bill had dismissed it without due consideration. The debate which followed was cut short when the lord lieutenant, the Duke of Grafton, adjourned Parliament for a month. The brief life of the bank project came to an end on 9 December when the House of Commons backed its earlier decision and the House of Lords, on 16 December, passed a further resolution condemning the bank.[25]

The Irish bank pamphlets published during the November recess of 1721 defended and opposed the bank venture using the same 'court' and 'country' rhetoric employed in the Bank of England debate during the 1690s. Opponents contended that land provided the only secure foundation for trade and that an increase in financial power would lead to

---

[22] Kelly, 'Harvests and Hardship', pp. 89–103; idem, 'Swift', p. 28.

[23] *LJ*, ii, 712.

[24] *Journals of the House of Commons for the kingdom of Ireland* [hereafter *CJ*] (4th edn, 21 vols, Dublin, 1796–1802), xiii, 267–8.

[25] *LJ*, ii, 684; Michael Ryder, 'The bank of Ireland, 1721: land, credit and dependency' in *Historical Journal*, xxv (1982), 559–69.

corruption: the vast sums of money earned would allow the 'monied' men to influence elections unduly and consequently remove the trustworthy, landed interest from their position of political hegemony. The South Sea Company proved a potent symbol of the corruption and deception that large companies were capable of. The collapse of its grossly, and perniciously, over-inflated share prices led to the first major crash of the British stock market. Many South Sea investors lost large amounts of money, especially those speculators who had bought shares when the prices were high (between early May and late June 1720, South Sea stock rose from 350 to 1050) in the hope of selling on their stock for a profit. One such person was the Irish peer, Lord Percival, who lost over £10,000. In response, supporters of the bank claimed that the interests of trade and land were identical. Henry Maxwell argued, in his pamphlet *Reasons offer'd for erecting a bank in Ireland; in a letter to Hercules Rowley* (1721), that public credit would be restored by the erection of a national bank, which in its turn would encourage trade and raise the value of land. These developments would work together to enhance the political and social power of landowners. The proponents of the bank may have supported trade and the new finance, but they were also vehement critics of financial abuse and its perpetrators.[26]

Those who opposed the bank also often argued that Catholics, who were banned from investing in land, would invest all their money in financial ventures and would thus win back economic power. They also suggested that, in contrast to wealth invested in land, money which was created by high finance was easily shipped out of the country; this would leave Ireland short of gold and silver, and a financially weak country was a country which was easy prey to a Jacobite invasion force. On the other hand, the bank supporters argued that the English national bank had in the past served to protect the country from the military might of the Pretender, and that the Protestant interest in Ireland could be strengthened by a similar institution.[27]

During the brief life of the bank project, Hutchinson emerged as one of its staunchest supporters. He not only defended the project in the Irish House of Lords but subscribed somewhere between £500 and £2000 to it in October 1721.[28] He also penned *A letter to the gentlemen of the*

---

[26] Ryder, 'Bank of Ireland', pp. 564, 570–81; Sean Moore 'Satiric norms, Swift's financial satires and the Bank of Ireland controversy of 1720-1' in *Eighteenth-Century Ireland*, liv (2002), 26, 29–31, 38–41; Hoppit, *A land of liberty*, p. 335; Patrick Kelly, 'Industry and virtue versus luxury and corruption': Berkeley, Walpole and the South Sea bubble crisis' in *Eighteenth-Century Ireland*, vii (1992), 59, 63–4.
[27] Ryder, 'The Bank of Ireland', p. 574.
[28] F. G. Hall, *History of the Bank of Ireland* (Dublin, 1949), pp. 18–24.

landed interest in Ireland, relating to a bank (1721). The pamphlet was designed to persuade the Protestant elite to reconsider their earlier dismissal of the bank bill when Parliament reconvened the following month. He aimed to do this by illustrating, using tried and tested court rhetoric, the erroneous nature of the country arguments upon which their opposition rested. Hutchinson consequently opened the *Letter ... relating to a bank* by declaring that it was the 'gentlemen of the landed interest, who seem to be the great enemies and opposers to the bank intended'.[29] He went on to deny that a national bank would 'greatly increase the interest and power of the money'd men ... and make them bear a greater sway than the landed'.[30] In his opinion, the economic fortunes of both interests were so intimately related as to be codependent: 'yet I hope there is never a gentleman in Ireland who has so little acquaintance with the world, as not to know, that land and money, or the landed interest, and the money'd interest, are like Hippocrate's twins, and stand and fall together'.[31] Thus, if traders, merchants and financiers prospered, so would the landed interest, because it was to them that the others paid rent and from whom they bought provisions.[32]

Hutchinson's pamphlet also contained an extended discussion of the South Sea Company. He felt that this was necessary because 'its very name, like a gorgon's head, benums people's brains' and takes 'away the use of their reason', leading them into blind opposition of financial schemes.[33] His defence of new financial institutions began with the suggestion that the comparison that the opponents of the bank made between the South Sea fiasco and the bank venture was absurd:

> wherein do a bank and the South-Sea resemble one another? Their names are as different as land and water, and their natures are as far from any likeness. One is the nation's paying its debts, the other is a partnership for lending money, and increasing credit, by strengthening the security, and safety of exchanges.[34]

He was also at pains to point out that joint-stock companies, such as the South Sea Company, were not by definition dangerous or corrupt, but only became so through imprudence or greed. According to Hutchinson, it was the avarice of the directors of the South Sea Company, combined with the actions of 'imprudent people' who had bought their shares 'without

[29] Hutchinson, *Letter ... relating to a bank*, p. 4.
[30] Ibid., p. 10.
[31] Ibid.
[32] Ibid., p. 11.
[33] Ibid., p. 23.
[34] Ibid., pp. 23–4.

money' and 'sold what they had not', which had spoiled the project.[35] Furthermore, he correctly argued, it was those who had invested late in the scheme, and sold their expensive shares cheaply in the panic of 1720–1, who had lost the most money. By contrast, those investors who had weathered this financial storm and had bought their shares early and at a low price saw the value of their stock rise by up to 8 per cent in the two years after the South Sea crisis.[36] This argument was based on personal experience. Hutchinson had bought £560 of South Sea stock early in 1720, before turning half of his stock into annuities a couple of years later, by which time it was worth four times its original value. He sold the rest of his capital in 1725 for £890, after enjoying five years of regular and healthy returns on his original investment. He sold his remaining annuities in 1728 for £842.[37]

Finally, in common with other bank supporters, Hutchinson also argued that a national bank could provide the government with the funds it would need to thwart a Jacobite rebellion, which he stated 'all past histories show' and what reason teaches 'us to expect again, when new occasion offers'.[38] He went on to state that 'if Ireland in 1641, had had a bank . . . with its credit [it] could have lent the government ten thousand pounds', which, in turn, would have 'prevented that popish and inhuman massacre'.[39] Having mentioned the Catholic threat, he called on Irish Protestants to apply themselves 'to the conversion of the natives, and make it a Protestant nation'.[40]

Hutchinson defended the bank project in almost hackneyed court terms, but beneath the rhetoric lay a sincere belief that founding a Bank of Ireland was an essential step in Ireland's economic development. It would provide the Irish landlord class with the capital they so badly needed to 'begin new manufactures . . . make our rivers navigable, drain our bogs . . . and search the bowels of our numerous hills for coals and other minerals'.[41] Finally, paper credit would act as a potent symbol of Ireland's increasing economic sophistication; without it, Ireland could never become equal to other, more developed European nations such as England.[42]

---

[35] Ibid., p. 20.
[36] Ibid., p. 23.
[37] Hutchinson's commonplace book, 1721–30 (P.R.O.N.I., MS DIO/1/22/1, pp. 11–13, 37, 39, 56–7 [2nd pagination]).
[38] Hutchinson, *Letter . . . relating to a bank*, p. 26.
[39] Ibid., p. 28.
[40] Ibid., p. 27.
[41] Ibid., p. 31.
[42] Ibid.

IV

The bank project may have attracted public attention in late 1721, but by the mid-1720s it was the shortage of low-denomination silver coin in the country, along with the proliferation of beggary and vagrancy, that dominated economic discussion. Hutchinson's *A letter to a member of parliament, concerning the imploying and providing for the poor* (1723), Robert, Viscount Molesworth's *Some considerations for promoting the agriculture of Ireland and employing the poor* (1723) and Sir William Fownes' *Methods proposed for regulating the poor, supporting of some and employing others, according to their several capacities* (1725) constituted the most significant contributions to this latter debate.[43]

Utilising a long-established Irish distinction, Hutchinson divided the poor into two categories: those who chose not to work, the undeserving poor, and those who could not work, the deserving poor. The deserving poor were to be cared for in their parish of origin. If parish vestries could not find other means of support for their orphans and foundling children, the churchwardens were to provide for them, using church money.[44] The practice of levying taxes to maintain foundling children had become the norm for Irish parishes by the 1720s.[45] 'Aged widows', and 'decay'd tradesmen', along with those 'over-burden'd with children', were to be placed in English-style workhouses, hospitals and single almshouses, all owned, maintained and run by the parish.[46] Hutchinson gave no indication by what practical means these institutions were to be set up, given the fact that in Ireland, unlike in England, there was no legal requirement for parishes to support their own poor. Hutchinson's plans were unsurprisingly never realised. Until the 1770s Ireland possessed only one house of industry, the Dublin Workhouse. Established in 1703 by an Act of Parliament (2 Anne c.19), the Dublin Workhouse by the 1720s was largely populated with orphans and foundling children.[47] In Hutchinson's schema, the undeserving poor, vagrants, beggars and thieves, were to be denied charity of any kind and whipped. This harsh treatment of the homeless would force young people to find employment and accommodation before entering into marriage. In utterances

---

[43] Kelly, 'Swift', p. 13.

[44] Hutchinson, *Letter . . . for the poor*, p. 12; Joseph O'Carroll, 'Contemporary attitudes towards the homeless poor, 1725–1775' in David Dickson (ed.), *The gorgeous mask: Dublin, 1700–1850* (Dublin, 1987), p. 69.

[45] David Dickson, 'In search of the old Irish Poor Law' in Rosalind Mitchison and Peter Roebuck (eds), *Economy and society in Scotland and Ireland, 1500–1939* (Edinburgh, 1988), pp. 151–2.

[46] Hutchinson, *Letter . . . for the poor*, p. 12.

[47] O'Carroll, 'Homeless poor', pp. 64–6, 70; Dickson, 'Irish Poor Law', pp. 150–1, 154–6.

almost Malthusian in character, he claimed that this would have the cumulative effect of slowing down population growth among the poorer sort.[48]

Those members of the poor both able and willing to work were to be set to work on schemes to develop Irish trade, agriculture and the fisheries, as well as mining and manufacturing.[49] Agriculture was to be improved in a number of ways. Acres of arable land were to be reclaimed by draining bogs, a feat he noted that had been carried out in Lincolnshire and Bedfordshire by cutting new water courses and setting up sluices.[50] Soil quality was to be bettered by introducing into Irish fields the types of crops and fertilisers used by English farmers, such as marls, lime, bog-earth, shells and ashes.[51] The mining industry was to be expanded by allowing projectors to locate and work mines anywhere they wished on condition they split their profits with the appropriate landlord. Trade was to be fostered by guarding against restrictive monopolies and financial fraud. Finally, he called for Irish fishing and manufacturing industries to be developed and nurtured. Unfortunately he neglected to state how this was to be achieved in a practical way.[52]

Although the *Letter . . . for the poor* was dedicated to a member of Parliament, as were the other main pamphlets which made up the poor debate of 1723–5, the bank project had left Hutchinson cynical as to the value of leaving economic development solely in the hands of MPs. Consequently he hoped that the above 'improvements' to agricultural, fishing and manufacturing industries would be implemented by privately financed initiatives set up and run by the Protestant gentry.[53] The gentry were also to be entrusted with fostering trade, either through individual initiative or collectively while serving on grand juries, by searching out and punishing 'pettifoggers', 'proctors', 'monopolizers' and 'forestallers of the markets'.[54] Parliament was not totally precluded from a role in economic development by his tract. Legislation was to be used to solidify projectors' rights in locating and working mines, and to compel landlords to ensure that rivers which traversed their land did not stagnate and turn the surrounding banks into bog or fen land.[55] Hutchinson's faith in the landed gentry had some historical precedent. In the 1650s,

---

[48] Hutchinson, *Letter . . . for the poor*, p. 14.
[49] Ibid., pp. 2–9, 15.
[50] Ibid., p. 5.
[51] Ibid.
[52] Ibid., pp. 6–9.
[53] Ibid., pp. 2–3, 5–9.
[54] Ibid., p. 9.
[55] Ibid., pp. 3–4, 6.

Samuel Hartlib and his circle had aimed to develop Ireland economically by collating, collecting and applying, in a practical manner, useful knowledge.[56]

It is only by contrasting its content and ideological undertones with those of Molesworth's *Some Considerations* and, to a lesser extent Fownes' *Methods*, that the distinctiveness of the *Letter . . . for the poor* becomes apparent. The *Letter . . . for the poor* was not only the first of these tracts to utilise a complex multi-layered approach to the problem of vagrancy, but it also displayed an unusual latitude in its prognosis of what areas of the Irish economy offered the most development potential. Singular in its implicit defence of the Whig administration at Westminster, it also eschewed the political approach to economic problems so favoured by contemporaries, in which responsibility for directing economic change was to be placed in the hands of either statesmen or the legislature; a fact which makes the title of Hutchinson's pamphlet somewhat ironic.[57]

In the period 1721–3, Hutchinson's involvement with improvement went beyond the publication of the bank and poor tracts. As was argued in the previous chapter, his conversion schemes possessed an improving aspect. Firstly, he regarded conversion as a way to remove the final barrier to improvement, Catholicism being seen as inimical to economic development. Secondly, he regarded his phonetic Irish as an improvement on traditional literary Irish, as well as being a conversion tool. Furthermore, both the *Catechism* and the *Almanack* were designed to improve their readers by teaching them not only how to read the native language, Irish, but also how to speak and read what he perceived as a more perfectly formed language, English. Furthermore, the *Almanack* contained useful knowledge, which he believed would enable Irish-speaking Catholics to become more efficient at organising their private business affairs, as well as to instruct them on improved husbandry techniques.[58]

V

After the controversy created by the shortage of coin and the proliferation of the poor, a discursive silence descended upon economic matters during much of 1726 and 1727. The subsistence crisis of

---

[56] Barnard, 'The Hartlib circle', pp. 284–5, 291–2.
[57] For an extended discussion of these pamphlets, see Andrew Sneddon, 'Bishop Francis Hutchinson (1660–1739): a case study in the culture of improvement' in *Irish Historical Studies*, xxxv, no. 139 (May 2007), 300–3; for a discussion of political economy in mid-eighteenth-century Ireland, see Patrick Kelly, 'The politics of political economy in mid-eighteenth-century Ireland' in S. J. Connolly (ed.), *Political ideas in eighteenth-century Ireland* (Dublin, 2000), p. 113.
[58] See Chapter 7.

1728–9, however, prompted economic authors to flood the market with pamphlets.[59] These tracts, along with the dozens of others published in the period 1728–40, have recently been studied in detail by Patrick Kelly. Kelly argues that most of these writers came from merchant or lesser gentry backgrounds, or from the established clergy. Their tracts betrayed a political approach to economic problems and were concerned with forwarding concrete schemes for the exploitation of Ireland's indigenous resources, while working within the confines of existing English, mercantilist restrictions. The main areas on which they wrote were currency, trade and agriculture, and more specifically on employment, poor relief and luxury.[60] One of these contributors was Hutchinson who, in April 1729, published the only pamphlet dedicated to the Irish fisheries, namely *A second letter to a member of Parliament, recommending the improvement of the Irish fishery*. The print run of the *Second letter* was 750 copies, a relatively common amount for an early eighteenth-century first edition printed in Dublin.[61] Although it was published just as Ulster was escaping from famine, it had actually been written when the crisis was at its height. Internal evidence makes this fact readily apparent: starvation, price increases and emigration are all spoken of in the present tense and with a sense of immediacy.[62]

All civilised peoples, Hutchinson argued, from the ancient Athenians to contemporary Venetians, had at one time or another exploited the seas for economic advantage.[63] He was particularly taken with the Dutch nation, which – so Ephraim Chambers's *Cyclopaedia; or, an universal dictionary of arts and sciences* (1728) informed him – employed a thousand fly boats in herring fishing.[64] Hutchinson was not alone in admiring the very successful Dutch fishing industry. Eighteenth-century Scottish fishery development enthusiasts, who were a small but often influential voice in debates on economic development, consistently advocated copying Dutch methods of herring fishing (in deep seas, using large vessels), curing and packing, to develop Scotland's relatively small fishing industry. An improved fishing fleet, they argued, would increase national security, wealth, maritime strength and employment.[65]

[59] Kelly, 'Swift', pp. 23, 31.
[60] Kelly, 'Political economy', pp. 107, 112–13, 108.
[61] Hutchinson's commonplace book, 1721–30 (P.R.O.N.I., MS DIO/1/22/1, p. 23 [1st pagination]); Pollard, *Dublin's trade in books*, pp. 119–20.
[62] Francis Hutchinson, *A second letter to a member of Parliament, recommending the improvement of the Irish fishery* (Dublin, 1729), pp. 6, 21.
[63] Hutchinson, *Second letter*, p. 27.
[64] Ibid., pp. 29–30.
[65] Bob Harris, 'Scotland's herring fisheries and the prosperity of the nation, c.1660–1760', *Scottish Historical Review*, lxxix, no. 27 (2000), 39–43, 60.

Hutchinson was in no doubt that Ireland possessed the natural resources to exploit its seas and inland waterways for economic advantage. He deduced from the fact that England, Scotland and Ireland shared the same temperate climate that the Irish seas were 'as full of fish as the Brittish'.[66] 'Mr Chambers', he stated proudly, 'saith the Irish herring are counted next to the Dutch'.[67] However, in order to harvest this natural bounty, Parliament would have to change the way that the Irish fishing industry operated by enforcing old, and introducing new, legislation. Although of great value to local economies, nationally it was, in the late seventeenth and early eighteenth centuries, underdeveloped, seasonal and uncertain in its returns.[68]

In the period between the publication of his *Letter . . . for the poor* in 1723 and his *Second letter* in 1729, Hutchinson had begun to have new respect for the political approach to solving Ireland's economic problems. This change in attitude was largely the result of the Irish political elite's renewed willingness to address Ireland's economic problems. This had been demonstrated in the 1727–8 session of Parliament, when acts were passed to regulate corn, bread and coal prices, to enhance the workhouse system, to increase the amount of land given over to tillage, to facilitate bridge repair throughout Ireland and to improve the linen industry.[69] The deterioration of the Irish economy, and by consequence the condition of the poor, since the previous session of Parliament, convinced many MPs sitting in the 1727 session of the need for political intervention in order to solve their country's current problems.[70]

In the *Second letter*, Hutchinson urged privy councillors, churchwardens, constables and justices of the peace to work together to enforce certain dormant laws relating to fishing. He first of all wanted to see a law enforced, originally passed in the second year of the reign of Edward VI (1547–53), to dissuade coastal landlords from charging fisherman every time they took to the seas.[71] He also wanted constables and churchwardens, under warrants issued by justices of the peace, to fine fishermen who deliberately caught spawn or fry of fish, or used nets whose mesh was not large enough to ensure only mature fish were trapped. By

---

[66] Hutchinson, *Second letter*, p. 17.
[67] Ibid., p. 27.
[68] T. C. Barnard, 'Fishing in seventeenth-century Kerry: the experience of Sir William Petty' in *Journal of the Kerry Archaeological and Historical Society*, xvi (1989), 14; James Kelly, 'William Burton Conyngham and the north-west fishery of the eighteenth century' in *Journal of the Royal Society of Antiquaries of Ireland*, cxv (1985), 65.
[69] Hutchinson, *Second letter*, pp. 3–4; *CJ*, iii, 570.
[70] Kelly, 'Harvests and hardship', p. 79.
[71] Hutchinson, *Second letter*, p. 22.

enforcing these Elizabethan and Jacobean laws, Hutchinson believed, healthy stocks of sea and freshwater fish could be maintained all year round.[72] In his capacity as a justice of the peace for County Antrim for the period 1730–33, Hutchinson himself persuaded some fishermen from the hamlet of Portglenone to promise on oath that they would 'kill no mother salmon or trout this season . . . till after Christmas day'.[73] County justices were the bottom level of the judiciary, appointed by the Lord Chancellor, usually from the local landed gentry, clergy or professions, and the main agents of law enforcement in rural areas.[74]

Hutchinson called for Parliament to enact new fishing legislation, appointing official fish days (Wednesday, Friday, Saturday), when people would be expected to eat fish for their main meal. This would, he conjectured, increase consumption of and demand for fish.[75] Parliament was also to help keep fish stocks at an optimum level by giving 'encouragement and premiums to those that destroyed the natural enemies or devourers of . . . fish', such as ospreys, otters and seagulls.[76] Financial incentives were also to be given to entrepreneurs willing to set up and run pilchard farms, an industry he claimed had been neglected in Ireland since before the 1641 rebellion.[77]

The subsistence crisis of 1728–9 ensured that the majority of the MPs who took their seats in the 1729–30 session of the Dublin Parliament were as convinced as those of the previous session of the need to take a prominent role in tackling Ireland's economic problems. Deeply influenced by recent economic pamphlets, most of the improving legislation they subsequently passed had been advocated previously in the improving literature: acts were passed that taxed absentee landlords, increased import duty on French wine, introduced measures to increase tillage, provided public money for inland navigation and re-animated a dormant 1716 act to drain and improve bogs and unprofitable land.[78] Despite this increased awareness of their economic role, there remained during the 1720s a significant number of Irish MPs reluctant to allocate public money to economic development programmes as long as the national debt remained sizeable and government expenditure continued to rise.[79]

---

[72] Ibid., pp. 13–15.
[73] Hutchinson's commonplace book, 1731–9 (D.R., p. 131).
[74] Neal Garnham, *The courts, crime and the criminal law in Ireland, 1692–1760* (Dublin, 1996), pp. 32–3.
[75] Hutchinson, *Second letter*, pp. 12–13.
[76] Ibid., pp. 15–16.
[77] Ibid., pp. 20–1.
[78] Kelly, 'Harvests and hardship', pp. 95–100.
[79] Magennis, 'Coal, corn and canals', pp. 71–86.

Unfortunately for Hutchinson, those Irish MPs who were anxious to develop the Irish economy did not share his enthusiasm for the fisheries. The Lords and Commons journals, as well as the English privy council registers, suggest that the development of Irish fishing industry was never discussed during the 1729–30 session of Parliament.[80] This is unsurprising, given the fact that it was generally afforded little attention by the Irish political elite during the first half of the eighteenth century. The bulk of the legislation passed in that period was concerned with the survival and propagation of freshwater salmon, with legislation relating to sea fishing being largely regulatory and restrictive. In the 1737/8 session of Parliament, for example, an act 'for the further improvement and encouragement of the fishery of this kingdom' was passed which prohibited sea fishing from sunset on Saturday nights to sunset on Sunday evenings, in accordance with Sabbath observance (11 Geo II, c.14).[81]

This indifference to the fisheries was not apparent in other parts of the British Isles. Although the years 1707–26 were ones of relative stagnation for the Scottish fishing industry and efforts to promote it, the year 1727 marked an new era of public support, by virtue of the establishment of the Board of Trustees for the improvement of manufacturers and fisheries. In a bid to compete with the Dutch herring fishing industry, the Board channelled most of its resources into providing premiums to fishermen prepared to fit out large vessels for deep-sea fishing. Its measures proved of little practical benefit, as few came forward to take advantages of the premiums.[82]

VI

The early 1730s bore many of the hallmarks of the economy of the late 1720s. Even though harvests had improved and the number of Ulster Presbyterians emigrating to the American colonies had fallen significantly, it was nonetheless a period marked by epidemics, falling population and a deterioration in the living standards of the poor. The 'proto-industrial' economy of Ulster and the grassland economy of the south were still extremely depressed. It was not until the mid-1730s that anything resembling economic growth came to Ulster, far less the

---

[80] Privy Council Registers, 1 June 1729 to 16 June 1732 (T.N.A., PC 2/91); *LJ*, iii, 86–147; *CJ*, iii, 575–652.
[81] Kelly, 'William Burton Coyngham', pp. 64–5.
[82] Harris, 'Scotland's herring fisheries', pp. 47–52.

rest of Ireland.[83] During the course of the 1730s, Hutchinson moved beyond pamphleteering, to embark on a more practical improvement programme, by disseminating a culture of improvement on his newly purchased private estate near Portglenone and by playing a prominent and active role in the newly founded Dublin Society. The Society met initially in Dublin on 25 June 1731, and afterwards every week, to encourage experimentation and to disseminate useful knowledge concerning the newest techniques in agriculture and manufacturing. The Society was regarded by contemporaries as a perfect practical complement to the efforts of Parliament and the Irish gentry to develop Ireland. Within the space of two or three years, the membership grew from 14 to around 300 members, and became one of Ireland's most important improving bodies. In its early years, its ranks were stocked primarily with members of the higher clergy and influential Irish gentry, some of whom, including Arthur Dobbs and William Maple (its secretary and treasurer from its inception until 1762), had already shown their improving mettle in the 1720s as authors of economic tracts.[84]

Hutchinson was yet another member of Dublin Society who had enjoyed an earlier career as an economic pamphleteer. Given the fact that his respect for the Royal Society in England was founded on the fact that it had improved England in tangible ways, it is not surprising that he joined its Irish equivalent almost as soon as it was founded. He was elected a member on 18 November 1731 and thereafter regularly attended its meetings whenever he was in Dublin to attend Parliament, which, in the 1730s, generally began in October and ended in March or April.[85] When in attendance, Hutchinson played a very active role in the daily running of the Society. He regularly chaired sessions, took part in special committees and suggested ways in which the Society could be improved.[86] Hutchinson's commitment to the Society was by no means a universal trait of its membership. In the late 1730s, the Society began experiencing, along with financial difficulties, falling attendance rates.[87] This laxity was not restricted to the Society's rank and file. The Archbishop of Armagh, Hugh Boulter, its vice president from 1731, attended

---

[83] David Dickson, *New foundations, Ireland 1660–1800* (2nd edn, Dublin, 2000), pp. 115–16; Patrick Griffin, *The people with no name: Ireland's Ulster Scots, America's Scots Irish, and the creation of a British Atlantic world, 1689–1767* (Princeton, 2002), p. 97.

[84] *A list of the members of the Dublin Society* (Dublin, 1734), pp. 3–9; Connolly, *Religion, law and power*, p. 57.

[85] Minute book of the Dublin Society, 1733–41, pp. 1–87; ibid., 1731–3, pp. 17–18, 1–80.

[86] Minute book of the Dublin Society, 1733–41, pp. 33, 62, 65; ibid., 1731–3, pp. 31–3, 45–6, 60, 22, 36.

[87] Clarke, *Thomas Prior*, pp. 34–7.

only one meeting (4 December 1731) and one formal dinner (7 December 1731) during his 11 years of membership, while the Rev Dr Samuel Madden only ever attended one meeting (7 February 1740).[88] It is generally accepted that while Madden helped to revive the flagging fortunes of the Dublin Society's after 1739, by suggesting ways in which the Society could raise both funds and its public profile, he was never a made a formal member.[89] The minutes of the Society, however, clearly state that Samuel Madden was 'proposed as a candidate by Mr [Thomas] Prior' on 12 April 1733[90] and 'balloted for and elected' a member on 26 April 1733.[91]

The initial rules of the Society were drawn up in a lengthy meeting held on 18 December 1731. Chief amongst these resolutions was the dictate that each member was to become learned in some aspect of natural history, manufacture, gardening or agriculture. They were to do this either through study or by experiment and were expected to inform the Society of the results of their enquiries in writing. If the Society approved of what they read, they were to publish their findings.[92] Hutchinson was allocated bog reclamation as his principal area of specialisation in a Society meeting of 10 February 1732. A week later he delivered to the Society a paper on the subject.[93] Four years later, in 1736, he presented another paper on bogs, entitled 'Some observations of the draining of bogs'.[94] These papers were eventually published in spring 1738 as the first part of *The state of the case of Lough Neagh and the Bann*.

Hutchinson main interest was in Ulster bogs. He was particularly taken by a bog which he claimed ran from Portglenone to Toome, measured over five miles long and was nurtured by water flowing along subterraneous passages from Lough Neagh.[95] This preoccupation with Ulster (in particular those parts of located closest to Lough Neagh) is reflected in the fact that the *The state of the case of Lough Neagh and the Bann* is dedicated 'to the members of Parliament of the five counties of Armagh, Derry, Down, Antrim and Tyrone' and the 'nobility and gentry, and all good people that are landowners or inhabitants near it'.[96] In it, he

[88] Minute book of the Dublin Society, 1731–3, pp. 23, 24; ibid., 1733–41, pp. 1, 40, 60, 73, 91, 98.
[89] See Terence De Vere White, *The story of the Royal Dublin Society* (Tralee, 1955), p. 23, and Livesey, 'The Dublin Society', p. 617, 10n.
[90] Minute book of the Dublin Society, 1731–3, p. 70.
[91] Ibid., p. 72.
[92] Clarke, *Dobbs*, pp. 28–9.
[93] Minute book of the Dublin Society, 1731–3, pp. 45–7.
[94] Minute book of the Dublin Society, 1733–41, p. 33.
[95] Hutchinson, *The state of the case of Lough Neagh and the Bann* (Dublin, 1738), p. 9.
[96] Ibid., p. 3.

contended that if the water level of Lough Neagh was lowered this would prevent water flowing along these passages and allow the surrounding bog-land to dry out. This would provide local farmers with acres of valuable arable land and could be achieved by creating a fast-flowing water outlet, by widening the River Bann at strategic points and by removing obstructive sand-banks, eel nets and dams.[97] It was for this reason Hutchinson had his own 'eyle wires in the Bann' removed in 1731, even although he had just rented them for a year for the not inconsiderable sum of four pounds.[98] The reclamation of good arable land from bogs, along with the introduction of soil improvement techniques, was a particularly worthwhile endeavour in eighteenth century Ulster, as much of the land there was of poor quality.[99]

Hutchinson's expertise on methods of bog reclamation had been built up over a number of years. In the early 1720s, he took careful notes from *Ireland's Natural History* (1652) on the types of bogs found in Ireland and how each type was best drained.[100] *Ireland's Natural History* comprised a survey of Ireland's natural resources, was compiled by the Dutch brothers Gerard and Arnold Boate and published under the auspices of Samuel Hartlib.[101] Hutchinson put this knowledge to the test in September 1725 by conducting experiments with various bog draining techniques on his property in the townland of Drumaghlis, which lay in the parish of Kilmore, Co. Down. Hutchinson bought a three storey house there in late 1723, along with an immediate demesne of 460 acres, for £1400. He paid tax for thirteen hearths for the house and, during the period 1737 to 1738, rented land out to at least eight tenants.[102] Furthermore, in 1737, he noted in his commonplace book that he had just paid some 'expenses ... towards draining the bog in Galway's Farm'.[103] James Galway rented land from Hutchinson in the townland of Ballnashee, in the parish of Rashee, Co. Antrim during the mid to late 1730s.[104]

Hutchinson's second area of expertise was the fisheries, and when an unknown hand passed some observations to the Society concerning

---

[97] Ibid., pp. 3–12.
[98] Hutchinson's commonplace book, 1731–9 (D.R., p. 159).
[99] Peter Roebuck, 'Landlord indebtedness in Ulster in the seventeenth and eighteenth centuries' in J. M. Goldstrom and L. A. Clarkson (eds), *Irish population, economy and society: essays in honour of K. H. Connell* (Oxford, 1981), p. 150.
[100] Hutchinson notes, c.1726 (R.I.A., Dublin, Antrim Box 14, Lisburn, pp. 116–18).
[101] Barnard, 'The Hartlib Circle', pp. 296–7.
[102] Hutchinson's commonplace book, 1731–9 (D.R., pp. 136–7, 401, 403); idem, 1721–30 (P.R.O.N.I., MS DIO/1/22/1, pp. 57, 216 [2nd pagination]).
[103] Hutchinson's commonplace book, 1731–9 (D.R., p. 9).
[104] Ibid., p. 25.

new methods of curing fish in October 1733 he was asked to judge whether or not they were worthy of further consideration. His conclusions on the matter were unfortunately never recorded.[105] However, in 1738 he presented to the society 'a new treatise on the fishery's'.[106] This paper appeared in print a month or so later as the second part of the *State of the case of Lough Neagh and the Bann*. Although advertised as a new treatise, the *State of the case of Lough Neagh and the Bann* was almost identical in content to the *Second letter*.[107] It did, however, contain three new suggestions with regards to the development of the fisheries. First of all, it suggested Parliament make it illegal to fish in rivers, seas and loughs from mid-April to early July every year, in order to give fish spawn and fry a chance to reach maturity. Secondly, it called upon the country's fishermen to devote more time and effort to pearl fishing.[108] Finally, in an apppendix, Hutchinson implored the then lord lieutenant, William Cavendish, 3rd duke of Devonshire, to 'incorporate a company of fishermen, and open a voluntary subscription for building a house and a mid-rate ship', both of which were to be 'the property of that company, and [to] be used either in fishing or exploring the sea'.[109]

Hutchinson also made his own household on his estate in Co. Antrim, near Portglenone, epitomise hospitality, civility and charity. He filled his new mansion house with fine furniture, draped the beds with expensive linen, stocked his large kitchen with every kind of utensil, and had it painted regularly.[110] By the early 1730s, his library contained over 700 titles dedicated to divinity, law, history, witchcraft and magic.[111] Hutchinson also catered for the more Epicurean appetites of his guests, and during 1730 he spent nearly £1000 on food and drink.[112] His household also epitomised Christian charity. In addition to individual hand-outs to the poor of Ulster, he regularly donated money to the Dublin workhouse and foundling hospital during the 1730s.[113] Hutchinson was also one of the first subscribers to the charter school system, but as this

[105] Minute book of the Dublin Society, 1731–3, p. 79.
[106] Ibid., p. 65.
[107] Hutchinson, *State of the case of Lough Neagh and the Bann*, pp. 16–19, 23.
[108] Ibid., pp. 20–3.
[109] Ibid., p. 24.
[110] Hutchinson's commonplace book, 1731–9 (D.R., pp. 13, 96).
[111] *A catalogue of books: being in the library of the right Rev. Dr Francis Hutchinson, late Bishop of Down and Connor*; Wheeler, 'Bishop Francis Hutchinson: his Irish publications and his library', p. 147.
[112] L. A. Clarkson, 'Hospitality, housekeeping and high living in Ireland in eighteenth-century England' in C. Lennon and J. R. Hill (eds), *Luxury and austerity* (Dublin, 1999), p. 88.
[113] Hutchinson's commonplace book, 1731–9 (D.R., pp. 129, 424).

patronage was the product of professional obligation it cannot be seen as further evidence of his charitableness.[114]

Hutchinson also beautified the grounds of his estate, by building a cluster of outhouses (which were finally completed in 1737 at a total cost of £222) and by filling his orchards with special varieties of trees purchased in Dublin.[115] He noted with dismay in the 1730s that before he bought the estate there was no sign that 'any one spade . . . had been used in the way of good husbandry'.[116] Consequently, on his demesne farms, he introduced new varieties of potato, beans, and cabbages, and improved soil quality through the introduction of minerals such as lime.[117] From July 1729 onwards, after the fashion of the day, Hutchinson left the day to day running of his estate to his agent. This agent was none other than his younger brother, Samuel, an occupation for which he was given an annual salary, paid in quarterly instalments.[118] By the 1730s, it was normal for Irish landowners to employ the services of an agent to manage their estates for them. An agent's principal duties were to collect or sue for rent money and debts, appoint bailiffs (a minor estate official), sign documents, issue receipts and pay surplus monies to the landlord. Agents in this period were usually afforded the status of the lesser gentry and were quite often the landlords' younger siblings.[119] Samuel was probably able to carry out the duties of an agent to a high degree of competency, having worked on, and managed, several lands for his father in Derbyshire in the 1690s.[120]

VII

The three pamphlets Hutchinson wrote in the 1720s helped redirect Irish economic discourse away from the restrictive impact of British mercantilist regulations towards one that suggested ways in which Ireland could exploit her indigenous resources and develop her economy. Unlike those of contemporaries, Hutchinson's pamphlets were devoid of 'patriot' or anti-English sentiments and demonstrated a particularly wide view of

---

[114] See pp. 173–4 above.
[115] Hutchinson's commonplace book, 1731–9 (D.R., pp. 403, 418–19).
[116] Ibid., p. 13.
[117] Hutchinson's commonplace book, 1731–9 (D.R., pp. 401, 403).
[118] Hutchinson's commonplace book, 1721–30 (P.R.O.N.I., MS DIO/1/22/1, pp. 11, 20 [1st pagination], p. 121 [2nd pagination]); Hutchinson's commonplace book, 1731–9 (D.R., pp. 400–27).
[119] Rosemary Anne Richey, 'Landed society in mid-eighteenth century County Down' (PhD thesis, Queen's University, Belfast, 2000), pp. 66–8.
[120] See p. 10 above.

what areas of the Irish economy were ripe for development. He was not only a particularly strong advocate of the development of Irish agriculture and fisheries, but also called for Ireland to increase the size and output of her mining and manufacturing industries. He also employed a multi – layered approach to dealing with vagrancy and poverty, and was among the sizeable minority for whom a national bank and a paper credit was an attractive proposition, being convinced that it would provide the capital needed for landowners to initiate industrial and agricultural improvement programmes throughout Ireland. It was in the hands of such private improvers that Hutchinson initially laid the responsibility of stimulating Ireland's economic recovery, only becoming convinced of the worth of the political approach to economic problems in the late 1720s, after the Irish Parliament passed a number of improving bills. He even helped to get one of these bills through Parliament and was not adverse, in the early 1720s, to attaching an improving element to his conversion campaigns.

Hutchinson's purchase of his Ulster estate at Portglenone in 1729, along with the advent of the Dublin Society in 1731, allowed him to expand his improving activities beyond the production of economic pamphlet literature. In contrast to many clerical members of the Society, Hutchinson's membership proved to be an unusually active one in which he regularly attended and chaired sessions and conducted research on its behalf. Furthermore, he ensured his clerical household epitomised charity, civility, and hospitality, by introducing new varieties of crops and trees on to his estate and by filling his manor house with books and fine furnishings.

Hutchinson's attachment to improvement lay in the fact that, as an ideology, it fitted perfectly with his wider, enlightened, Latitudinarian – Whig, world view, an outlook becoming increasingly widespread in English elite culture after the Glorious Revolution. Ireland, a severely under-developed country, regularly caught in the grip of economic crisis, provided Hutchinson with the opportunity and resources to demonstrate his support of improvement in a practical way for the first time. The fact that it complemented his other main concern of the period, the political pacification of Irish Catholics by means of mass conversion, only served to increase this support.

Conclusion

Between 1683 and 1739, Hutchinson had three main concerns in life: to protect the privileged position of the established Church in society; to help the Whig and Hanoverian regime achieve, and after 1714 maintain, their political hegemony; and to bring about the social, cultural and economic improvement of Ireland. Ideals and institutions he defended in ways characteristic of a moderate, principled, career-minded, Latitudinarian-Whig.

I

In the parliamentary elections of the 'rage of party', Hutchinson consistently voted for Whig candidates, and used his Suffolk pulpit to support the party stance on the great issues of the day, such as the 1707 Union with Scotland and the need for prolonging the War of the Spanish Succession. Once the Whigs gained political ascendancy, after the accession of George I in 1714, Hutchinson became an apologist for a Whig regime intent on turning their political ascendancy into political hegemony by building a solid basis of public support: he not only espoused the new Whig ideology of order, in various pamphlets and sermons, but produced two prominent anti-Jacobite and anti-Catholic books. He defended the Whiggish social and cultural ideology of politeness, and its vision of an improved, stable, ordered and hierchicial society, a social order mirrored for him in the Newtonian view of the universe. He did this in two main ways: by lauding a sociable form of religion, namely Anglicanism, of which he considered belief in God's providence and the existence of good and evil spirits to be vital parts; and by decrying those forms of belief regarded by his contemporaries as enthusiastic or unsociable, namely astrology, modern miracles, prophecy and those parts of angel belief considered heterodox.

Hutchinson attacked witchcraft for the very same reason: he regarded it as a dangerous, unsociable and enthusiastic belief system, a disposition hardened by first-hand experience of witchcraft trials and the effects they had on small communities. Although the methodology he employed in the *Historical essay* was similar to that used by other English sceptics, the structure of the book was shaped by his attempt to influence two sectors of English society, the literate lower orders and the judiciary. Hutchinson argued that the prosecution rate for witchcraft would remain low if the judiciary continued to regard the accusations and evidence of witchcraft brought before them with caution and scepticism. He was also convinced that the power to prevent witchcraft trials occurring in the first place lay with the lower orders, for it was they who made the bulk of witchcraft accusations. He consequently designed the *Historical essay* so as to appeal to this target audience and convince them of the erroneous nature of their witchcraft beliefs. Although the book ultimately created glory for its author, it proved a controversial work upon its publication in 1718.

For such a defender of the Whig order of things, it was not unusual to find that Hutchinson's brand of churchmanship was that of a Low-Church Latitudinarian. This outlook manifested itself in his theology, his sermon style, his support of the Toleration Act of 1689, and his advocacy of bringing Protestant Dissenters back into the Anglican fold both by comprehension and by persuasive means using voluntary societies and missionising. He also wanted religion placed on a reasonable basis as much as he could without straying outwith the realms of Anglican theological orthodoxy. Hutchinson's Latitudinarianism also underlay his decision to fight on the Low-Church side (while representing the archdeaconry of Suffolk and Sudbury as a diocesan proctor) in the 'party'-fuelled 1701–2 session of the Convocation of Canterbury. He unsuccessfully tried to reprise this latter role at two further sessions of Convocation, those of 1705 and 1710. He was beaten on both occasions in the proctorial elections by a local High-Church Tory, Henry Hasted.

In common with many post-Revolution Church of England clergymen, beneath Hutchinson's partisanship was a deep commitment to serving the needs of the Church. This is demonstrated by the pastoral improvement programme he initiated and sustained in his parish of St James' in Bury St Edmunds in the late seventeenth and early eighteenth century. Like most Anglican clergymen, Hutchinson was convinced that pastoral reform would enable the parish clergy to draw Protestant Dissenters back into the Anglican fold, which in turn would help to raise the status and authority of the established Church in society.

Hutchinson's pastoral improvement programme took two forms. Firstly, he maintained a high standard of public worship by conducting regular services and Holy Communions, and by providing frequent, high-quality sermons. Secondly, he employed a number of educational strategies designed to inculcate his parishioners with an understanding of their Anglican faith. He not only set up and ran three charity schools but tried, on various occasions, to catechise the adult poor of his parish. He also distributed religious pamphlets among the local Quaker population and kept his parochial library well stocked. These activities he carried out in conjunction with the S.P.C.K, as the corresponding member of that society for the county of Suffolk.

Hutchinson's Low-Church Whig credentials, in conjunction with the patronage of certain Whig grandees and a smattering of self-recommendation, ensured that he rose swiftly up the clerical ladder after the Hanoverian accession in 1714: he was made chaplain in ordinary to George I in 1715 and created Bishop of Down and Connor in January 1721. Hutchinson's first few years in Ireland proved troublesome. He was disliked by the largely Irish-born lower and higher clergy for his ethnicity, his Latitudinarian-Whig religious politics (especially his lack of concern with the large numbers of Presbyterians in his diocese) and his surprisingly lax attitude to the spiritual needs of his diocese. He was also universally disliked by an Irish episcopate normally polarised on English–Irish lines. English-born bishops, such as Bishop John Evans of Meath, were disturbed by his lack of social grace and his reluctance to socialise with them. The controversy created by his efforts to proselytise the Catholic population using the Irish tongue did little to change these opinions.

On a surface level, then, Hutchinson seemed to fulfil the prophecies of this 'Irish interest' during his first decade in Ireland by displaying less concern with clerical reform and the dispatch of his relatively light diocesan duties, and more with attending the House of Lords as a spiritual peer. In reality, however, Hutchinson was equally concerned with maintaining the welfare of the Church of Ireland as he was with serving the Whig and Hanoverian regime, being convinced that both could be best served by devising ways to remove that which threatened their very existence, the mass of the population's adherence to Roman Catholicism.

Hutchinson came to Ireland convinced that the Catholic majority there were on the brink of overthrowing both Protestant religion and rule. Political anti-Catholic ideology had convinced him that all Catholics were disloyal to their Protestant monarchs and intent on placing James III, the Old Pretender, on the throne. Hutchinson argued that the only way to neutralise this threat was to convert the Irish Catholic population to Protestantism. He believed that the only way to effect mass conversion was to proselytise the natives using the medium of the Irish tongue.

The reason why past attempts to do this had failed, he claimed, was because the vast majority of Irish Catholics could not read their own language. In order to overcome this obstacle he devised a new form of Irish designed to enable monoglot Catholics to read Irish, and then English, both quickly and easily. In order to make this practicable, Hutchinson concentrated his efforts on those Irish children already attending charity schools. Hutchinson was well aware that there was little enthusiasm among the Irish Protestant elite for printing in Irish. Therefore, in order to encourage charity schools throughout Ireland to proselytise their pupils using his new 'phonetic' form of Irish, he set up a pilot scheme on Rathlin Island.

His scheme was condemned by Catholics and Protestants alike, and his *Catechism* was only ever used on Rathlin. A few years later, he tried once again to advertise his new form of Irish by printing a bilingual almanac. Unfortunately for Hutchinson, the almanac was met by almost universal indifference on its publication in 1724. Even though he was still convinced of the converting power of his new Irish, this failure persuaded him to pursue conversion in a less controversial and ambitious manner. In 1729, he published *Advices . . . receiving popish converts*, the main purpose of which was to furnish his own clergy with a set of guidelines on how Catholics could be encouraged to join the Established Church, by making the process of transferring from one denomination to the other as easy and unsettling as possible.

The experience of living in his newly purchased castle on his estate at Portglenone in County Antrim during a period of famine and general economic distress (1729 to 1731) taught him that only a minority of Irish Catholics were intent on, or capable of, overthrowing Protestant religion and rule in Ireland. The poverty-stricken majority were to be more pitied than feared. Once the sense of Catholic threat retreated in Hutchinson's mind, he became less concerned with devising and implementing conversion schemes and instead set about defending the Whig/Hanoverian regime and the established Church in much the same way as he had done in England a decade earlier: through the exercise of his pen and increased effort in the dispatch of his spiritual duties.

During the 1720s, Hutchinson published a number of influential pamphlets suggesting ways in which Ireland could escape its economic backwardness by developing its indigenous resources. For the most part, these were written in response to specific economic events, such as the attempt in 1721 to launch a national bank and a paper credit, and the severe economic crises of 1720–3 and 1727–9. In the 1730s, he widened his 'improving' activities beyond the production of pamphlets, to expounding the culture of improvement and becoming involved with improving societies. He was able to widen his improving repertoire as a result of his purchase of an estate at Portglenone in 1729 and the creation of the Dublin Society for the improvement of husbandry and other useful arts in 1731. In addition to being one of the very first members of the Dublin Society, Hutchinson also played a very active role in the daily business of running the society. He was its first expert on the Irish fishing industry and the proper methods of draining bog-land.

Finally, in common with many of his contemporary clerical brethren, Hutchinson regularly expounded the culture of improvement by making his clerical household, first in Lisburn and then in Portglenone, a model of civility, hospitality and charity, and by implementing a sustained programme of agricultural and estate improvement. It has been suggested that wealth, opportunity, religious impulse and a non-political sense of patriotism fuelled zeal for improvement among the Irish Protestant clergy and laity. New-found wealth and resources, and the fact that he now lived in a country so obviously in need of economic regeneration, provide necessary rather than sufficient explanations for Hutchinson's unusual zeal for improvement. On the other hand, his particular brand of Whiggery and Churchmanship, along with his interest in matters 'scientific', supplies an entirely sufficient explanation. That combination provided the mental context in which ideas of improvement found a natural home.

II

As well as providing a rare and much-needed portrait of an early eighteenth-Irish bishop and witchcraft theorist, it is hoped this book has helped to shed at least some light on important areas of eighteenth-century historiography. Chapters 4 and 5, for example, illustrate how one of the main sceptical witchcraft texts was constructed and what its relationship to the wider intellectual and literary context of the time was. It has also been argued that the *Historical essay* proved controversial upon publication in 1718. This in its turn suggests that witchcraft was not as dead an issue among the educated of England as once thought. The fact that Hutchinson's scepticism was hardened by first-hand experience of witchcraft trials makes it even harder to justify the recent historiographical trend of studying belief and trials as two separate, even unrelated, phenomena.

Hutchinson was an unusually active cleric and the detailed study of his clerical career in Chapter 2 yields a rare insight into how the national directives of the Church of England at the centre were implemented in the localities by reforming clergy. This research takes on new force when one takes into the account the locale for this study, Suffolk. This is a county that has been largely neglected by recent Church historians. Chapter 2 also pries into another area of ecclesiastical history that warrants further research, the party-fuelled clashes between 'high' and 'low' clergymen in the early eighteenth-century sessions of the Convocation of Canterbury.

The examination of Hutchinson's later clerical career conducted in Chapter 6 deepens what is known about how, and in what circumstances, members of the English clergy were promoted to Irish sees and what they did once they took up residence in them, in terms of performance of spiritual and temporal duties. This is particularly worthwhile considering the fact that the Church records enabling this to be done systematically are no longer extant. Furthermore, the unflattering portrait painted in this chapter of the relationships between English-born, Whig bishops and their Irish-born, Tory clergy adds weight to Patrick McNally's contention that the Irish Episcopate was polarised across English–Irish lines in the early eighteenth century.[1]

Although T. C. Barnard has highlighted the role of clergymen in bringing about the improvement of Ireland and the Irish, there has been little research done on individual improvers. This oversight has tended to lend their methods and motivations for improvement more homogeneity than they possessed in actuality, a tendency that has been offset slightly by an examination of Hutchinson's 'improving' activities, the range and variety of which were unusual by contemporary standards. Furthermore, by examining Hutchinson's motivations for becoming involved in improvement we delve into the ideological reasons as to why only some of the Irish Protestant clergy and laity became active improvers. Furthermore, recent research has suggested that the last serious attempt to convert the native Irish population using the Irish language occurred during the first years of the reign of George I. In actuality, Hutchinson sustained a campaign to convert the Irish Catholic population in this manner throughout the early 1720s, albeit with little encouragement or success.

Perhaps more than anything else, this study of Hutchinson has helped to warn of the dangers of defining an historical figure by one aspect of their life or literary output, especially when that writer was involved in an area, such as witchcraft, that our culture regards as particularly interesting or thought-provoking.

---

[1] See McNally, 'Irish and English interests'.

Select bibliography

Printed primary sources

Ady, Thomas, *Candle in the dark, or a treatise concerning the nature of witches and witchcraft*... (1665)

Andre, Francois de Saint, *Mr. de St André... lesenwürdige briefe an einige seiner freunde uber die materie von der Saubery... gedruckt zu Paris 1725 ... statt eines suplements zum Hutchinson aus dem Frantzosischen ins Teutsche übersetzt... von Theodoro Arnold* (Leipzig, 1727)

Anon., *An excellent new ballad* (Dublin, 1725/6)

Boulton, Richard, *A compleat history of magick, sorcery, and witchcraft* (2 vols, London, 1715, 1716)

Clayton, Robert, *A letter to the Right Reverend the Lord Bishop of *******, concerning his defence of the ancient historians, &c. Which may serve as a postscript to his lordship's preface* (Dublin, 1733)

Cotta, John, *The triall of witch-craft, shewing the true and right methode of the discovery: with a confutation of erroneous wayes*... (London, 1624)

Daubichon, J., *A French grammar: or, a new and easy method for to learn to speak French in a short time* (Dublin, 1721)

Ecton, John, *Valor benficiorum, or a valuation of all ecclesiastical preferments in England and Wales to which is added, a collection of choice presidents, relating to ecclesiastical affairs* (London, 1695)

—— *Liber valorum and decimarum; being an account of the valuations and yearly tenths of all such ecclesiastical benefices in England and Wales, as now stand chargeable with the payment of first-fruits and tenths*... (London, 1711)

—— *Liber valuorum and decimarum Thesaurus rerum ecclesiasticarum: being an account of the valuations of all the ecclesiastical benefices... in England and Wales, as they now stand chargeable with, or lately were discharged from the payment of first-fruits and tenths* (London, 1742)

Filmer, Sir Robert, *An advertisement to the jury-men of England, touching witches. Together with a difference between an English and Hebrew witch* (London, 1653)

Fownes, Sir William, *Methods proposed for regulating the poor, supporting of some and employing others, according to their several capacities* (Dublin, 1725)

Gaule, John, *Select cases of conscience touching witches and witchcrafts* . . . (London, 1646)

Glanville, Joseph, *A blow at modern sadducism in some philosophical considerations about witchcraft. To which is added, the relation of the fam'd disburbance by the drummer in the house of Mr John Mompesson: with some reflections on drollery and atheisme* (London, 1668)

Hopkins, Matthew, *The discovery of witches: in answer to severall queries, lately delivered to the judges of assize for the county of Norfolk . . . by Matthew Hopkins, witch-finder* . . . (London, 1647)

Hutchinson, Francis, *A sermon preached at Beccles in Suffolk before the Right Reverend Father in God, John, Lord Bishop of Norwich, at the second session of his Lordship's primary visitation held there, May 27. 1692. By Francis Hutchinson, M.A. vicar of Hoxne. Imprimatur, Aug. 3. 1692* (London, 1692)

—— *A sermon preached at the publick commencement at Cambridge. Sunday in the afternoon July iij 1698. By Francis Hutchinson, D.D. preacher at St. James's in Bury St. Edmunds* (Cambridge, 1698)

—— *A sermon preach'd at the assize at Bury St Edmunds in Suffolk, March the 25th, 1707* . . . (London, 1707)

—— *A sermon preached at St Edmund's-Bury, on the first of May, 1707. Being the day of thanksgiving for the union of England and Scotland* . . . (London, 1707)

—— *A short view of the pretended spirit of prophecy, taken from its first rise in the year 1688: to its present state among us* . . . (London, 1708; repr. Edinburgh, 1709)

—— *A defence of the clergy's liberty, in the choice of their proctors for convocation: . . . In a letter to the reverend the clergy of the Archdeaconry of Sudbury* (London, 1710)

—— *A compassionate address to those papists, who will be prevail'd with to examine the cause for which they suffer. In five letters* . . . (London, 1716)

—— *The life of the Most Reverend Father in God John Tillotson . . . Compiled from the minutes of the Reverend Mr. Young . . . with many curious memoirs communicated by the late Right Reverend Gilbert, Lord Bishop of Sarum* (London, 1717)

—— *An historical essay concerning witchcraft with observations upon matters of fact; tending to clear the texts of the sacred scriptures, and confute the vulgar errors about that point. And also two sermons: one in proof of the Christian religion; the other concerning good and evil angels* (1st edn, London, 1718)

—— *A defence of the Compassionate address to papists. Being an answer to the Queries of a papist, relating to that address. In a sixth letter* . . . (London, 1718)

—— *An historical essay concerning witchcraft with observations upon matters of fact; tending to clear the texts of the sacred scriptures, and confute the vulgar errors about that point. And also two sermons: one in proof of the Christian religion; the other concerning good and evil angels. The second edition, with considerable alterations* (2nd edn, London, 1720)

—— *A sermon preach'd by the Right Reverend Father in God, Francis, Lord Bishop of Down and Connor, at his primary visitation, held at Lisburn, May 3rd, 1721, and published by at the unanimous request of his clergy* (Dublin, 1721)

—— *A sermon preached in Christ's-Church, Dublin, on the first of August, 1721. Being the anniversary of his Majesty's happy accession to the throne* (Dublin, 1721)

—— *A letter to the gentlemen of the landed interest in Ireland, relating to a bank* (Dublin, 1721)

—— *The state of the case of Raghlin* (Dublin, 1721)

—— *The church catechism in Irish, with the English placed over against it in the same karakter. Together with prayers for sick persons, and some texts of scripture, and a vocabulary explaining the Irish words that are used in them* (Belfast, 1722)

—— *A sermon preached in Christ-church Dublin, on Thursday the 30th day of January, 1723. Being the anniversary fast for the martyrdom of King Charles the First, before . . . Charles Duke of Grafton . . . And the Lords spiritual and temporal, . . . By Francis Lord Bishop of Down and Connor . . .* (Dublin, 1723)

—— *A letter to a Member of Parliament, concerning the imploying and providing for the poor* (Dublin, 1723)

—— *An Irish–English almanack for the year, 1724. Being bissextile, or leap-year. And from the creation of the world, about 5686* (2nd edn, Dublin, 1724)

—— *Advices concerning the manner of receiving popish converts, and encouraging both priests and others to live in unity with the Church of Ireland . . . In a letter to a reverend clergy-man of the diocese of Down and Connor* (Dublin, 1729)

—— *A second letter to a Member of Parliament, recommending the improvement of the Irish fishery* (Dublin, 1729)

—— *A sermon preached in Christ-Church, Dublin, on Friday, November 5th 1731. Being the anniversary . . . of . . . the gun-powder plot: . . . before His Grace Lionel Duke of Dorset, Lord Lieutenant of Ireland, and the Lords Spiritual and Temporal in Parliament assembled. By Francis, Lord Bishop of Down and Connor. Published by command of his Grace the Lord Lieutenant, and by order of the House of Lords* (3rd edn, Dublin, 1731)

—— *A defence of the antient historians: with a particular application of it to the history of Ireland and Great-Britain* (Dublin, 1733)

—— *A defence of the antient historians: with a particular application of it to the history of Ireland* (Dublin, 1734)

—— *The state of the case of Lough Neagh and the Bann* (Dublin, 1738)

—— *The certainty of Protestants a safer foundation than the infallibility of Papists* (Dublin, 1738)

Kennet, White, *The present state of convocation in a letter giving the full relation of proceedings in several late sessions: beginning from Wednesday, January the 28th, and continued to Thursday, February the 19th, correcting the mistakes and slanders of the pretended faithful accounts, number, 1, 2* (1702)

—— *A reconciling letter, upon the late differences about convocational rights and proceedings as managed by those who have maintained the liberties of the lower clergy* (London, 1702)

Lewis, John and Richardson, John, *The church catechism explain'd by way of question and answer; and confirm'd by scripture proofs* (London, 1712)

Molesworth, Viscount Robert, *Some considerations for promoting the agriculture of Ireland and employing the poor* (Dublin, 1723)

Newcourt, Richard, *Repertorium ecclesiasticum parochiale Londinense: an ecclesiastical parochial history of the diocese of London* (2 vols, London, 1708–10)

Potts, Thomas, *The wonderfull discoverie of witches in the countie of Lancaster. With the arraignment and triall of nineteene notorious witches, at the assizes and general gaole deliverie, holden at the castle of Lancaster, upon Munday, the seventeenth of August last, 1612. Before Sir James Altham, and Sir Edward Bromley, Knights; barons of his Maiesties Court of Exchequer: and justices of assize, oyer and terminor, and generall gaole deliverie in the circuit of the north parts. Together with the arraignment and triall of Jennet Preston, at the assizes holden at the castle of Yorke, the seven and twentieth day of Julie last past, with her execution for the murther of Master Lister by witchcraft. Published and set forth by commandement of his Maiesties iustices of assize in the north parts* (London, 1613)

Richardson, John, *A short history of the attempts that have been made to convert the popish natives of Ireland, to the establish'd religion: with a proposal for their conversion* (London, 1712)

Scot, Reginald, *Scot's discovery of witchcraft: proving the common opinions of witches contracting with divels, spirits, or familiars . . .* (1584, repr. London, 1651)

Wagstaffe, John, *The question of witchcraft debated, or a discourse against their opinion that affirm witches, considered and enlarged . . .* (2nd edn, London, 1671)

Webster, John, *The displaying of supposed witchcraft, wherein is affirmed that there are many sorts of deceivers and impostors, and divers persons under a passive delusion of melancholy and fancy . . .* (London, 1677)

Willis, Browne, *Parochiale Anglicanum: or, the names of all the churches and chapels within the dioceses of Canterbury, Rochester, London, Winchester, Chichester, Norwich, Salisbury, Wells, Exeter, St Davids, Landaff, Bangor, and St Asaph . . . With an account of most of their dedications, their patrons . . .* (London, 1733)

Official publications and lists

The book of common prayer, and administration of the sacraments (Dublin, 1712)

A catalogue of books: being in the library of the Right Rev. Dr. Francis Hutchinson, late Bishop of Down and Connor. To be sold by auction, by William Ross, at the coffee house . . . the House of Lords, on Monday, the Twenty-sixth of April 1756. The sale to begin every day at eleven o'clock in the forenoon (Dublin, 1756)

A copy of the poll for the knights of the shire for the county of Suffolk, taken at Ipswitch, May 9th, 1705, Thomas Kerrage, Esq High Sherrif (London, 1705)

A copy of the poll for the knights of the shire for the county of Suffolk, taken at Ipswich, Oct. 18. anno dom. 1710. Stephen Bacon, Esq; High Sheriff. George Harrington, gent under sheriff. Candidates, Sir Thomas Hanmer, Sir Robert Davers, Barts. Sir Philip Parker, Baronet (London, 1711)

Journals of the House of Commons for the kingdom of Ireland (4th edn, 21 vols, Dublin, 1796–1802)

Journals of the Irish House of Lords (8 vols, Dublin, 1779–1800)

A list of the members of the Dublin Society, for the improvement of husbandry and other useful arts for the year 1733 (Dublin, 1734)

A true and exact list of the names of the gentlemen, and others, free holders, that voted for . . . the Earl of Dysart, Sir Robert Davers, Bart, Sir Dudley Cullum, Bart, and Samuel Barnardiston Esq; to be knights of the shire for the county of Suffolk . . . as the same was taken at Ipswich, the fifth day of August, 1702 . . . (London, 1702)

Secondary sources

Books

Adams, J. R. R., *The printed word and the common man, 1700–1900* (Belfast, 1987)

Almond, Philip C., *Heaven and hell in Enlightenment England* (Cambridge, 1994)

Barnard, T. C., *The kingdom of Ireland, 1641–1760* (Basingstoke, 2004)

Bartlett, Thomas, *The fall and rise of the Irish nation: the Catholic question 1690–1830* (Dublin, 1992)

Bennett, G. V., *Tory crisis in Church and State, 1688–1730: the career of Francis Atterbury, Bishop of Rochester* (Oxford, 1975)

—— *White Kennet, 1660–1728, Bishop of Peterborough: a study in the political and ecclesiastical history of the early eighteenth century* (London, 1957)

Brown, Michael, McGrath, Charles Ivar, and Power, Thomas P. (eds), *Converts and conversion in Ireland, 1650–1850* (Dublin, 2005)

Burns, Robert E., *Irish parliamentary politics in the eighteenth century, 1714–30* (2 vols, Washington DC, 1990)

Capp, Bernard, *Astrology and the popular press: English almanacs 1500–1800* (London, 1979)

Clark, Stuart, *Thinking with demons: the idea of witchcraft in early modern Europe* (Oxford, 1997)

Cruickshanks, Eveline, Hayton, David William, and Handley, Stuart, *The House of Commons, 1690–1715* (5 vols, London, 2002)

Cullen, L. M., *An economic history of Ireland since 1660* (2nd edn, London, 1972)

Curry, Patrick, *Prophecy and power, astrology in early modern England* (Cambridge, 1989)

Davidson, L., Hitchcock, T., Keirn, T. and Shoemaker, R. B. (eds), *Stilling the grumbling hive: the response to social and economic problems in England, 1689–1750* (New York, 1992)

Davies, Owen, *Witchcraft, magic and culture, 1736–1951* (Manchester, 1999)

Dickinson, H. T., *Liberty and property: political ideology in eighteenth century Britain* (London, 1977)

Garrett, Clarke, *Spirit possession and popular religion: from the Camisards to the Shakers* (Baltimore, 1997)

Gaskill, Malcolm, *Crime and mentalities in early modern England* (Cambridge, 2000)

Gregory, Jeremy and Chamberlain, Jeffrey S. (eds), *The national Church in local perspective: the Church of England and the regions, 1660–1800* (Cambridge, 2003)

Hayton, D. W. (ed.), *The Irish Parliament in the eighteenth century: the long apprenticeship* (Edinburgh, 2001)

Heyd, Michael, *'Be sober and reasonable': the critique of enthusiasm in the seventeenth and early eighteenth centuries* (New York, 1995)

Holmes, Geoffrey, *Augustan England: professions, state and society, 1680–1750* (London, 1982)

—— (ed.) *Britain after the Glorious Revolution, 1689–1714* (London, 1978)

—— *The making of a great power: late Stuart and early Georgian Britain, 1660–1722* (Harlow, 1993)

Jacob, Margaret C., *The Newtonians and the English Revolution, 1689–1720* (New York, 1976)

Jacob, W. M., *Lay people and religion in the early eighteenth century* (Cambridge, 1996)

Klein, Lawerence E. and Vopa, Anthony (eds), *Enthusiasm and the Enlightenment* (San Marino CA, 1998)

McNally, Patrick, *Parties, patriots and undertakers: parliamentary politics in early Hanoverian Ireland* (Dublin, 1997)

Marshall, Peter and Walsham, Alexandra (eds), *Angels in the early modern world* (Cambridge, 2006)

Milne, Kenneth, *The Irish charter schools, 1730–1830* (Dublin, 1997)

Mullet, Michael A., *Catholics in Britain and Ireland, 1558–1829* (London, 1998)

Poole, Robert (ed.), *The Lancashire witches: histories and stories* (Manchester, 2002)

Pruett, John H., *The parish clergy under the later Stuarts: the Leicestershire experience* (Urbana IL, 1978)

Schwartz, Hillel, *Knaves, fools, madmen and that subtle effluvium: a study of the opposition to the French Prophets in England, 1706–1710* (Gainesville FL, 1978)

Sharpe, James, *Instruments of darkness: witchcraft in England, 1550–1750* (London, 1996)

—— *Witchcraft in early modern England* (London, 2001)

Spurr, John, *The Post-Reformation: religion, politics and society in Britain, 1603–1714* (Harlow, 2006)

Stewart, Larry, *The rise of public science, rhetoric, technology and natural philosophy in Newtonian Britain, 1660–1750* (Cambridge, 1992)
Sweet, Rosemary, *The English town, 1680–1840: government, society and culture* (London, 1999)
Thomas, Keith, *Religion and the decline of magic: studies in popular beliefs in sixteenth- and seventeenth-century England* (London, 1971, repr. 1973)
Walker, D. P., *The decline of hell: seventeenth century discussions of eternal torment* (London, 1964)
Walsh, John, Haydon, Colin, and Taylor, Stephen (eds), *The Church of England c.1689 to c.1833: toleration to Tractarianism* (Cambridge, 1993)

Contributions to edited volumes

Barnard, T. C., 'The Hartlib Circle and the cult and culture of improvement in Ireland' in Mark Greengrass, Michael Leslie and Timothy Raylor (eds), *Samuel Hartlib and universal reformation: studies in intellectual communication* (Cambridge, 1994), pp. 281–98
—— 'Improving clergymen, 1660–1760' in Alan Ford, James McGuire and Kenneth Milne (eds), *As by law established: the Church of Ireland since the Reformation* (Dublin, 1995), pp. 136–51
Borsay, Peter, 'The culture of improvement' in Paul Langford (ed.), *The eighteenth century* (Oxford, 2002), pp. 183–212
Crawford, W. H., 'The creation and evolution of small towns in Ulster in the seventeenth and eighteenth centuries' in Peter Borsay and Lindsay Proudfoot, *Provincial towns in early modern England and Ireland* (Oxford, 2002), pp. 97–120 at 102–3
Elmer, Peter, 'Towards a politics of witchcraft in early modern England' in Stuart Clark (ed.), *Languages of witchcraft: narrative, ideology and meaning in early modern culture* (Basingstoke and New York, 2001), pp. 101–18
Gillespie, Raymond, 'Women and crime in seventeenth-century Ireland' in Margaret MacCurtain and Mary O'Dowd (eds), *Women in early modern Ireland* (Edinburgh, 1991), pp. 43–52
Hayton, David, 'The "country" interest and the party system, 1689–c.1720' in Clyve Jones (ed.), *Party management in parliament, 1660–1784* (London, 1984), pp. 37–55
Kelly, Patrick, 'The politics of political economy in mid-eighteenth-century Ireland' in S. J. Connolly (ed.), *Political ideas in eighteenth-century Ireland* (Dublin, 2000), pp. 105–29
Roebuck, Peter, 'Landlord indebtedness in Ulster in the seventeenth and eighteenth centuries' in J. M. Goldstrom and L. A. Clarkson (eds), *Irish population, economy and society: essays in honour of K. H. Connell* (Oxford, 1981) pp. 135–54
Wheeler, Gordon, 'Bishop Francis Hutchinson: his Irish publications and his library' in John Gray and Wesley McCann (eds), *An uncommon bookman: essays in memory of J.R.R. Adams* (Belfast, 1996), pp. 140–58

Journal articles

Barnard, T. C., 'Reforming Irish manners: the religious societies in Dublin during the 1690s' in *Historical Journal*, xxxv, no. 4 (1992), 805–39

—— 'Protestants and the Irish language: c.1675–1725' in *Journal of Ecclesiastical History*, xliv (1993), 243–72

Blackey, R., 'A war of words: the significance of the propaganda conflict between Catholics and Protestants, 1713–1743' in *Catholic Historical Review*, iv (1973), 534–55

Cressy, David, 'Levels of illiteracy in England, 1530–1730' in *Historical Journal*, xx, no. 1 (1977), 1–23

Davies, Paul C., 'The debate on eternal punishment in late seventeenth- and eighteenth-century English literature' in *Eighteenth-Century Studies*, iv, no. 3 (Spring 1971), 257–76

Falvey, Jeremiah, 'The Church of Ireland episcopate in the eighteenth century: an overview' in *Eighteenth-Century Ireland*, viii (1993), 103–14

Gibson, William T., ' "Unreasonable, and unbecoming": self-recommendation and place-seeking in the Church of England, 1700–1900' in *Albion*, xxvii (1995), 43–63

Guskin, P. J., 'The context of witchcraft: the case of Jane Wenham (1712)' in *Eighteenth-Century Studies*, xv, no. 1 (1981), 48–71

Hayton, D. W., 'From barbarian to burlesque: English images of the Irish, c.1660–1750' in *Irish Economic and Social History*, xv (1988), 5–31

Kelly, James, 'Harvests and hardship: famine and scarcity in Ireland in the late 1720s' in *Studia Hibernica*, xxvi (1991–2), 65–106

McNally, Patrick, 'Irish and English interests: national conflict within the Church of Ireland episcopate in reign of George I' in *Irish Historical Studies*, xxxix (1995), 295–314

Mischler, G., 'English political sermons 1714–1742: a case study in the theory of "divine right of governors" and the ideology of order' in *Eighteenth-Century Studies*, xxiv, no. 1 (2001), 33–62

O' Dochartaigh, Cathair, 'The Rathlin catechism' in *Zeitschrift fur Celtische Philologie*, xxxv (1976), 175–233

Peltonen, Markku, 'Politeness and Whiggism, 1688–1732' in *Historical Journal*, xlviii, no. 2 (2005), 391–414

Rose, Craig, 'Evangelical philanthropy and Anglican revival: the charity schools of Augustan London, 1698–1740' in *London Journal*, xvi (1991), 35–65

Ryder, Michael, 'The Bank of Ireland, 1721: land, credit and dependency' in *Historical Journal*, xxv (1982), 557–82

Sneddon, Andrew, 'Bishop Francis Hutchinson (1660–1739): a case study in the culture of improvement' in *Irish Historical Studies*, xxxv, no. 139 (May 2007), 289–310

Theses

Clark, Richard, 'Anglicanism, recusancy and Dissent in Derbyshire, 1603–1730' (PhD thesis, Oxford University, 1980)

Crawford, W. H., 'Economy and society in eighteenth century Ulster' (PhD thesis, Queen's University, Belfast, 1983)

De Valera, Ann, 'Antiquarian and historical investigations in Ireland in the eighteenth century' (Master's thesis, University College Dublin, 1978)

Fitzpatrick, Bridgit A., 'The development of the Irish Almanac, 1612–1724' (Master's Thesis, T.C.D., 1990)

Murrel, Patricia E., 'Suffolk: the political behaviour of the county and parliamentary borough from the Exclusion Crisis to the accession of the House of Hanover' (PhD thesis, University of Newcastle Upon Tyne, 1982)

Richey, Rosemary Anne, 'Landed society in mid-eighteenth century County Down' (PhD thesis, Queen's University, Belfast, 2000)

Sneddon, Andrew, 'The life and thought of Bishop Francis Hutchinson, 1660–1739' (PhD thesis, University of Lancaster, 2002)

Index

Note; 'n' after a page reference indicates the number of a note on that page

Act of Union (1707) 57, 64–8, 95, 100
Ady, Thomas 116
almanacs 72
  see also An Irish–English Almanack (1724)
An historical essay concerning witchcraft (1718, 1720)
  see witchcraft
An Irish–English Almanack (1724) 164–8, 189
Angels 24, 83–5, 89, 92
anti-Catholicism
  in England 33, 45, 72–6, 81, 84
  in Ireland 131, 148, 150, 152–4, 166–74 *passim*, 184, 186
astrology 94, 166–7
Atterbury, Francis, Archdeacon of Exeter 38–9, 46

Ballycastle, County Antrim 180
Bann, river 196
Barnardiston, Sir Samuel 55–7
Baxter, Richard 105
Belfast, County Antrim 1n.1, 3, 142, 142n.71
Berkeley, George, Bishop of Cloyne 152
Boate, Arnold 196
Boate, Gerard 196
Bodin, Jean 101, 105

Bostridge, Ian 2, 93, 95–6, 99, 109, 119, 121, 123
Boulton, Richard 114–16, 121, 123–4
Boultor, Hugh, Archbishop of Armagh 137, 142, 151, 182, 194–5
Boyd, Hugh 180
Boyle, Robert 150, 155
Bury St Edmunds, Suffolk 5, 17–18, 26–7, 29–34, 46, 55, 59, 67–8, 132, 161
  see also charity schools
  witchcraft trials, in 100, 115

Carsington, Derbyshire 3–4, 10–11
Casaubon, Meric 105
Catholicism
  see also anti-Catholicism; conversion of Catholics
  in England 22, 34, 74–5
  in Ireland 153–4, 156, 166
  see also Penal Laws
charity schools 34–5, 151, 155–6, 160
  in Bury St Edmunds 36
  on Rathlin Island 156–7, 164
Charlett, Arthur, master of University College, Oxford 122–3
charter schools 151–2, 174, 177, 197–8

Church catechism in Irish (1722) 119n.136, 156, 158–63
Church of England
  Church courts 22, 30, 45–7
  see also Convocation
  educational initiatives of 21, 30–5
  see also Latitudinarianism
  see also S.P.C.K.
  pastoral care 25–7, 29–30
Church of Ireland
  see also anti-Catholicism; conversion of Catholics
  High-Church party 133, 136, 140, 146
  pastoral care 20–1, 25–30, 49
Churchill, John, first duke of Marlborough 59–61
Clagett, Nicholas, Archdeacon of Sudbury 36, 43–4
Clark, Stuart 97, 101–2, 107
Clayton, Robert, Bishop of Killala and Achonry 173
conversion of Catholics
  in England 33, 75–6
  in Ireland 131, 136, 151–76 *passim*
Convocation
  of Canterbury 36–52 *passim*, 57
  in Ireland 139, 150
Crispe, Samuel 44
Cullum, Sir Dudley 55–7
cunning-folk 106, 112

Davers, Sir Robert 55, 57–8
Davies, Owen 96, 126
Declaratory Act (1720) 131, 143
demonic pact 112–13
demonology 101, 103, 105–7, 112–13, 116, 118
demons 86–8, 103, 108, 110, 113, 122
  see also evil spirits; familiars; Satan

devil, the *see* Satan
devil's mark 106, 114, 116, 120
  see also familiars; Satan
Dissent (Protestant), 11, 35, 37–8, 41, 45, 53, 55–8, 65, 131, 140, 169
  comprehension 23–5, 42, 47
  Toleration Act (1689), 21–2, 67
Dobbs, Arthur 179–80, 194
Down and Connor, diocese of 124–5, 129–30, 133–43, 163
  see also Smythe, Edward, Bishop of Down and Connor
Downes, Henry, Bishop of Elphin 135
Dublin Society for the Improvement of Husbandry and Other Useful Arts 178, 194–7

Ellis, Welbore, Bishop of Kildare 135, 138
Elmer, Peter 97–8, 125
emigration 182–3, 190
enthusiasm 82–3, 86–7, 90, 95, 99, 102, 166
  see also Angels; astrology; French Prophets; millenarianism; miracles; politeness; witchcraft
Evans, John, Bishop of Meath 134–5, 140, 163–4
evil spirits 83, 88, 92, 102–3, 108, 113, 118
  see also demons; familiars; Satan

Fairfax, Charles Brandon, Dean of Down 140–1
familiars 113–14, 116, 120
  see also devil's mark; Satan
famine 174, 181–3, 190
  see also subsistence crisis
Fitzroy, Charles, second Duke of Grafton 134
French Prophets 80–91 *passim*, 107

Gaelic *see* Irish language
Gaskill, Malcolm 96–7
George I, King 11, 68, 75, 117, 130, 132, 143
George II, King 117, 168–9
Gifford, George 102n.42, 110
Glanvill, Joseph 114–15
Godolphin, Sidney 59–60, 65, 132
Gore, Ralph, Chancellor of Irish Exchequer 134
Gore, William, Dean of Clogher 134–5

Halsted, Henry, rector of Stansfield, Suffolk 37, 43–52
Hanmer, Sir Thomas 57–8
Harley, Robert 59, 65
Hartlib, Samuel 189, 196
Haydon, Colin 72–3, 76
heaven 29, 88–9
hell 29, 92, 103–4
Hervey, John, first earl of Bristol 132
Hopkins, Matthew 99–100, 118
Hort, Josiah, Bishop of Ferns, Kilmore and Ardagh vi.n.3, 135
Hoxne, Suffolk 15–18, 29–30, 56, 99–100
Hutchinson family 3–5, 9–12

illiteracy 32, 155, 167
improvement 78–80, 124, 139, 160–1, 167, 175, 177–81
  agricultural 177, 188, 190, 194
  Bank of Ireland 183–6
  bogs 186, 188, 192, 195–6
  culture of 197–8
  see also Dublin Society for the Improvement of Husbandry and Other Useful Arts
  fisheries 188, 190–3, 196–7
  mining 188
  poor, employment of 187–9

Incorporated Society for promoting English Protestant working schools in Ireland see charter schools
Irish language 144–5, 150–68 *passim*, 175–6

Jacobite rebellion 69, 73–5, 90, 149, 184, 186
Jacobites 38, 60, 172
James II, King 11, 60, 67, 70, 73
  see also Jacobites
James III, King 60, 73
  see also Jacobites

Kennet, White, Bishop of Peterborough 40, 43, 46
King, Sir Peter, Lord Chief Baron of Exchequer 117
King, William, Archbishop of Dublin 125, 131, 134–5, 137–8, 152, 156–7, 162–3, 179

Latitudinarianism 23–5, 27–9, 39, 41–2, 78–9, 95, 103–4, 169, 199
  see also Dissent (Protestant); comprehension
Leadbetter, Charles 166
Lindsay, Thomas, Archbishop of Armagh 135
Lisburn, County Antrim 138–9, 174
Lough Neagh 139, 195–6

McCollum, Archibald, curate of Ramoan and vicar of Loughguille, County Antrim 161–3
MacNeice, Louis 1n.1
Macro, Dr Cox 26, 163
Macro family 17
Macro, Susan 68
Macro, Thomas 17, 36, 68

Madden, Samuel 195
Maynard, Thomas, MP for Eye and West Looe 15, 18
Maynard, William 15–19
millenarianism 80–1, 86, 88–9
see also French Prophets
miracles 24, 75–6, 80–4, 86, 88, 94, 100–3, 171
Moore, John, Bishop of Norwich 16, 26, 28, 35, 95

Newton, Sir Issac 77, 79, 119–20
see also Newtonian science; Philosophiae naturalis principia mathematica (1687)
Newtonian science 77, 80, 87, 92, 95, 109, 119–20
see also Newton, Sir Issac; Philosophiae naturalis principia mathematica (1687)
Nicolson, William, Bishop of Derry 135, 137, 144–5
Nine Years' War 60, 63

Palliser, William, Archbishop of Cashel 135
Parker, Thomas, Lord Chief Justice of England 117–18, 122–3, 132–3
parliament
Dublin 130–1, 139, 141–52 passim, 172, 178, 183–8 passim, 191–7 passim
Edinburgh 64, 66
see also Privy Council
Westminster 10, 14, 23, 45, 47, 56–60, 64–5, 68, 118

Passenham, Northamptonshire 16, 18–19, 30
Penal Laws
England 75
Ireland 131, 148–50, 153–4, 164, 170–2

Perkins, William 112, 118
Philosophiae naturalis principia mathematica (1687) 89, 109, 119
see also Newton, Sir Issac; Newtonian science
politeness 18, 28, 76, 78–80, 95, 99, 102, 135, 166
popular magic see cunning-folk
Porter, Roy 96, 99
Portglenone, County Antrim 6, 139, 141, 174, 192, 195, 197–8
Powell, Sir John 100–1, 116–17, 122
Poynings' Law (1494–5) 143–4
Prideaux, Humphrey, Archdeacon of Suffolk 43
Prior, Thomas 195
Privy Council
in England 143, 193
in Ireland 143, 157, 191

Quendon, Essex 15

Ramoan, County Antrim 161
Rathlin Island, County Antrim 156–8, 163–4
see also charity schools
Reformation, the 25, 136, 154–5
Richardson, John, rector of Belturbet 150–2, 155, 157–161
Royal Society, the 79, 95

Satan 86, 88, 94–5, 101–3, 106–8, 112–13, 119–21
see also demonic pact; demonology; devil's mark; familiars
Schwartz, Hillel 86
Scot, Reginald 101, 102n.42, 105
Scotland 11, 91, 95, 100, 110–11, 144, 156, 160, 190–1, 193
see also Act of Union (1707)
Sharpe, James 2, 93–7, 99, 112, 125

Sloane, Sir Hans 95, 100, 165
Smythe, Edward, Bishop of Down and Connor 133–4
Smythe, James, prebendary of Cairncastle 163
Smythe, William, Bishop of Raphoe 163
South Sea Bubble 182, 184–6
S.P.C.K. 4, 21, 26–7, 30–4, 36, 150–1, 157
subsistence crisis, 174, 181–3, 189–90, 192, 203
  see also famine
Swift, Jonathan vi, 145
Swimming test 116–120
Synge, Edward, Bishop of Raphoe and Archbishop of Tuam 131, 135, 152

Tallents, Francis 11, 49
Tenison, Thomas, Archbishop of Canterbury 38, 91, 95
Thorn, Ann 108
Tillotson, John, Archbishop of Canterbury 23–5, 27–9, 104
Toland, John 41–2, 173
Tollemache, Lionel, Earl of Dysart 55–7
Tories
  in England 15–16, 38, 45, 47, 53–69 *passim*, 93
  in Ireland 133, 140–1, 146, 150, 157

Trimnell, Charles, Dean of Peterborough and Bishop of Norwich 26, 30–1, 40, 42n.114, 43

Wake, William, Archbishop of Canterbury 11–12, 91, 121–2, 124–5, 133, 140, 163–4
War of Spanish Succession 53, 59–64
Webster, John 102n.42, 105
Wenham, Jane 93, 95, 98–101, 108, 114, 116
Whigs
  in England 11–12, 15–19, 22, 41, 45, 47, 52–80 *passim*, 91–100 *passim*, 103, 109, 117, 132–3
  in Ireland 130–4, 136, 140, 143–4, 149, 149, 151–2, 182, 189
Widdington, Essex 13–15, 19
Wilson, Thomas, Bishop of Sodor and Man 162
witchcraft
  in England 1–3, 80, 88, 92–126 *passim*
  in Ireland 124–5, 197
  in Scotland 95, 100
  see also demonic pact; demonology; demons; devil's mark; familiars; Hopkins, Matthew; swimming test; Wenham, Jane

EU authorised representative for GPSR:
Easy Access System Europe, Mustamäe tee 50,
10621 Tallinn, Estonia
gpsr.requests@easproject.com

www.ingramcontent.com/pod-product-compliance
Ingram Content Group UK Ltd.
Pitfield, Milton Keynes, MK11 3LW, UK
UKHW021945200326
4879IPUK00005B/104